PRACTICAL
TEXT ANALYTICS

STEVEN STRUHL

PRACTICAL
TEXT ANALYTICS

Interpreting text and unstructured data for
business intelligence

MARKETING SCIENCE SERIES

LONDON PHILADELPHIA NEW DELHI

First published in Great Britain and the United States in 2015 by Kogan Page Limited

2nd Floor, 45 Gee Street	1518 Walnut Street, Suite 1100	4737/23 Ansari Road
London EC1V 3RS	Philadelphia PA 19102	Daryaganj
United Kingdom	USA	New Delhi 110002
www.koganpage.com		India

© Steven Struhl, 2015

The right of Steven Struhl to be identified as the author of this work has been asserted by him in accordance with the Copyright, Designs and Patents Act 1988.

ISBN   978 0 7494 7401 0
E-ISBN   978 0 7494 7402 7

British Library Cataloguing-in-Publication Data

A CIP record for this book is available from the British Library.

Library of Congress Cataloging-in-Publication Data

Struhl, Steven M.
    Practical text analytics : interpreting text and unstructured data for business intelligence / Steven Struhl.
        pages cm. – (Marketing science)
        ISBN 978-0-7494-7401-0 (paperback) – ISBN 978-0-7494-7402-7 (ebk)   1. Marketing–Data processing.   2. Big data.   3. Business intelligence.   4. Marketing research.   I. Title.
    HF5415.125.S77 2015
    658.4'72–dc23
                                                                                                                    2015016005

Typeset by Graphicraft Limited, Hong Kong
Print production managed by Jellyfish
Printed and bound by CPI Group (UK) Ltd, Croydon, CR0 4YY

*This book is dedicated to
my wife Debra and my mother Lydia.*

CONTENTS

Test banks, slides and useful web links are available online at:
www.koganpage.com/PracticalTextAnalytics

PREFACE

Although Chapter 1 and the table of contents will tell you all about what you will find in the rest of the book, this preface still has its uses. It can give you a first inkling of the author's writing style, as historian Frank Muir aptly noted. You can get some sense of whether the person doing the writing is going to drag you on heedlessly until you are smothered in tedium, or if this is somebody who will at least occasionally think about what you as a reader are likely to be experiencing.

You certainly can get some sense about the likely pace of the book – whether it will go quickly, or perhaps not, or if this is one to be read late at night when nothing else gets you to sleep.

In fact, this is a place where you can meet the author on neutral ground, without having to wonder if you are misunderstanding him because you are somehow lacking in the subject area. It is your chance to start forming some good opinions about who this person is anyhow, who is asking you to journey through territories that could be fraught with complexity, obscurity and obfuscation.

If you are flipping through a preview online, or (rarity of rarities) looking at this in a bookstore, here could be your spot to decide if you want to continue to the next peek inside. If you opened this book by mistake, then this could be a good spot to realize that this was a serendipitous stroke after all.

One intention of this book is to cut through as much of the recondite language, the murky formulations, the jargon, and even utter nonsense surrounding this field. We will go over vocabulary, but only so you will be prepared when you encounter such terms as 'named entity' and know that they are nothing to fear.

We will steer around equations, subscripted notation and Greek letters whenever possible. If you were hoping to see all of those, then you definitely have sat down in the wrong theatre.

We hear that unstructured data is a really 'hot' topic. Also, that in the arena of unstructured data, text is one of the hottest of areas. (This holds just in certain circles, though – don't try it as an ice-breaker at your next party.) Text has received a lot of attention from friendly vendors as a result.

While this book will focus on the types of analyses that you can do within your organization, we also want to arm you to deal with this strong promotional interest that text analysis has accrued.

This book is not a guide to the types of services that vendors typically supply, including document retrieval, document search, and organizing a document library. Reading this book, though, should help you deal with sellers as they bombard you with their newest, latest things. The information you get here should enable you to evaluate their claims in an informed and suitably inquiring way.

Looking at other prefaces, it seems this is the place where the book needs to take a turn into the first person, and I tell you a little about myself. You may be questioning what my *bona fides* are to write a book like this in the first place. Here's what I can come up with. I have been working in applying data and data analysis to practical problems for over 25 years. My clients have included many Fortune 100 companies, but also a host of mid-size and smaller entities, along with charitable, educational and non-profit organizations. I have written over 25 articles and another book, which has been in print for over 20 years – and which you can see (and even buy, not that I am hinting at anything) on Amazon. I have taught advanced statistics to bored doctoral students who had to take it to get their degrees, given numerous other courses and seminars, and continue to teach certification courses online.

In education, I have an MBA (University of Chicago), doctorate in psychology (Chicago School of Professional Psychology) and an MA in language and linguistics (Boston University). This combination does seem to fall into place with the topic of the book, and also gives rise to the question of why, when I was younger, I didn't just get a job.

Concerning text analytics, I have been working with this for over 10 years. It started while I was at a major market research company, when a somewhat shifty colleague came to me, asking if we couldn't do something better than was possible with the latest text analytics software we had licensed. This massive program had automatically categorized thousands of comments from a large online community, after somebody had manually trained it over the course of a couple of weeks. (Things were comparatively primitive as recently as a decade ago.) The program's big gimmick was printing out a list of words that occurred most often near a word that you entered. This co-worker was not satisfied, and should not have been.

After a few false starts, I came up with a predictive model using the categories (or codes) this program generated. The method was classification trees, which are discussed in Chapter 7. Neither I nor the other fellow had ever seen anything like this, but it worked. He said something like, 'Gee this is great', and then did the equivalent of packing his bags and climbing out of a window at midnight. I didn't hear from him for a couple of weeks. It was a very busy time, and when I finally went over to his side of the building to talk about the next steps, I found he had cleared out his office and vanished. Soon afterwards, he turned up as a Wandering-Genius-Scholar type at a major software company. Apparently, this was based on his expertise in analysing text. They must have really liked that predictive model.

However, this story does turn out well for all involved. I learned that analysing text could be useful in a number of ways, and of course I now have the great opportunity to write this book.

Many thanks are in order here. We should start with Melody Dawes at Kogan Page, and agent Richard Burton, for making this possible. I owe particular thanks to my editor Jasmin Naim for being a constant delight to work with and the most courteous and professional possible of colleagues. Also, many thanks to Anna Moss at Kogan Page for being unfailingly helpful and patient in dealing with all the official materials related to getting this book ready.

I would like also to give particular thanks to my wife Debra for tolerating months of very late nights and working weekends – and in particular for her acting as a kind of royal food taster for you the readers, trying out various sections of the book to find whether they were particularly indigestible.

Lastly, more thanks to several colleagues who talked about points in this book, offered expert advice and were early readers of various chapters. These include Professor Josh Eliashberg at the Wharton School of Business, Larry Durkin, Well Howell, John Jeter and Edward Zyvith.

This book always aims always to follow the advice set forth by former US President Gerald Ford:

'When a man is asked to make a speech, the first thing he has to decide is what to say.'

Now let's go on to what we decided, and see where this journey takes us.

IMAGE 0.1

SOURCE: Victor Garaix, French aviator in cockpit of plane with dog: 1914 March. Reproduction Number: LC-USZ62-48802, LOT 10818, Library of Congress Prints and Photographs Division Washington, DC 20540 USA.
http://www.loc.gov/pictures/item/2001704143

WHO SHOULD READ THIS BOOK?

And what do you want to do today?

KEY QUESTIONS

Who should read this book? What can you expect from it? What are the ground rules for successful text analytics?

This chapter explains who should read the book and discusses the basics of text analytics. Here we discuss data itself, the types of text that you can analyse, the basic guidelines for any analysis, the types of text analyses and their natures, and what you can expect to get from reading this book.

Who should read this book

This book is for anybody who wants to understand text analytics, and how to use it – and who is interested in practical applications. This is not a book for somebody who wants instructions in programming, or who wants to read a lot of mathematical notation. If you are hoping for a great many Greek letters, subscripts and complex equations, you will be disappointed.

You might be anybody with these needs:

- You want to understand what text analytics means, what it does, and the practical applications that you can use;

- You want to cut through the jargon and claims that surround this topic, and so learn what you really can expect and what is hype;

- You are learning about text analytics in a course and want to see how academic concerns become actual applications;

- You want to understand the powerful analytic methods that you can use with text and with other data;

- You want to understand what makes for sound practices in analysing text (and other data, for that matter) and what does not;

- You want to see some real data being analysed and the uses of the output explained;

- You work with people who analyse text and unstructured data, and want to understand better what they are talking about;

- You are already digging into text analytics and want to see what else you might be doing.

Why read this? Text can have real value

Hearing from people in their own words can give you tremendously valuable insights that you could not get anywhere else. Text can be used alongside numerical measures to build predictive models that are stronger than are possible with either the measures alone or text alone. On the converse side, you really need to understand the ground rules and pitfalls. People can be terrifically disappointed if they rush into applying text analytics without considering what they need to do, how to do this, and where to find the right text. This brings us to part 2 of 'Why read this?'

Why read this? (Part 2) Understand advanced analytics as well as dealing with text

This book will serve as more than a guide to analysing text. It provides a necessary bridge between the person who must put text analytics to use and the increasingly rarefied community of experts who do the actual analysis. This book will provide a practical and accessible guide to many of the remarkable advances that the specialists are discussing among themselves. We will talk about a number of powerful analytical and predictive methods, their uses, strengths and weaknesses.

We also review valuable pointers on good practices to use when analysing text – and any other data – that may somehow slip away in the rush of pursuing a dynamic and rapidly growing field. Getting useful information from text may well be more challenging than with other forms of data, so staying grounded is important.

Where we find text

We can find text to analyse in many places, but by far the fastest growing and most massive repository is the internet. Text in many varieties explodes in torrents through the web, including: reviews, postings, tweets, blogs, news, articles, responses to surveys, advertisements, product descriptions, scholarly papers, emails, comments collected for insurance, retail, health care and research (to name a few), recapitulations, aggregations and summaries of other information – and so on. There is an immense amount out there, and what to do with it is a critical, ongoing question.

The conundrum of online text

As Tim Berners-Lee, the inventor of the World Wide Web, has pointed out, the internet now is a web of documents. However, documents, as we will see, are not structured in the same ways as the numeric data for which analytical methods were first devised. This lack of a common structure makes documents not readily amenable to analysis. We will be discussing how we try to overcome this problem. Berners-Lee has advocated that the internet should evolve towards being a web of analysable data, meaning that the text it contains would need to accumulate a great deal of other information, largely hidden from the reader, that makes the text behave more like data. (We will talk more about this idea in Chapter 5). Until this massive transformation happens, though, the internet will continue as a largely unstructured mass. Therefore, as the information it contains grows rapidly, it paradoxically will remain difficult to tap and use.

Data vs information

Anything that can be collected in any fashion counts as **data**. Noise from a cell phone tower is data. Mistranslated text is data. Propaganda is data. Data exists, but may not have any purpose. It is not **information.** The distinction is essential. **Information** conveys valuable new insights, telling us about something that we did not expect, or allowing us to deal with an unusual contingency.

We often encounter the belief that having a great deal of data also means that we must have something interesting. Some writers have even made a point of saying, apparently earnestly, that more data is always better. This is not true. In many cases, this assertion can be completely backward.

If the data you have at hand mainly is not useful, more of it makes it **harder** for you to find what you need, not easier. As valuable items get overrun by useless ones, they become more elusive, and may even vanish from sight entirely. Knowing where to look, as well as how to do the analysis, becomes critical with data that is not structured.

IMAGE 1.1   I know what I want is in here somewhere

SOURCE: Kitchen midden at Elizabeth Island, 1888, Stefan Claesson. Image ID: fish7827 from NOAA's Historic Fisheries Collection. Gulf of Maine Cod Project, NOAA National Marine Sanctuaries; Courtesy of National Archives. http://en.wikipedia.org/wiki/Midden#mediaviewer/File:Kitchen_midden_at_ Elizabeth_Island_1888.jpg. Licensed under public domain via Wikimedia Commons.

What is unstructured data?

Most simply, unstructured data does not follow a regular pattern that fits easily into a table. When people talk about unstructured data, most of the time they actually are talking about text. Text of course is divided into words, phrases and paragraphs, not into neat cells as in a spreadsheet. For now, it is important to understand that you must do a great deal to text before you can start to analyse it – including removing parts that are completely useless in an analysis and somehow transforming the rest so that you can do something with it. We will talk more about the ways unstructured data becomes structured in Chapter 2.

How big data relates to text, and what it is exactly

Big data is a term surrounded with confusion. For a time it was the epi-centre of a storm of hype and impossible-to-fill promises. It is still generally described in terms that do not appear immediately helpful. For instance, the Massachusetts Institute of Technology (MIT) found at least six conflict-ing definitions. One of the best known comes from a company named Gartner, and talks about volume, velocity and variety. They also mention 'innovative forms of information processing for enhanced insight'.

From this, we would conclude that if you just had an enormously large dataset, you still would not have big data – unless it arrived quickly and had a lot of variety. And apparently, if you had very quickly arriving data, but it did not pass the threshold for volume (whatever that might be), then your data would still not count as big, and... presumably, you get the idea.

> **Big data** does not have a consistent and concise definition. We might say somewhat lightheartedly that it appears to involve more data than you can handle comfortably with whatever software and hardware you now own. **You do not need to have big data to do text analytics.** The methods work with large, medium and small datasets.

One thing we can say with some confidence is that big data is hard to manage, and this in part is because there will be more of it than you can handle comfortably. The definition seems to be shifting. A few years ago, terabytes of data seemed to suffice. Now that we can process at least a few terabytes with a powerful enough PC, perhaps we need to have petabytes. (A petabyte is 1,000 terabytes. Next up is the exabyte, 1,000 petabytes.)

One slightly facetious conclusion is that big data is whatever requires new big storage, big software, and big expenses. Also, this means it is something that many friendly vendors are very interested in your getting – immediately.

You do not need to cross the barrier into big data to analyse text. The methods work admirably with smaller datasets, and can be scaled up to handle as much data as your computing equipment (and budget) will allow.

Perhaps one last point about big data is that a great deal of caution is prudent. Articles with titles like 'Why most big data projects fail' are appearing with some frequency. Also, using Google searches as a yardstick, the results are not terribly reassuring. The terms 'big data' and 'success stories' do return some 1.4 million results. However, 'big data' and 'failure stories' bring back over 77 million.

Sense and sensibility in thinking about text

A few key points require very careful consideration before you embark on analysing text. Starting with monetary considerations and working through procedural ones, they follow below:

- Analysing text has more costs than you may expect;
- You need to have good reasons for analysing text;
- Text analytics needs to follow good analytical principles;
- You need to look in the right places to find text to analyse.

Analysing text has more costs than you may expect

It has been wrongly said that 'information wants to be free'. (This is wrong because, as Gladwell pointed out, **information** does not want anything. The people who use it may want it gratis, but that is another matter.) However, there is no confusion about text analytics: it requires investment.

Software for text analytics ranges in price all the way from free to **enterprise level**, with 'enterprise level' being a secret code for 'costing

IMAGE 1.2   Suddenly, you may need a few people like these

SOURCE: Von Braun's rocket team in 1961, anonymous photographer. This image catalogued by NASA, headquarters of the United States National Aeronautics and Space Administration (NASA), under photo ID: GPN-2000-001660 AND Alternate ID: 1963ADM-1.
http://en.wikipedia.org/wiki/Rocket#mediaviewer/File:VonBraunTeam1961.jpg.

five to six figures'. Free software unexpectedly still has costs because it typically requires a considerable amount of time and effort to learn – and may require a specialist to learn it. Almost invariably, free software involves output or processes that are tedious to deal with, and so has costs of time. Free programs typically also have scanty or no support, so if you get stuck, you are really stuck. Insuperable problems can arise no matter how much experience you have. (There is a sad note of personal experience here. Not all things work at all times.)

Also, if you have great masses of text, you likely have great masses of other data. You may indeed need to invest in new storage, new hardware and new software to handle this. You may also need to invest in somebody scientific-seeming, or perhaps even a few individuals, to deal with all the resources you have on hand.

You need to have good reasons for analysing text

The costs mentioned are one key factor for needing good reasons. As importantly, you do not want to be seen as wasting your time, and especially not management's time (should you need to contend with management). The motivations for doing the analysis should flow from the needs of the people who are going to apply it to making decisions (the 'stakeholders', as they are sometimes called). Without the involvement of an interested person or group who can act on your findings, even the most startling insight will have little if any value.

Text analytics needs to follow good analytic principles

It almost seems strange to address this specifically, but reports about the ways text gets analysed sometimes reveal that basic rules have been broken in arriving at a conclusion (which then becomes highly questionable). You can of course still reach a reasonable answer (at times) when you ignore a few minor rules – and may even come out well enough disregarding an important rule or two. But the odds of success must go down if you do not follow sound principles. Here are a few to keep in mind:

- Work on a well-defined problem;
- Expect that you will need to invest time making the data suitable for analysis;
- Know what is important and what is not;
- Go for the simplest model that explains what is important.

Work on a well-defined problem

This means that you need objectives for what you are doing and intended uses for the results. This may seem self-evident, but some language surrounding unstructured data suggests that useful information will rise up out of the data and wave to get your attention. For instance, this is hinted at in the quote we mentioned earlier, which 'linked innovative information processing' with 'enhanced insight'. This is misleading because insight comes from knowing what you need to find out and thinking about what you find in the data. While some new method may help you answer your questions, the processing cannot do so by itself.

We have been here before. This wishful formulation appeared in the early days of data mining, around 1990. There even was what amounted

IMAGE 1.3   Babies and beer (1916): perhaps the source of a legend?

SOURCE: Advertisement, 1916, author unknown, from *The Dubuque Telegraph Herald*, 1 July 1916, page 12.

to a data-mining urban legend. It had to do with a 'major retailer' (whose identity changed depending on who was telling the story). Beer and diaper sales, it was said, were discovered to rise together before weekends. Some highly clever person realized that recent dads, while stocking up on Pampers, also would stop to pick up a six pack or two of beer. The store then put beer promotions near the diaper aisle, or maybe vice versa. (It makes more sense to think that really heavy beer drinkers might find the diapers handy.) Sometimes the story is embellished with a set of related factoids, like saying sales went up some specific amount, say 27 per cent.

There is one problem: this is absolutely untrue. The person who started this story has been located. He said it was all a joke. He intended it to point out how foolish claims for unplanned insight discovery can be.

Expect that you will need to invest time making the data usable for analysis

Any trip into unstructured data will yield surprises, not of the beer and diaper type, but rather unexpected messiness, if not chaos. You typically will spend more time than you might anticipate addressing data problems and irregularities. Computer science is making some progress in automating clean-up, but the old adage often may hold that most of the time you spend in a project will go into preparing the data so that you can analyse it.

Know what is important and what is not

We need more than intuition to know when something we believe we are seeing is real. Unless we have every shred of data possible, we have a **sample** – and samples have error associated with them. That is, because we are not measuring everything, we are uncertain about what the measurement would be if we in fact had all the data. Formal tests can help, but are not infallible by any means – as we will discuss.

Those of us with more academic experience have heard a great deal about **statistical significance**. This also is used often in reporting about research, of the scientific and market varieties. Yet this term is not well understood. We hope to clear that up now.

> **Statistical significance** is often mentioned, but its meaning is not well understood. When a result is significant, it means you are very confident that you are not making a false claim. Significance does not measure how likely you are to be missing something real, which is determined by the much less-used **statistical power**. Testing for significance tends to break down with huge samples or with hundreds of comparisons. You need to use **the test of what is sensible** along with statistical significance testing.

Perhaps you recall the term **null hypothesis**. In non-formal terms, this means the belief that nothing is happening. We go from there to **rejecting the null hypothesis**, with apologies to those of you who still have tremors when thinking back to statistics class. This means **not saying that nothing has happened.**

That convoluted-seeming formulation is at the heart of significance testing. Statisticians want to be sure that they are **not falsely claiming something is happening** when it is not. Making that kind of mistake is sometimes called a **Type I error**. Statisticians in fact have decided something is **significant** only if they are **95 per cent certain** they are not making a false claim.

Why is the threshold 95 per cent? The best answer that seems available is: **just because**. This is a just a convention, if a very solidly established one. Based on the number of scientific papers that go through incredible contortions to reach this 95 per cent level, you might think there is some magic behind it, but there is not.

However, traditional **significance testing** breaks down with very large samples. If you have enough data, everything starts seems significant. This effect occurs well below today's threshold for big data. For instance, looking at about 12,000 people who answered the NORC General Social Survey, we found that people with the astrological sign Leo watched significantly more television than anybody else. However, don't go and chide your Leo friends. This is simply an artefact of testing for significance with a large sample – you can find random-seeming items passing the test.

> **Significance testing can break down** with huge samples or with hundreds or thousands or comparisons. Alternative methods of testing models are used by some procedures. Other methods involve testing how well the model works on new data, or on data put to one side before the model has been made.

Traditional significance testing also can stretch past its limits while doing hundreds or thousands of comparisons, trying to find which effects or values are larger. Some methods, such as the Bayesian networks we discuss in Chapter 8, may use **a value of information** approach rather than traditional statistical testing to overcome this problem. Other methods, such as the classification trees we discuss in Chapter 7, can deal with this issue by using highly sophisticated testing, advanced enough to have once been called artificial intelligence.

A few authors have even advocated abandoning statistical significance in favour of what they call searching for 'repeatable patterns', which boils down to seeing how well the model holds up on other data, or perhaps some part of the data that you have set to one side before you made the model. Testing on other data, even data you have put to one side before making the model, is a sound idea – but it also is worth keeping the extra guidance that significance testing can give you on what should definitely **should not** go into a model.

Passing a test of statistical significance does not prevent you from missing something that is real. Testing helps you avoid saying something by mistake, but you could be remaining silent when you should not. Another statistical test, called **statistical power**, is more closely related to the idea that what you are apparently seeing really is happening. Testing for **statistical pow**er is used far less than testing for **significance**, although ideally these two should be used together. Missing something that actually is happening is that other type of error mentioned in statistics class, **Type II error.**

Statistical tests of any kind cannot determine if what you seem to be seeing makes sense. For instance, in Chapter 6, we use significance testing but do not accept all the results the computer identifies as passing the test – because it did not make sense to include all of them. (This problem arose partly due to using a large sample and partly due to a known problematic tendency of regression modelling.) Especially with huge swaths of data, you will be most prudent to use statistical significance testing as suggesting a threshold below which you do not want to go, rather than as forming the final decision.

Go for the simplest model that explains what is important

Complexity may be impressive, but ultimately, what influences outcomes is the simplest explanation that reveals what is happening. We will be talking a great deal about statistical **modelling** as a means of explanation. There have been many definitions for a mathematical or statistical **model**. We will take it to mean a way of representing how one or more variables influence another variable and how variables relate to each other. **Variables** usually are considered discrete items that can change from one person or observation to another. Text can be broken down into words and phrases that are counted as variables.

Going for the simplest working model is an extremely well-established practice in the sciences. It is sometimes called **Ockham's razor.** (Ockham was William of Ockham, who lived around 1300, so this idea has a great deal of history. The razor, going along with the idea that you should cut away everything extraneous, apparently came into this around 1840. It is not clear whether William actually even saw a razor.)

If you have a liking for fancy charts, the temptation to use a gee-whiz graphic can be very strong indeed. And there are many who say that complex graphics are the best way to display data.

IMAGE 1.4   Wow! But now what do I do with this?

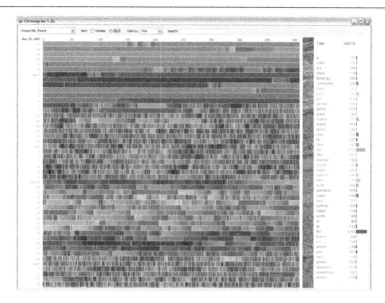

SOURCE: Visualization of all editing activity by user 'Pearle' on Wikipedia (Pearle is a robot), uploaded 2009, F B Viégas.
http://en.wikipedia.org/wiki/Big_data#mediaviewer/File:Viegas-UserActivityonWikipedia.

However, while the more ornate of these depictions may stun an audience into silence, they generally do not make the point in a way that is acted upon. An important part of any analysis of complex and messy data – often as important as the analysis itself – is figuring out how to get the points across in ways your audience will understand.

Overall, then, it is best not to aim for highly intricate patterns just because somebody has said that is the nature of data (especially the 'big' variety). Rather, it works better to ensure that you include everything that is needed and no more. Whatever you find by analysing text should reduce the risk in decisions and make those decisions simpler. Text analytics should add insights that improve your organization's ability to respond to – if not lead – changes.

Know which text to analyse

The web has such an abundance of text that it may be tempting to believe you merely need dig into it enough and you will find meaning. Social media platforms, with their wealth of commentary, can look particularly enticing. Yet, unless you are planning to advertise on those platforms, they might not be the right places to investigate. Whether the text you investigate

FIGURE 1.1   Alternative frames: right and wrong

Frame is correct   Frame is incorrect

SOURCE: A view of Arles with Irises, 1888, Vincent Van Gogh.
http://commons.wikimedia.org/wiki/File:VanGogh-View_of_Arles_with_Irises.jpg#mediaviewer/
File:VanGogh-View_of_Arles_with_Irises.jpg. The frame was photographed by the author and the
images assembled by the author.

will work for you depends on how well the people who express opinions there match the people who you need to understand and who you hope to influence.

Getting the wrong people, no matter how many you find, can lead to stunningly mistaken conclusions. This problem is known somewhat more formally as choosing the wrong **sample frame**. You can think of a sample frame as the boundaries of where you look for information. Alternatively, you can think of it like framing a picture. Figure 1.1 shows this in action.

Getting the frame right means that you can see the picture clearly, as on the left side of Figure 1.1. Having the frame wrong means you may see part of the picture, but you also see something else that you do not want to see, as on the left side of the figure.

Getting the right sample frame really matters. The question of using an accurate frame should have been settled nearly 80 years ago – while simultaneously putting to rest the notion that more data always is better. Here is the story.

In 1936, George Gallup and the magazine *Literary Digest* both forecast the results of the US presidential election, based on different samples of people likely to vote. The Literary Digest poll was huge by any standard, some **2.4 million people**. Adjusting for inflation, this was perhaps the most expensive poll ever conducted. Gallup used a scientifically selected sample of about 50,000.

Gallup got the results right, predicting that Franklin D Roosevelt would win handily. The *Literary Digest* got things terribly wrong, predicting a landslide for Roosevelt's opponent, the now largely forgotten Alf Landon. They called the results at 57 per cent of the vote for Landon against Roosevelt's 43 per cent. The actual results of the election: an overwhelming 62 per cent for Roosevelt vs 38 per cent for Landon.

The *Literary Digest* poll was off by some 19 per cent. This is reportedly the largest error ever made in a major public opinion poll. Practically all of this error came from picking the wrong sampling frame.

This error is also called **sample bias.** In 1936, this problem generally was not understood. The *Literary Digest* thought they had everything covered well enough to be accurate within a fraction of a per cent. They sent out some 10 million invitations by mail to cast a mock election ballot, using lists such as their own subscribers, telephone directories, and club memberships. Unfortunately for them, this meant their sample strongly represented middle-class and upper-class people (only about 40 per cent of US households had a telephone in 1930, and with the Great Depression in full force, many did not subscribe to magazines or belong to clubs). Their sample frame did not include the many poorer people who (in 1936) voted in large numbers – leading to the terrible results we saw.

The different places on the web where you might find text are also **sample frames**. Somewhat facetiously, you need to be sure that the person who just finished posting 'Thisbe is such a chunker' is also the person who will want to use your fine product or service.

> **Sample frames** are the locations where you gather data. Using the wrong sample frame can lead to grievously wrong predictions, no matter how much data you gather. We need only recall Alf Landon, who did not win the 1936 US presidential election, even though a sample of 2.4 million (from the wrong sample frame) predicted he would in a landslide.
> **Text from the web must be vetted very carefully** to make sure you are analysing text from the right people.

One more point about online commentary bears some consideration. People who volunteer their opinions online (without anybody asking) even may not reflect the opinions of all people at that site. Freely offered opinions can represent both the negative and positive extremes. They also simply may want to say something, for the attention they expect, without much knowledge of the product or issue. People who are neutral, moderately pleased and even moderately displeased rarely have much to say about their experiences. This ties in with the next point as well.

Carefully controlled sources, including well-conducted surveys and closed professional online communities, have generated the text that has been most useful for predictions. These sources have two key points in common. First, the people who participate in them must meet certain criteria, such as (for instance) actually being software engineers who understand the product in question, or being professionals who understand and use the service of interest. Also, forums like these allow for direct questions. These can ask both for free commentary and for scaled measurements. We have found the combination of text and scaled measures can have particularly strong power to predict an outcome.

Uses for text from social media if you are not advertising there

Still, there can be circumstances in which monitoring social media sites becomes important, even if the people you find on a given site largely are not the people most vital to the success of your product or organization. If you are concerned about any negative publicity, or if something controversial has happened, then careful observation could be in order.

IMAGE 1.5   Actually nothing Satanic under the sun or moon

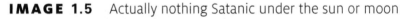

SOURCE: Flammarion Woodcut, 1888, Camille Flammarion, *L'Atmosphere: Météorologie Populaire*, p 163.
http://commons.wikimedia.org/wiki/File:FlammarionWoodcut.jpg#mediaviewer/
File:FlammarionWoodcut.jpg.

For instance, around 1990, Procter and Gamble (P&G) changed the man-in-the-moon logo they had used for over 100 years because a small group of people were spreading false rumours about supposed Satanist associations in the image. The company did not want any breath of the negative, so the logo had to go. If an issue like this arises, social media could conceivably serve as an early warning signal. If you are considering this type of temperature-taking, any of the more descriptive methods we discuss in Chapters 3 and 5 would probably alert you to an incipient problem.

A few places we will not be going

Text analytics is a vast field. We are covering key methods and approaches that will help you find meaning and solve practical problems. No one book could possibly cover everything associated with this field, and that includes this one. The areas we cannot cover include these:

- Information retrieval, which is largely a programming problem;
- Things companies like Google and Amazon do already extremely well, like searching, indexing, scoring and recommendation systems;
- Some analytical methods proposed for use with text, particularly those not producing a model you can interpret (such as neural networks and so-called ensembles);
- Attempting to capture meaning on the fly from continually arriving text.

The last two of these may need some additional explanation. First, there are a host of analytical methods that we could apply, and we cannot cover all of them. The book *Data Mining*, for instance, discusses about 100 methods that fall under the heading of **machine learning**, and there are more methods still. Some procedures, such as the two we mentioned, do not produce models you can see. Neural networks involve tangles of hidden connections and cannot tell you exactly what they are doing. Ensembles may perform well, but they typically involve mixing advanced methods that most audiences find baffling – and so are extremely difficult to diagnose and explain.

Concerning streaming text, there are systems in place that gather text frequently and search for key words. Systems like this will tell you, for instance, which topics appear most topical on Twitter. They generally use

IMAGE 1.6
We cannot cover
continuous processing

SOURCE: 1944, author unknown. This image is available from the United States Library of Congress's Prints and Photographs division under the digital ID fsa.8e02902.
http://commons.wikimedia.org/wiki/File:Airacobra_P39_Assembly_LOC_02902u.jpg.

very large samples, but samples nonetheless, and even these appear to pause before reporting.

All the methods we explain work on text you have gathered in a database or a file. You can, of course, go back and gather text frequently, but the text needs to be stored and settled before the analytical methods we discuss can work. It also takes time to reach good answers with the more advanced analytical methods, particularly ones where we look for likely influences on outcomes such as liking, preference, time spent on a web page or shopping and buying behaviour. Good analytics never are instant.

Where we will be going from here

The book follows a progression, starting with what you need to do with text to analyse it, then moving through more descriptive approaches and finally arriving at some powerful and new predictive methods. Chapter 2 discusses the basics of processing text so you can do anything analytical with it. We then go on to some approaches that give you more general patterns or descriptions, starting with ways you can depict text pictorially, in Chapter 3. Chapter 4 extends some of the concepts explained there, dealing with gathering similar text items, as well as comparing and contrasting groups of items.

From there we will talk about counting and enumeration, including sentiment, in Chapter 5. The next three chapters comprise methods that build predictive models, showing how they can work with text. We start with one probably more familiar, regression, in Chapter 6. You are likely to learn some surprising facts there. We conclude with two highly powerful methods that should be in everybody's analytical armamentarium – whether you are analysing text or any other data – classification trees and Bayesian networks. What you encounter in these chapters should open new approaches giving you better ways to direct action and reach successful outcomes. We conclude with a look forward to what might be coming next, including some expert opinions, and a wrap-up that compares the methods and how they might best be applied.

Summary

In addition to giving you the preview in the section immediately above, we discussed a number of key considerations that will help all your analytical work, including text analytics, reach successful outcomes. You should keep these in mind of these before you start any investigation of data. First, though, we talked briefly about data vs information, followed by the difficulties we have in defining **big data** (except that it always seems to be more data than you can manage with whatever software and hardware you now have). Also we passed along the reassuring pointer that **you do not need to have big data** to do text analytics – the methods work on small, medium, large and monstrous data sets.

This was followed by a review of basics that still may get overlooked. Text analysis requires time, expense, and expertise that you must develop or hire. We discussed the importance of starting with **well-defined needs**, and **well-defined problems**. We talked about the importance of using **the simplest explanation** that covered all the facts.

This was followed by a review of ways you can know that what you have found is real and is important. We made a necessary visit to a subject that made many of us vow never to become statisticians, **statistical significance.** We also mention of its underappreciated counterpart, **statistical power**.

A substantial section of the chapter addressed the topic of choosing the right places to find text, or more formally **choosing sample frames**. This topic received some extra attention because it is quite tempting just to dig in, after seeing all the data out there – even though much of the text you find will lead you to erroneous conclusions. Even mountains of data can steer you down the wrong path, if it comes from individuals who do not represent your audience or the people who use your fine brand or institution. We asked you to recall, if ever so briefly, Alf Landon – who a sample of 2.4 million predicted would win the US presidency handily vs Franklin Roosevelt. This massive group of people happened to be the wrong ones to use as the basis for this conclusion, and the result was horrendously incorrect.

Finally, we stressed the fact that success in building strong models has come much more readily from text gathered in **controlled environments**, such as surveys and curated online communities. In these settings, the people involved at least needed to know something about the topic on which they express opinions – and we have the opportunity to ask important questions.

Now, onward to what you actually can do with text. We should have some fun along the way, and with luck there will be much that is both good and new.

References

Berners-Lee, T (2009) The next web, TED talks (February) [online] http://www.ted.com/talks/tim_berners_lee_on_the_next_web [accessed 11 February 2015]

'Big data' [accessed 11 February 2015] Definition, Wikipedia [online] http://en.wikipedia.org/wiki/Big_data

Biggs, D, DeVille, B and Suen, E (1991) A method of choosing multiway partitions for classification and decision trees, *Journal of Applied Statistics*, **18** (1), pp 49–62

Cohen, J (1988) *Statistical Power Analysis for the Behavioral Sciences*, 2nd edn, Erlbaum Publishers, Mahwah, NJ

DeTurck, D [accessed 11 February 2015] Case Study 1: The 1936 *Literary Digest* Poll, University of Pennsylvania [online] http://www.math.upenn.edu/~deturck/m170/wk4/lecture/case1.html

Espy, W R E (1978) *Thou Improper, Thou Uncommon Noun*, William N Potter, Inc, New York, NY

Floridi, L (2010) *Information – A Very Short Introduction*, Oxford University Press, Oxford

Gladwell, M (2009) Priced to sell, *The New Yorker*, 6 July 2009 [online] http://www.newyorker.com/magazine/2009/07/06/priced-to-sell?currentPage=1 [accessed 11 February 2015]

Hirsch, P (1980) The scary world of the non-viewer and other anomalies: A re-analysis of Gerbner *et al*'s findings on cultivation analysis, part 1, *Communication Research*, **7** (4), pp 403–56

Jessen, R J (1978) *Statistical Survey Techniques*, Wiley, Edison, NJ

Kish, L (1995) *Survey Sampling*, Wiley, Edison, NJ

McCullagh, P (2002) 'What is a statistical model?', *Annals of Statistics*, **30** (5), pp 1225–310

MIT Technology Review (2013) Undefined by data: a survey of big data definitions, Cornell University Library, 20 September 2013 [online] arxiv.org/abs/1309.5821 [accessed 11 February 2015]

Miner, G, Elder J, Hill, T, Nisbet, R, Delen, D and Fast, A (2012) *Practical Text Mining and Statistical Analysis for Non-structured Text Data Applications*, Academic Press, Waltham, MA

Oram, A (1998) The land mines of data mining, Praxagora, 1 September 1998 [online] http://www.praxagora.com [accessed 11 February 2015]

Sapsford, R and Jupp, V (2006) *Data Collection and Analysis*, Sage, New York

Shannon, C E and Weaver, W (1998) *The Mathematical Theory of Communication*, University of Illinois Press, Champaign Illinois

Shearer, C (2000) The CRISP-DM model: the new blueprint for data mining, *Journal of Data Warehousing*, **5** (4), pp 13–22

Stamper, L (2013) In spite of old, false Satanist accusations, P&G put a moon back into its new logo, *Business Insider*, 21 May 2013 [online] http://www.businessinsider.com/pg-puts-moon-in-new-logo-despite-satanist-accusations-2013-5?op=1#ixzz3KxnXxSAN [accessed 11 February 2015]

Struhl, S (2008) Data mining comes of age: overcoming the myths and misconceptions, Hospitality Net, 9 June 2008 [online] http://www.hospitalitynet.org/news/4036261.html [accessed 11 February 2015]

Smiley, G (2004) US Economy in the 1920s, *EH.Net Encyclopedia*, ed R Whaples [online] http://eh.net/encyclopedia/the-u-s-economy-in-the-1920s/ [accessed 11 February 2015]

Witten, I, Frank, E and Hall, A (2011) *Data Mining*, 3rd edn, Morgan Kaufmann, Burlington, MA

GETTING READY   02

Capturing, sorting, sifting, stemming and matching

KEY QUESTION

How do we get text ready for analysis?

This chapter discusses the key first steps in a text analytics project. As with any in-depth analysis, getting the data ready to use is critical. Here are some of the steps that need to be taken, and some software that can help greatly, or even do the dirty work for you. This section also introduces some of the key language that we (alas) must learn to understand what is happening as we prepare to do the analysis.

What we need to do with text

When you hear about unstructured data, it is very likely that text is actually being discussed. Perhaps the first thing we can say about **text** and **analytics** is that until roughly 1975 these words could not logically occur together in a sentence. Text does not follow any regular pattern amenable to being analysed using standard statistical methods.

That is, in text we may encounter organization by sentences and paragraphs, and even an overall outline and a progression of arguments, but these do not fall into the specific, neat slots that allow us to apply well-established analytical techniques. Anything we analyse using these methods must be broken down into discrete units, and ultimately fit into a space resembling a spreadsheet. Everything must be organized by rows and columns, with specific requirements for how the contents are divided and treated.

Before we get too far, let's divulge a secret: **text analytics** includes activities that involve little to no analytics. For instance, counting words gets lumped into **analytics**. Similarly, looking for words within some set distance from a word of interest (such as 'wellness' or 'illness', to pick two disparate examples) also gets included under the heading of analytics. So too does simply recognizing that a word is a name or belongs in some other specific category. These activities present computer programming challenges, but only in the realm of text do these become 'analytics'.

But then, text is difficult to analyse. The challenges we encounter with analysing text are summarized in Figure 2.1. There we see some actual verbatim text resembling comments you may encounter, and what must happen to these before we can approach the text with more advanced analytical methods. Free-form comments must be disassembled and split into elements in a form that can be treated numerically.

For each person, we have one row of data containing the words they used. (These words are in truncated form, as we will discuss in a moment.) Sentence structure, punctuation, and word groupings all are eliminated.

In a statistical analysis program, each row would be simply be called a row or perhaps a case. When dealing with text, each row typically represents a **document.** A **document** most commonly is just the comments from one person. Alternatively, a document could be a single review, or an entire book. Large or small, it is one block of text we want to examine as a unit. We could gather the comments of any number of people into a single document, but that is not usually done.

> A **document** most simply holds the comments made by one person or otherwise is a single collection of text. The **word vector** model captures the text in a document as a collection of words on a single row of a spreadsheet or other database, without reference to word order or syntax.

Reading down the columns at the bottom of Figure 2.1, we see whether the word was used by each person or not. A code of '1' means that the person used that word, and a blank means that he or she did not use that word. In statistical parlance, the columns of words are **variables**. As we look down each column, we can see that their presence and absence do indeed **vary** from one person (or row, or document) to the next – and that is what the term **variable** means.

The way we see the words represented in this figure sometimes is referred to as **word vectors**. (That is, a row is also considered a **vector** of words.) This terminology may be somewhat confusing – in normal parlance a vector might indicate a direction of forces, or something that carries a disease. With words, this takes another meaning from computer science: a one dimensional **array**. An **array** is simply a set of rows and columns, and in that array, each row (or column) is considered one dimension. The fact that each record is on one row makes this one dimensional.

You can see that the rows in Figure 2.1 are mostly empty spaces. We can think of a word vector as something like a long string of Christmas lights, where nearly all of the lights are off. Every possible word captured across all the documents goes into the length of the **word vectors** going across, but each document will contain relatively few words out of the total. In this example, people on average used only about five of the words captured in the vectors and never more than 22. There are dozens of key words (in truncated forms) represented, so all the rows or **vectors** are mostly unoccupied spots. (We will talk about limiting words and truncation shortly.)

Recall that treating words as vectors means that we are ignoring the order of the words and the meanings that they might take from the words around them. This may seem like a great deal to disregard, but in the more advanced forms of analysis, and in particular **predictive analytical methods**, the ways words are present (and absent) alone can give us a great

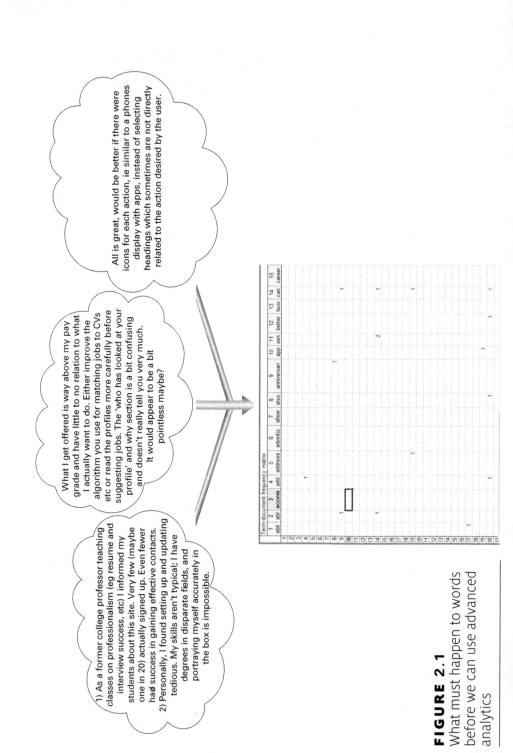

FIGURE 2.1
What must happen to words before we can use advanced analytics

deal of information, and allow us to build powerful models that can forecast or predict liking, preference and even behaviour.

Perhaps this is a good time to introduce a topic that we will review throughout this book. Most of what gets included in text analytics falls under the heading of **descriptive analysis**, rather than **predictive analysis**. The difference between these is critical.

Descriptive analytics methods show patterns of similarity, discuss what is near an item of interest, count how often something occurs, and give an overall view of patterns. They do not show you what influences an outcome and do not generate models that can forecast the value of some target variable. For instance, knowing that some word comes up frequently in connection with your product or service, even a word that intuitively seems negative, will not show you whether this word has any influence on use patterns or even on overall liking of your product. You will know that the word is there and that it may signal a problem, but that is where your knowledge stops.

> **Descriptive analytics** makes up a very large part of text analytics. These methods show broad patterns, count items, or shows what is near another item. This form of analytics does not show what influences an outcome and by how much. The business of **predictive analytics**, however, is doing just that – showing what leads to a change in some target variable, such as liking, preference or behaviour, and how strong those influences are likely to be.

Predictive analytical methods take the needed next step of showing whether we can see any influence on an outcome based on a specific comments, or coded comments (more on coding will follow). This type of model can be used to determine levels of influence and to forecast or predict changes in some target variable, such as liking, preference or sales.

There is considerable confusion about how much descriptive analytics can do. Even the most detailed description is just that, a description. It does not tell us what will happen if we can change one of the elements that we describe. And unfortunately, the act of looking and guessing, while sometimes the default method for decision-making, does not follow from an understanding of what is likely to change, and by how much.

Descriptive methods and the difficulties in dealing with text

Perhaps part of the confusion about descriptive methods (and their limitations) arises from the heavy computer programming that often goes into generating anything intelligible from text. Another part may arise from the incredible intricacy of some descriptions. (We will see some highly complex descriptive methods in Chapter 3.)

It remains difficult getting computer-based systems simply to recognize what is present in text. You may encounter the terms **information extraction** and **natural language processing** in connection with text analytics. These are the baseline activities required to get the information out of text and into some usable form, like translating the commentary at the top of Figure 2.1 into the tabular form at the bottom of the figure.

> **Natural language processing** and **information extraction** are terms you may encounter and are the baseline activities required to get text ready for analysis.

Back to terminology: cleaning up text

Perhaps one reason text analytics can seem so daunting is that it involves so much terminology. As the verbiage flies fast and furious, it is easy to feel as if you really understand very little – and that all this must be working at an almost mystical level.

There was indeed a time when much of this seemed like magic. But hardware and software have raced forward, and we now need concern ourselves mainly with understanding and applications – and of course, in not getting snowed under along the way.

IMAGE 2.1   The latest in computation is always changing

SOURCE: Babbage's Analytical Engine, 1834–71, uploaded 2013.
http://de.wikipedia.org/wiki/Analytical_Engine#mediaviewer/File:Babbages_Analytical_Engine,_
1834-1871._%289660574685%29.jpg. Wikimedia Commons. Modified by the author.

Programs need to do more than simply finding words. They must follow a
number of steps to make text analysable, including these:

- First, **stop words** (such as **the, of, and, a, to**, and so on) must be
  removed. These words do not contain any meanings that will help
  the analysis, and they can occur so frequently that that they swamp
  all the words that do have meaning.

- Next words must be made regular, by a process sometimes called
  stemming.

- Spelling errors need to be corrected using a dictionary. Plurals must
  be singularized. Idiomatic expressions need to be resolved. Tenses
  need to be made uniform so that the same word does not reappear
  many times with minor variations.

  - **Lemmatization** is a special type of stemming that regularizes
    words while trying to figure out their part of speech. How words
    get reduced to a stem may differ depending on how the words
    are used. For instance, the noun 'moped' should not be
    stemmed into the form 'mope', while the verb 'moped' should.

- With text that people have typed in themselves online, we will need to remove all the nonsensical or obviously non-useful comments, such as 'nothing' or 'what?' or 'no comment' or 'fjjfjfjfjfjfj', that we find appearing in commentary. Phrases such as these make up a surprisingly large percentage of online responses.

- Depending on the stemming program, we may also look for word pairs or larger groups of words (eg 'not good' or 'not bad' or 'South Gas Works'). We will discuss this process directly below.

- Programs may remove infrequent words. Some have a setting you can adjust to screen words based on how often they appear. For instance, the 100 or so words that made up the entire table excerpted in Figure 2.1 all appeared in at least 1 per cent of all individual documents. Eliminating infrequent words helps reduce the overall analytical burden considerably.

The words taken from a block of text sometimes are called **tokens**, and the process of identifying the words is sometimes called **tokenization**. **Named entity extraction** aims to overcome a problem in separating words by using blank spaces. For instance, an expression such as 'Mr Sand' contains two tokens ('Mr' and 'Sand'), and the computer must recognize that they belong together to identify the poor fellow as a person. Similarly, 'the Hill Corporation' either has three tokens that belong together ('the', 'Hill' and 'Corporation') or two tokens that require attention and one item ('the') that we can ignore as a **stop word.**

> **Tokens** are the words taken from a block of text once it has been cleaned. This process is sometimes called **tokenization. Entity extraction** means identifying a set or group of words so that the computer understands they have a single meaning. It often is used to identify people or organizations.

Named entity extraction is done with a special **dictionary or lexicon** that is applied to the text being analysed. The software recognizes phrases in the dictionary as single items. This is a step that not all text analytics software takes. Some more expensive programs, such as SAS Text Miner and SPSS Text Analytics recognize phrases as well as single words. (SAS and SPSS are well-established programs that are very well known to data analysts and statisticians of all stripes. The acronyms mean something but the programs have long been referred to solely by their initials.) The free programs Apache NLP (Natural Language Processing) and RapidMiner can do this as well. The SPSS program, which we will discuss more fully, also encodes text, grouping comments by topic heading.

Ways of corralling words

Once we have words cleaned and prepared, we need some further way of reducing them so they can be analysed and compared. When we deal with a large number of documents, even after cleaning the text as described, we typically still have too many words to fit into most analytical methods. A useable predictive model rarely contains more than 70 to 80 variables, and even descriptive models will become incomprehensible if we include much more than a hundred. There are several other ways to manage words so that they become more usable in addition to removing less commonly used words. We will be discussing three of these: sliding windows, automated coding and the factor analysis of words.

Sliding windows

A **sliding window** (or as it is sometimes called, an **n-gram window**), gives us one way to address the question of which words occur together other than named entity extraction. Think of the sliding window as a box that is a certain length (say seven words) that moves through the text, one word at a time, and which keeps a count of how many times words fall together in that moving box.

An approach like this would be useful for analysing a collection of documents, and looking for the strongest themes expressed across this set. (This might be useful in looking at a single document if it was very long, say a long blog post or article. Some published examples even use an entire book as one document.)

Figure 2.2 represents how a sliding window moves through text (the box is displaced vertically so you get a better sense of how it progresses). It would continue on this path until it reached the end of the block of text. As it moves, it keeps count of how many times words fall together in the box.

FIGURE 2.2   Two steps of a sliding n-gram window on text that has been cleaned

former college professor teach class professional resume interview success inform student site few actual sign fewer success gain effective contact personal find set update tedious skill aren't typical degree disparate field portray accurate box impossible

Sliding windows can be different lengths, and changing the size of the window may change the results you get. If you pick a larger window, words will occur together more often. Longer windows tend to pick up phrases that are more like regular writing, so could be better for more lengthy comments. (No definite rules exist for choosing the length of a window. More words will get flagged as belonging together in a longer window. Therefore a longer window could help find patterns of similarity that appear sparse with shorter windows. Windows from six to 11 words long seem to work well with most text.)

The first output from this window is in fact a spreadsheet-like table. Both the rows and the columns of this table are defined by the words that were used. Each box (or cell) in the table shows how often the words occurred together across all the documents. This is sometimes called a **similarities matrix.** Figure 2.3 shows a similarities matrix with counts of how often words occur together across a few documents. The bottom triangle in the table is blank because it would duplicate the information in the top triangle – for instance, we know how often 'also' occurs along with 'able' and do not need to see this repeated as how often 'able' occurs along with 'also'.

With a sliding window, the text takes a roundabout route to a table, but finally appears in one. This table in turn can lead to other, still more compact forms of data representation. Use of sliding windows is a key part of generating the pictorial representations you can find in Chapter 3.

Automated coding

For many years, if we wanted to understand the themes in text, **hand coding** was the best method available. That is, a person or people sat with the documents and developed a coding scheme, aiming to capture

FIGURE 2.3   Similarities matrix showing how often words occur together

	able	also	benefit	best	busi	can	career	colleague	connect	contact
able		1	2	0	4	0	3	0	0	1
also			0	0	1	0	1	0	1	0
benefit				0	5	1	6	0	5	2
best					1	3	1	0	1	3
busi						1	4	2	4	4
can							1	2	3	1
career								1	5	5
colleague									2	2
connect										5
contact										

the underlying ideas in the text. Documents were then encoded, these codes were attached to the documents, and the number of times a code occurred was counted among a total sample and various groups.

More specific codes could be gathered into a larger umbrella code. For instance, negative comments about software and negative comments about hardware could be gathered or **netted** into a larger code capturing **all** negative comments.

Even for a survey having a few hundred responses, this could grow into a time-consuming and expensive process. With many thousands of

IMAGE 2.2   People once used these for hand coding

SOURCE: Hand-operated card punch (manufacturer: ICT), uploaded 2009 by 'Jkbw'.
http://commons.wikimedia.org/wiki/File:Hand-operated_Card_Punch-2.jpg.

responses, this could became too costly to be practical except with the largest budgets. As you might expect, interest in automating this process has existed for many years.

The encoding of text went through an intermediary phase, where a person needed to set up the coding scheme using perhaps 100 to 200 documents, and then the computer could take over, applying those rules to many thousands of documents in a short time.

Finally, we are close to seeing machines able to do coding unsupervised. Several programs can make substantial headway without any instruction. One remarkable program that can do this is SPSS Text Analytics. (This is a stand-alone program, not the regular SPSS that we discuss later, which does traditional statistical analysis. Also, this is not an endorsement, but just a program that your author has seen in action and that has produced some strong results. You are best served by reading online comparisons, testing those programs that have trial versions, seeking other users for advice, and selecting the one program most suited to your particular needs.)

In our example, we gave SPSS Text Analytics over 3,900 verbatim comments provided by users on the web, most showing indifference to grammar, spelling, punctuation and sentence structure. It analysed the text and returned a list of over 300 codes, including main codes and sub-codes.

A truncated list of some of these codes appears in Figure 2.4. These codes could be appended to the data file from which the raw text responses came. To understand how this would work, each of the individual items within, for instance, section 5.5 would be assigned a 'yes' or '1' in a column corresponding to code 5.5 in the data file. Similarly, each of the items within section 5.16 would get assigned a 'yes' or '1' in a column corresponding to that code.

All of the items shown would also get a 'yes' (or '1') for code 5 (the broader heading 'people'). The items that appear just in section 5 (such as '_random people') would get **only** a code 5. Any other items would get both a code 5 and the sub-code of the section into which they fall.

In this small example, we can see a remarkable combination of ability to discriminate and to combine. We can call this artificial intelligence without straining the term. Still, no matter how powerful the software, you will want to check what it has done carefully, and in all likelihood will at least make some adjustments.

FIGURE 2.4   Some automatically generated codes

5 people
_random people
_people to use
_liberties of some people
_anonymous people
_people from different areas
_check people
_times people
_people to enter
_quality of the people
_encourage people
_block people
_people's profile
_communication from people
_notices from people
_employee people
_people troll to connect
_academic people
5.5 people to connect
_people to connect I connecting with people
_service to connect people
_opportunity to connect with people
_connecting to people in field
_connect to other like-minded people
_help people connect
5.16 contact people
_barriers to contacting people
_contact base of people
_contact particularly people
_contact people
5.2 requests from people
_requests to link to people
_requests from people
_linkedin request from people
_request from sales people
5.1 meet people
_site to meet peope
_meet people I meeting people
_employees to meeting people
_meeting people from a variety

This program also allows you to change the coding scheme. It even includes **sentiment analysis** as an extra ingredient. **Sentiment analysis** may be one of the best-known activities related to text, and we will discuss this in Chapter 5.

Encoding with or without sentiment provides several strong benefits. It allows you to determine the actual meanings revealed by groups of words, and to see how ideas are expressed in different ways. You can isolate key ideas as codes and use these for further analysis, including in predictive analyses, as we will show in later chapters.

Factor analysis: introducing our first analytical method

Yet another method exists for reducing the number of words in a set of documents to a more manageable level. This is the statistical method called **factor analysis.** Factor analysis originally was developed (over 100 years ago) because responses to questions on intelligence tests seemed highly related. The factors teased out the ways responses were similar. The first theories about intelligence were in fact based on factor analysis. This method also has been used to develop and refine psycho-logical scales for many years.

An important practical use of factor analysis is finding common underly-ing **ideas or themes** in a set of scaled questions. This type of application is where some of you may have encountered this method. That is, sup-pose we have asked people 20 to 30 questions on a variety of topics. We can use factor analysis to develop a small number of **factors** that group the questions, capturing the basic ideas that each group of questions have in common.

> **Factors analysis** finds communalities in questions or other items, including the way text appears in documents. **Factors** can capture groups of questions that reflect some underlying idea, or groups of words that tend to appear together.

This may seem abstract, so let's look at a list of questions and the way in which we grouped them. Once we discuss this, we will show how this method applies to text. This example using scaled questions comes from a study about an insurance product.

One important point, which we will discuss later, is that we decided on the right number of factors and that we came up with the names. There

FIGURE 2.5 A factor solution with names for the factors and factor loadings

	Factor and loadings			
	1	2	3	4
Factor 1: care, concern and trust				
This product is a way companies show how much they value employees	.792			
Is a company that employers can trust	.665			
Is a socially responsible company	.659			
Offers online solutions for managing benefits	.640			
Is compassionate and respectful when working with employee	.549			
Is forward thinking	.513			
Factor 2: market leadership				
A market leader in supplemental coverages		.767		
Offers a broad range of employee benefits products		.762		
A market leader the employee benefit industry		.716		
Is financially strong		.703		
Offers innovative employee benefit products/solutions		.655		
Has a positive corporate reputation		.548		
Can be trusted to do the right thing		.542		
Factor 3: employer service focused (easy to do business with)				
			.746	
			.745	
			.729	
			.577	
Factor 4: employee-focused				
Offers face-to-face benefits counselling for your employees				.825
Is a leader in helping employees understand their benefits				.622
Is a leader in providing financial protection benefits				.602
Delivers superior customer service to your employees				.546

are 26 question items in total, and these were gathered into four groupings or factors. Figure 2.5 shows the items that went into each factor. You can see that each set does in fact relate to a broad concern or theme. We have put names on the factors which aim to represent the meaning of each theme.

The numbers in Figure 2.5, or the loadings, show us how closely each variable is related to the factor in which it falls. Loadings can range from zero to one. These are all over 0.5 and so are considered as strong loadings in their respective factors.

To make the chart easier to read, we have suppressed all the small loadings. Otherwise, there would be numbers in all spots on the chart, because individual variables will always have some loading in the factors other than the one to which they clearly belong. These are called **off-loadings**. The presence of a lot of strong off loadings suggest you may need to try again with another factor solution that allows more factors. The idea of choosing a solution may seem strange – but indeed you need to do this with factors. We will talk more about this once we clear up some terminology.

One word you may encounter in connection with figuring out the right number of factors is **eigenvalue**. You should at least be prepared in case somebody starts throwing this term around. It sounds very complex but it simply reflects the strength or size of a factor. Not all factors are equal, and a factor will be **stronger** when it picks up or explains more of the pattern of responses (or variance) for all the questions. A stronger factor will have a large eigenvalue.

You should not feel overwhelmed if analytical type says something like, 'We used an eigenvalue cutoff of 1 to determine the number of factors.' They may do so because it is the default behaviour for many statistics programs (meaning the program will do this unless you tell it otherwise). However, this value of 1.0 has **no statistical basis** for being chosen. It is just a convention that somehow got established without much justification.

Perhaps some people follow arbitrary rules because it can feel dis-comforting that factor analysis is a statistical method, and yet there is no ironclad way to know if you have chosen the best answer. Over 100 years of testing has not revealed a clear mathematical 'best', and so we can feel fairly confident that your judgment must be the final arbiter of what makes a good solution.

The **eigenvalues** of factors and measures of **total variance explained** by the factors are mechanical means for deciding on the number of factors you should elect to have. The scree plot is a graph that also provides a computer-driven means for reaching this decision. While some follow these strictly, and they may provide some preliminary guidance, your judgment in evaluating what goes into each factor should be the primary guide.

These are a few clues about whether you have settled on a good solution. If you choose to have too few factors, items will get crowded and you will see questions with no clear relationship being assigned to the same factor. You may also see a lot of large off-loadings, or places where items appear strongly associated with two or more factors. On the other hand, if you choose to have too many factors, you will see factors that are just small groupings of items – and you may even see quite a few factors that contain just one or two items.

Trying to come up with **short descriptive name** for the factors is an excellent way to determine if you have too many or too few. There should be a common theme to all the items that are grouped together. Looking at the names we developed for the factors in Figure 2.5, you can see that each of the items in the factor does in fact reflect something about the idea captured in the factor's name.

Two other more or less mechanical ways of deciding on the number of factors exist. One is called the **scree plot**. The other is a measure called **total variance explained** by the number of factors. Let's get into those with our text example, directly below.

Text in factors: an example

Our example comes from a large survey done among users of a social media site. Users were given a number of scaled questions and were asked to explain some of their overall ratings in their own words. (Three actual quotes from this survey appear in Figure 2.1 – there were over 3,900 comments like these altogether.)

Factors derived from text will have a somewhat different meaning from the factors that come from scaled questions. With text, the words that get grouped together are words that tend to appear with each other across all documents. These words should ideally refer to a common meaning, but may simply tend to occur together.

The first step in simplification came after words were cleaned, with corrections of misspellings, removal of punctuation and stop words, and stemming. Only words that appear in more than 1 per cent of the docu- ments were allowed into the analysis. This brought us down to some 112 different stemmed words. The program doing the stemming is Statistica. This is a comprehensive full-price program that does statistical analysis and text mining.

Figure 2.6 shows us a small corner of the data file containing the cleaned words. This is from SPSS, where we substituted zeros for the empty cells we saw in Figure 2.1. (SPSS is one of the oldest and comprehensive statistical programs – and along with SAS, one that you are highly likely to encounter in traditional statistical analyses.) You can

FIGURE 2.6   A small portion of a dataset containing cleaned text

	able	also	benefit	best	busi	can	career
1	0	0	0	0	0	0	0
2	0	0	0	0	0	0	0
3	0	0	0	0	0	0	0
4	0	0	0	0	1	0	0
5	0	0	0	0	0	0	0
6	0	0	0	0	0	0	1
7	0	0	0	0	1	0	0
8	0	1	0	0	0	0	0
9	0	0	0	0	0	0	0
10	0	0	0	0	0	0	0
11	0	0	0	0	0	0	0
12	0	0	0	0	0	0	0
13	0	0	0	0	0	0	0
14	0	0	0	0	0	0	0
15	0	1	0	0	0	0	0
16	0	0	0	0	0	0	0
17	0	0	0	1	0	1	0
18	0	0	0	0	1	0	0
19	0	0	0	0	0	0	0
20	0	0	0	0	0	0	0

see that the stemming routine cut back a great deal on one word, with the various forms of 'business' becoming 'busi'. The figure shows the first 20 rows or records, each corresponding to the comments by one person. The '1' values, meaning that the person used that word, remain from Figure 2.1. There are not too many of these '1' values. As we pointed out earlier, each person used relatively few of these words.

In theory, a grid containing just 1 and zero values like this should not work well in factor analysis. So one of the first steps we will take is to run a check of the suitability of this data to be reduced to factors. This is called the KMO test, and for statistics at least, it is somewhat humorous.

Values for the KMO run according to the formula in the table below. In SPSS, for instance, asking for this measure is as simple as checking a box saying that it should be included.

Our KMO value for this data set was 0.70, or just enough to be middling – but certainly well above the 'don't factor' level. So we can feel confident about going ahead with the analysis.

We also looked at the two mechanical means of screening that we discussed earlier. The first, the **scree plot**, shows the eigenvalue of each factor that might consider including in the final set. In this plot, we are supposed to look for the place where the lines in the plot start to flatten. If you are a skier, you will recognize scree as the place where the snow in the mountain flattens out – and that is what this chart looked like to its inventor. (Who said there is no adventure in statistics?)

TABLE 2.1   Meaning of KMO values

KMO value	Meaning
0.90 to 1.00	Marvellous
0.80 to 0.89	Meritorious
0.70 to 0.79	Middling
0.60 to 0.69	Mediocre
0.50 to 0.59	Miserable
0.00 to 0.49	Don't

The second measure, the **per cent of variance explained**, represents how much of the total pattern of scores we capture as we add more factors. That is, because there are fewer factors than actual questions, the factors lose some of the information present in the entire data set. We trade the loss of some information against the gain in being able to find common themes and in having fewer items to consider. This is a worthwhile trade with text because we typically start with too many items to study in most analytical methods. Finding the ones that are most important or most representative of the data should help us understand meaningful patterns.

Figure 2.7 shows these two diagnostic measures. The scree plot to the left shows that we could have had as many as 83 factors, nearly one factor per item. Also, you can see that there really is not a clear point at which the curve drops off sharply. (This output is a slightly simplified version of the output from the statistics program SPSS.)

In this case, we chose to override the mechanical defaults. You will notice the total variance explained chart shows the eigenvalue of each factor. For the eighteenth factor, where we decided this was enough, this is still well over the default cutoff of 1.0. In fact, if we were to keep adding factors until we reached one that weighed in at 1.0, we would have been left with some 55 factors. Looking at the number of words that appear in the first few factors when we stopped at 18, we can see that these factors already are somewhat sparse, with just a few variables loading into each. ('Component', by the way, is essentially another term for factor. There are

FIGURE 2.7 Diagnostic measures that may help find a factor solution

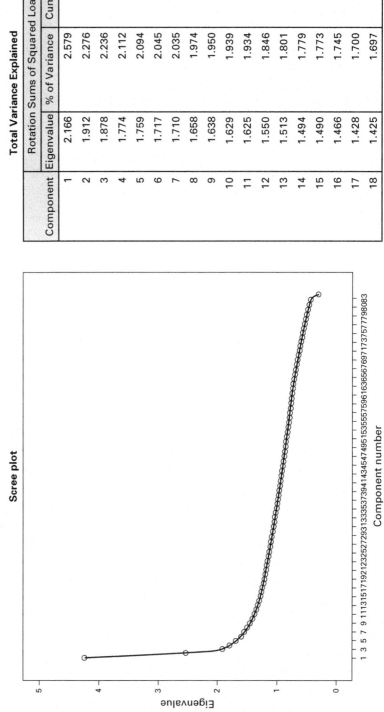

Scree plot

Total Variance Explained

| Component | Rotation Sums of Squared Loadings | | |
	Eigenvalue	% of Variance	Cumulative %
1	2.166	2.579	2.579
2	1.912	2.276	4.855
3	1.878	2.236	7.091
4	1.774	2.112	9.203
5	1.759	2.094	11.297
6	1.717	2.045	13.341
7	1.710	2.035	15.376
8	1.658	1.974	17.350
9	1.638	1.950	19.300
10	1.629	1.939	21.239
11	1.625	1.934	23.174
12	1.550	1.846	25.019
13	1.513	1.801	26.821
14	1.494	1.779	28.600
15	1.490	1.773	30.373
16	1.466	1.745	32.118
17	1.428	1.700	33.819
18	1.425	1.697	35.515

FIGURE 2.8 The first seven factors found

	Component						
	1	2	3	4	5	6	7
don't	.685						
much	.655						
use	.575						
really	.461						
media		.895					
socila		.884					
touch			.805				
keep			.729				
colleague							
email				.645			
get				.415			
recommend					.748		
would					.650		
friend					.431		
job						.766	
search						.718	
industries							.659
place							.422

some tiny technical differences between components and factors – but practically, these terms are interchangeable.) Adding more factors would have spread the variables out further, leading to very few in each factor.

Before we get to Figure 2.8, the chart showing the words in the first few factors, we also should consider the total variance explained. If we were look-ing at a set of questions and hoping to capture the key ideas in the factors, then coming up with factors that explained only 35 per cent of variance (or pattern in scores across the whole data set) would be quite disappointing. With words, this may not be such a bad thing. It will at least allow us to focus in on the most important groups of words that tend to occur together.

Meanings and uses of the factor analysed words

The factors in Figure 2.8 represent the most important ideas and group-ings appearing in the many words offered by the 3,900 people giving their opinions. We can see that the top of this list is the word group 'don't really use much', which is self-explanatory, and not a positive. The next grouping appears more neutral (social and media), while the third appears more positive (we can sort this to 'keep touch colleague'). You may have noticed that 'colleague' does not have a loading listed – this is because the value is under 0.40, or relatively weak. The word belongs in this group more than the others but the connection is not that strong.

These factors generate **scores** for each person. A **factor score** is a weighted composite of the items in the factor, and a document's score for a given factor would reflect how strongly the commentary in that document reflected that factor's idea or theme. These scores are **standardized** or rescaled in such a way that the average score across all documents is set to zero and so that two-thirds of the scores fall between +1 and −1. (This helps in interpretation if factors include items with different scales, and so is done by default.) We can use those individual scores just like any other variables. Factors work well in most predictive analytic methods. We will see the factor scores we just described used in this way in a regression in Chapter 6.

Summary

Before we can do anything analytical with text, we must change it from basically unstructured to structured data. Analytical methods expect data to appear in a format that is in neat columns and rows, something like a spreadsheet, with discrete items in each cell. Getting text into a form that can be analysed remains difficult. This may be one reason that a surprising number of activities called text analytics have little or no analysis in them. For instance, counting words, or finding which words are close to some word you are interested in, or even whether a word is a name or some other part of speech, all fall under the heading of 'text analytics'.

Text can be analysed either in a descriptive model or predictive model. These are very different and understanding the distinction is critical. **Descriptive models** show overall patterns, count items, show similarities, and find words that tend to appear with each other. Descriptive models can involve very difficult programming and can grow highly intricate. Seeing all that complexity, we might forget that these models are in fact just descriptions. They do not tell us what is likely to happen to some variable of interest if we change other ones. Rather it is **predictive modelling** that shows us what is likely to influence a target variable, such ratings, or intent to use, or time spent at a website, or purchasing behaviour – and how strong that influence is likely to be.

Descriptive models often provide an excellent foundation on which predictive models can build. These approaches are strongly complementary,

IMAGE 2.3
We should all take a deep
breath and stay calm

SOURCE: Mujer con abanico y manto. Carboncillo, tinta y lápiz, original done before 1916, uploaded 2009 by Poniol60.
http://upload.wikimedia.org/wikipedia/commons/3/35/Mujer_con_abanico_y_manto_-_Ulpiano_Checa.JPG.

working together to provide excellent guidance on how to get to a desired outcome. Neither substitutes for the other, though. Descriptive models, even the most elegant, leave us to look and guess about what might happen. Predictive models without a sound basic understanding can fail completely by searching in the wrong places or by trying to resolve unimportant problems.

You will encounter a lot of new terminology when dealing with processing text. The sheer number of terms can seem daunting, especially when an analytical type is throwing them around with abandon. The basic ideas are not difficult, though.

The units of text that we want to analyse sometimes are called **tokens.** The process of finding those units is sometimes called **tokenization**. In English, a blank space between words typically marks the boundary between tokens, but not always. Sometimes two or three word phrases must be considered as a single unit, for instance, the name of a person or a corporation.

Recognizing phrases as a single unit when needed, or even recognizing the category of thing in which a word belongs, is called **named entity extraction**. **Named entity extraction** uses a special dictionary or **lexicon** to identify any named entity as a single unit, or as a specific type of word.

A collection of words that we analyse as a single unit is referred to as a **document**. Most often a document is represented as a single line in a spreadsheet-like space. The row is the document and the columns are the words in the documents. The spreadsheet must hold every word being considered in many documents, with a code showing whether the word was present in a specific document. Most rows therefore are largely empty spaces, with the blanks indicating that the particular word was not present in that specific document. This model is called the **word vector model**, and just shows whether a word was used anywhere in a particular document, without regard to word order or the presence of other words that might be nearby.

Not all words get into the spreadsheet. Frequent words that carry no real meaning, such as 'a', 'the', 'and', 'although' and so on, are removed. These are called **stop words**.

Words also must be regularized, with misspellings corrected, punctuation removed, and tenses of verbs made the same. This process is called **stemming**. A more advanced form of stemming, called **lemmatization**, tries to determine each word's part of speech, because this can make a difference in how the word gets treated. The word 'moped', for instance, would be stemmed back to 'mope' if a verb, but left as is if a noun.

Some programs also eliminate words that do not appear often. For instance, we saw an application which included only words mentioned in more than 1 per cent of all documents. Restricting the number of words is a very good idea, because most modelling methods break down if you have too many items. It is rare to see a predictive model with more than 80 variables.

A number of methods to get words into more manageable form have been developed. We discussed three of these. The first, the **sliding window**, or **sliding n-gram window,** is like a box of fixed length (say six words long) that slides across text that has been cleaned for processing. Sliding windows count how often words occur together in the box as it moves through the document, and so are particularly valuable for finding patterns of similarity and association among words. The sliding n-gram window leads to all the pictorial representations of patterns in words that we find in Chapter 3.

Automated coding, another method of making text more manageable, has made tremendous progress in recent years. Now computers can break text down into meaningful groupings, encoding documents by the meanings of words and phrases. The program we highlighted actually was able to develop an intricate system of codes and sub-codes, with broader ideas holding more specific ones. It is not stretching terminology to call this real artificial intelligence. Smart as the computer is, though, even here you will want to check, and most likely will find some things that need adjustment.

The last method we discussed, **factor analysis**, groups words based on how they were used across documents. Words that go into a factor tend to reflect a common theme, although at times they can simply be words that occur together. Factor analysis, like automated coding, needs words to be cleaned according to the basic procedures we discussed.

Factor analysis requires you to figure out the best possible way to group words. There are some mechanical cutoffs designed to help you decide on how many factors you will want to form, but none of these is ironclad, and your judgment about what makes sense should be the final arbiter in deciding what works most effectively. You also are responsible for naming each factor based on the idea that the various words gathered in that factor seem to represent. Seeing whether you can find simple names for the factors is an excellent test for deciding whether the solution makes sense. The variables that are strongest in the factors (that have the strongest loadings) ideally should all refer to a single underlying concept.

Factor analysis creates **factor scores,** which can be used just like other variables in a predictive model. Factor scores show how strongly a given document reflects the idea represented by the factors. We will demonstrate how the factor scores described in this chapter work in a regression model, alongside scaled measurements, in Chapter 6.

References

Brogden, H E (1971) Further comments on the interpretation of factors, *Psychological Bulletin*, **75**, pp 362–63.

Eysenck, H J (1952) The uses and abuses of factor analysis, *Applied Statistics*, **1**, pp 45–49.

Green, P E and Carroll, J (1978) *Analyzing Multivariate Data*, Dryden Press, Hinsdale, IL

Harman, H H (1976) *Modern Factor Analysis*, University of Chicago Press, Chicago, pp 175, 176

Jackson, P and Mouliner, I (2007) *Natural Language Processing for Online Applications*, John Benjamins Publishing, Philadelphia, PA

Jurafsky, D (2009) *Speech and Language Processing*, 2nd edn, Pearson, NJ

Manning, C D and Schutze, H (2002) *Foundations of Statistical Natural Language Processing*, 5th edn, MIT Press, Cambridge, MA

McNemar, Q (1942) On the number of factors, *Psychometrika*, **7**, pp 9–18

Mitkov, R (2009) *The Oxford Handbook of Computational Linguistics*, Oxford University Press, Oxford

Nisbet, R, Elder, J and Miner, G (2009) *Handbook of Statistical Analysis and Data Mining Applications*, Academic Press, Boston, MA

Spearman, C (1904) 'General intelligence', objectively determined and measured, *American Journal of Psychology*, **15**, pp 201–93

Stewart, D W (1981) The application and misapplication of factor analysis in marketing research, *Journal of Marketing Research*, **XVIII**, pp 51–62

Thurstone, L L (1935) *Vectors of the Mind*, University of Chicago Press, Chicago, IL

Thurstone, L L (1947) *Multiple Factor Analysis*, University of Chicago Press, Chicago, IL

Velicer, W F (1976) Determining the number of components from the matrix of partial correlations, *Psychometrika*, **41**, pp 321–27

Weiss, S M, Indurkhya, N and Zhang, T (2010) *Fundamentals of Predictive Text Mining*, Springer, New York

Wilkinson, L, Blank, G and Gruber, C (1995) *Desktop Data Analysis with Systat*, SPSS Inc, Chicago, IL

IN PICTURES   03

Word clouds, wordles and beyond

KEY QUESTION

What are ways in which pictures can reveal the meaning of words?

The (moderately) famous wordle, or picture of words of different sizes piled on top of each other, is just the beginning of what you can do to display relationships in text. Examples of powerfully revealing diagrams will include word treemaps, word clouds, putting covers around word clouds, graph layouts of words and heat maps. These names will becomes clearer as we go through the chapter.

Getting words into a picture

The pictures or diagrams we talk about in this chapter nearly all come from statistical analyses which find patterns of similarities.

As a reminder, nearly all statistical analyses need the data in the form of a table – that is, a set of rows and columns. Text obviously does not look anything like that, so we will need to convert it to make it amenable to analysis.

IMAGE 3.1   Not our type of stop

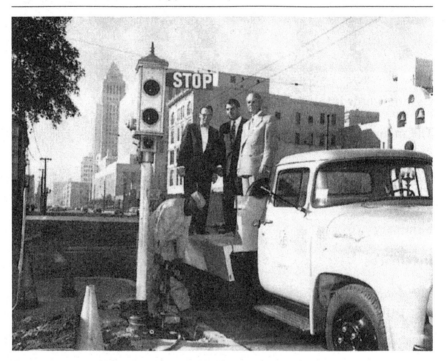

SOURCE: San Francisco traffic signal, circa 1935, author unknown.
http://corotates24.rssing.com/chan-12925746/all_p1.html.

There are several steps to this. First, we must clean up the text as we discussed in Chapter 2. As a reminder, we will follow several steps:

- First, **stop words** (such as **the, of, and, a, to**, and so on) must be removed. These words do not contain any meanings that will help the analysis, and they can occur so frequently that that they swamp all the words that do have meaning.

- Next words must be made regular, by a process sometimes called **stemming.** Spelling errors need to be corrected using a dictionary. Plurals must be singularized. Idiomatic expressions need to be resolved. Tenses need to be made uniform so that the same word does not reappear many times with minor variations.

- Depending on the stemming program, we may also look for word pairs (eg 'not good' or 'not bad').

- With text that people have typed in themselves online, we will need to remove all the nonsensical or obviously non-useful comments, such as 'nothing' or 'what?' or 'no comment' or 'xkxkxkxkxkx', that we find appearing in commentary that people provide. Phrases such as these make up a surprisingly large percentage of online responses.

The raw text becomes something usable. Then we can begin to analyse what we have.

The process that gets words into the stemming routines uses the **sliding window (or n-gram window)** that we discussed in Chapter 2. Think of this a box that is a certain length (say six words) that moves through the text, one word at a time, and which keeps a count of how many times words fall together in that moving box. You also can think of it as counting how often words occur within a few words of each other.

Sliding windows can be different lengths, and the size of the window may change the results you get. If you pick a larger window, words will occur together more often. Longer windows tend to pick up phrases that are more like regular writing, so could be better for more lengthy comments.

The many types of pictures and their uses

We will be discussing eight different types of pictures that can be made to show the relationships among words. One question that arises from this is: 'Which of these works best for a given problem or situation?' The simple answer is that only examination of many will tell which one works best. Each picture provides different shades of meaning, and we need to look at a good number of them to discern which one does the best at conveying the subtle patterns found in text-based data.

Fortunately, the programs that can perform these kinds of visualizations typically offer at least a half dozen alternatives. This allows you to weigh and compare, finding the one or ones that best convey the information your audiences need.

What exactly is a wordle?

A wordle is perhaps the most well-known single form of output from text. Basically, this amounts to words stacked into a box or some other shape, with the largest words being the most prevalent.

The wordle in Figure 3.1 comes from a research study of insurers done among professionals who administer insurance plans, summarizing the comments they typed in (online) about their concerns. (This will be our case study throughout this chapter.) This free online version simply arranges words, although others may be more advanced. Stemming routines in this

FIGURE 3.1   A wordle

free version are rudimentary. (You can see that the free program running the wordle was fooled by a plural, listing 'patients' in very large letters with 'patient' to the right in somewhat smaller letters.)

Nonetheless, you can see that **patients** and **providers** are very important topics. In making this diagram, not wanting to take any chances, we took care of the stop words such as 'a', 'the' and 'and' by the simple process of removing them before the text was processed. This ensured having a clearer wordle. You can get results like this by typing 'wordle' into your browser and uploading a simple text file to the make-your-own-wordle page.

Wordles simply count words. The way the words are arranged does not have anything to do with how the words relate to each other, but rather just reflects their frequency. We will go next to a set of methods that do more than this, but first, we need to explain another multivariate method, **clustering.**

Clustering words

To do more the complex analyses, we need to see how words relate to each other. The principal method we will use is **clustering. Clustering** finds patterns of similarities among people or objects. It seeks to create groups in which every member is very similar to all the other members of its own group – and at the same time, very different from the members of all other groups.

> **Clustering** comprises a set of methods that group words based on how similar they are to each other. It underlies many of the more advanced methods of putting words into pictures.

Those of you having experience with market research will recognize clustering as a critical early step in a segmentation study. The notion of clustering people may therefore be familiar – and if not, at least intuitive. When we think of what people do and how they consider the world, we can see many individuals falling naturally into groups.

For instance, considering food, we can find a clearly defined group of people who care a lot about nutrition, read ingredient labels, and eat a lot of natural foods. We can find another clearly defined group that eats just about anything at any time. Then we can find another group that wants to eat better and does at times, but not much of the time. We unfortunately can find another group that cannot afford to eat well. And so on.

If we asked people a lot of questions about their eating habits and preferences, we could then put them into groups like these based on their responses to the questions. Clustering is the pre-eminent method to do that.

Looking at words, though, all we have is how frequently words occur near each other in a block of text. We need to go beyond the wordle above to answer the question of how words are related, and which words are most closely related, or most similar.

What is similar and how can we tell?

As it turns out, the concept of **similarity** is quite elusive. Many mathematical definitions have been proposed, and most of those have found their way into a method for creating groups or clusters. There are enough different clustering routines to give us serious pause, especially since results from one method may disagree with another about how to form groups more often than not.

IMAGE 3.2
Mule's head or umbrellas? Apparent patterns can be deceiving

SOURCE: Society Portrait, vintage postcard circa 1900, George Watherspoon, publisher unknown.

This gives rise to many deep questions about which methods work best, and indeed what is a real pattern and not. In spite of many years' research into these questions, we only can get part of the way to answering them. We must finally realize that clustering does not give an ultimate answer about how to make groups. However, it can provide very valuable guidance by revealing strong patterns in the data, in spite of that limitation.

The two types or classes of clustering most commonly used are the **hierarchical methods** and the **K-means or iterative K-means methods.** The many hierarchical methods take one pass at the data and find what they consider to be the best structure, based on their criteria for what is 'best'. K-means takes a preliminary pass through the data, then goes back and checks to find if it can do better, and then does this again at least several times – hence the term **iterative.** This might make K-means seem like the automatic best choice, and in fact it often performs quite well when we are dealing with data concerning behaviours and opinions. However, the hierarchical methods produce a type of display that you will find very useful dealing with words.

This is a kind of tree-like structure showing which words are most closely related to each other, known as a **dendrogram** (Latinate for 'tree diagram'). It is sometimes called an agglomeration diagram.

In the very small diagram in Figure 3.2a, we have used the expedient of numbering the words. The similarity of the words is shown first by their locations (words close together usually go together) and more importantly, by the length of the lines bridging them. Longer lines mean less similarity.

FIGURE 3.2a   A dendrogram or tree diagram of how words are similar

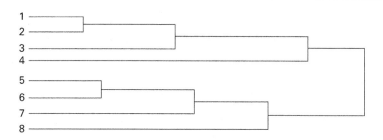

We can see, for instance, that there are two larger groups:

- The first group: words 1 to 4;
- The second group: words 5 to 8.

Within the first group, words 1 and 2 are most similar, and words 1 and 4 are least similar. In the second group, words 5 and 6 are most similar, while words 5 and 8 are least similar.

Given the very long line bridging the first group (words 1 to 4) and the second group (words 5 to 8), we can conclude that these two groups are dissimilar. We can say that each set is a **cluster** of words, that is, a group where the words are similar to each other and not similar to members of the other group.

To show word clusters in action we will discuss output from a remarkable program called **Advisor**, from **Skytree Software.** The larger text-mining packages (such as SAS, IBM and Statistica) can produce many of the same images. **Advisor** is unique in the large amount of explanation it offers along with the diagrams. It also has the advantage of being intuitively easy to use, once you get acclimated to its very sparse user interface. Basically, you load a text file, select a number of options from a spare screen display, and click 'go'.

Advisor uses a method of hierarchical clustering called **Ward's method**. This is one of the sturdier hierarchical methods. It also has a known tendency to favour making even-sized groups if possible. All clustering methods have their own tendencies, and this one is relatively benign. It produces useful diagrams, and works against the formation of tiny 'splinter clusters' of words.

Let's now take a look at how the words in our medical study were put into groups. Since this is a complex diagram, we will start with a small excerpt from the whole diagram, below. The darker words, 'specific', 'medication' and 'cost' are connected by lines that are relatively short going from right to left. A line that is much longer from left to right, pointed out by the arrow, connects this set of three to the set in lighter type ('try' and 'formulary'). We have put a box around all these words in the larger diagram that follows. (We talk about the other words that are circled in the diagram directly following it).

FIGURE 3.2b A portion of an actual tree diagram of how words are similar

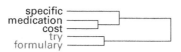

FIGURE 3.3 A full tree diagram showing how words are similar

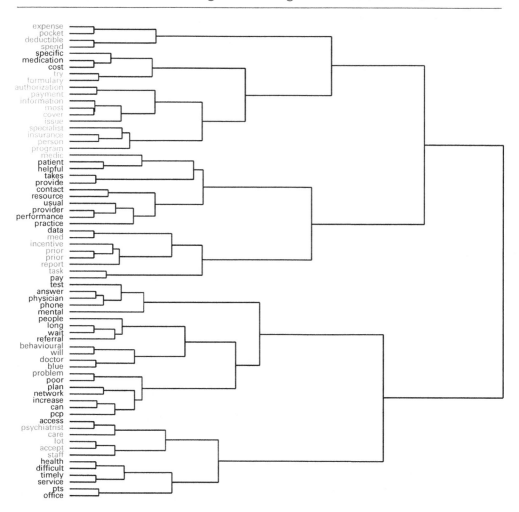

As mentioned, this is large and complex diagram. There are in fact 10 separate word clusters, or 10 groups, each containing words related to each other and not very related to the other groups of words. The grey-scale we use throughout this book makes it somewhat more difficult to

see where the groups separate than it would be to see with the default colour schemes that Advisor uses. Here, the darkness of the type sets off the different word groups.

We have circled one other group of words, which may be too small to read easily in its printed form. It contains **problem, poor, plan, network, increase, PCP, can** and **access**. (PCP is 'primary care physician' or family doctor.) Seeing that these words often fell together already says interesting things about how these medical managers feel about several ideas. The **plan** and the doctor **network** covered naturally go together, as do the **PCPs** or family physicians that make up most of the network. But the words **poor, problem, increases** and **access** also fall into this word group, showing that there are salient concerns about the plan and network, and that these likely have some relation to accessing the network.

Beyond simple diagrams: word treemaps

The clustering diagram, while repaying study, does not come across as particularly approachable to many audiences. Still, it is important as a first step leading other diagrams. So, rather than continuing to look at small sections of it, let's go on to those other displays.

The **word treemap** is an advance over the standard wordle. It does more than just packing words into a space. It puts similar words together, based on the clusters that were just formed. It is called a **treemap** because it is based on the **dendrogram,** or tree diagram that emerged from the clustering.

While this is still a complex display, it lays out the relationships among words and the frequency of words in a way that repays study. For instance, let's look at just the top left group of words in more detail.

Referral is by a small margin the largest word, enclosed in the largest box. It is closely associated with **wait, long, behavioural** and **problem.** Other words in this group are **blue** (as in Blue Cross, a major insurer in the area where the study was done) and **doctor**.

This cluster shows us that **referrals** from the family doctors to specialists often are associated with **problems**, and that these seem to arise when dealing with **behavioural** health (formerly mental health). **Referrals** often are associated with **long waits,** another **problem**. It appears that **Blue Cross** and **doctors** are part of the problem as well.

FIGURE 3.4 A treemap of words

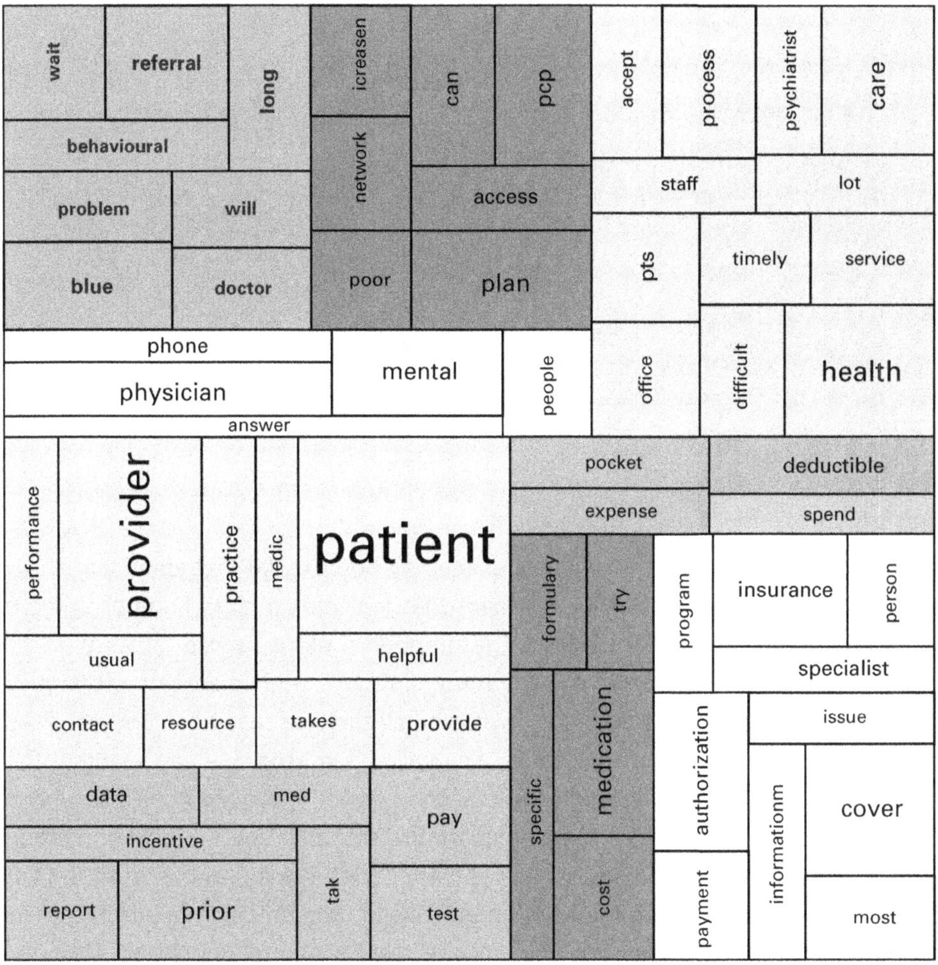

That is a great deal to learn from just this corner of a diagram. We could go back and look at other sections, but the usefulness of this diagram – when examined carefully – should already be apparent.

Seeing words in space: How word clouds show relationships

Word clustering uses a special type of table, showing how frequently words appear with each other. Each word is listed at the top of a column and at the start of a row. Each box or cell in the table shows how often a word appears with another word.

FIGURE 3.5 A section of the treemap of words

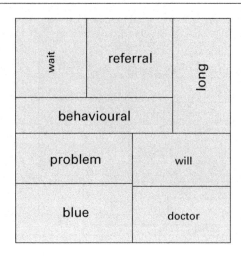

You can think of this type of table as something like the tables that show distances between cities, except that for cities a large number is more distant, and in this table a large number is more similar. Tables of word similarities have a great many zeroes in them, and so are not informative at a glance. Let's take a look at a small table of distances among cities instead. Looking at this table, also called a **matrix,** we can see that the two cities with the greatest distance between them are Apalachicola and Belle Glade, some 439 miles apart. We also can see that all information appears twice. (To show this we have circled the fourth box from the left in the top row, and the fourth box down in the first column, which convey precisely the same information: the distance from Apopka to Alachua.) And yes, these are all real cities, in Florida, USA.

This table has a lot of redundant information. We could in fact work with just the triangular part of the table above the zero boxes (these zeros are where the cities appear vs themselves). We also could use just the part of the table below the zero boxes. That is, half the information here is redundant. Sometimes, you will even see a matrix like this showing only the lower triangle or the upper triangle – either one is all you need.

There is a statistical method that can take a table like this and accurately recreate the regular map of the distances between the cities. This is called **multidimensional scaling** or **MDS**. This method also can work with a similar table that shows how often words occur together.

FIGURE 3.6 A table with distances (in miles)

CITY	Alachua	Altamonte Springs	Apalachicola	Apopka	Arcadia	Auburndale	Avon Park	Bartow	Belle Glade	Blountstown	Boca Raton
Alachua	0	119	180	110	196	138	174	147	268	171	308
Altamonte Springs	119	0	291	9	115	55	85	67	159	282	198
Apalachicola	180	291	0	282	358	307	345	309	439	71	479
Apopka	110	9	282	0	113	53	82	65	162	273	202
Arcadia	196	115	358	113	0	62	40	50	100	349	151
Auburndale	138	55	307	53	62	0	42	13	143	297	185
Avon Park	174	85	345	82	40	42	0	37	102	336	143
Bartow	147	67	309	65	50	13	37	0	139	300	180
Belle Glade	268	159	439	162	100	143	102	139	0	430	59
Blountstown	171	282	71	273	349	297	336	300	430	0	470
Boca Raton	308	198	479	202	151	185	143	180	59	470	0

> **Multidimensional scaling** takes a table of similarities among words and
> turns it into a visual display like a map showing distances among cities.

To get started, we just have to tell the procedure that larger numbers
mean more similarity. A table where larger numbers reflect more similarity
is sometimes called a **similarity matrix.** (The distances above are an
example of the opposite, a **dissimilarity matrix**.) At one time, multidimensional scaling was a terrifically difficult task, but it has been tamed
for many years, and now reliably produces excellent results.

Let's take a look at a diagram that uses multidimensional scaling, called
a **word cloud.** This can prove to be one of the most accessible displays

FIGURE 3.7   Word cloud

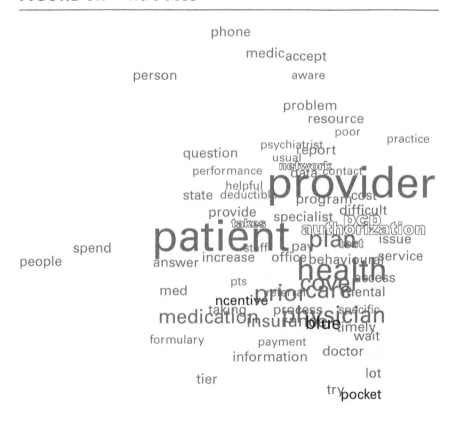

you will get from text analytics. Even if treemaps of words overwhelm an audience, they may find a word cloud approachable. As with treemaps, the bigger words are the ones that appear more often. So we once again have size and proximity to provide information, along with the colouring from the clusters to remind us of the word groupings. (This word cloud comes from analysis of another question in the survey, because the word relations appear more clearly in greyscale.)

Extending word clouds with covers

Nice as the word cloud is, there is a great deal going on in it, and so it still might seem unclear. The display also could puzzle some people because it in fact represents many dimensions in just the two we can use on a flat piece of paper (up vs down and left vs right is all we have). That is, the display is something like looking at a shadow (in two dimensions) and inferring how an object would look in three dimensions.

Worse, the computer can calculate in four, five, ten or twenty dimensions. There typically will be more information from this type of analysis than we can see in the diagram.

Drawing boundaries around groups of words is one way to get some of this information. These boundaries are called **covers. Covers** surround the places in the chart where similar words congregate together.

The idea of drawing these boundaries is intuitively appealing. However, as with clustering, when we draw covers, there is more than one way to do it – and again, no one clearly best choice. The most sensible approach you can take is to try the various options and see which one does the most in clarifying relationships.

Figure 3.8 shows what is called **convex hull covers**, which tend to be angular and fit fairly closely around the groups of words. These provide sharp demarcations for the regions in which similar words tend to group – and where word groups tend to overlap most. Remember we are in effect squeezing at least three dimensions into two dimensions – but fortunately the first two dimensions often convey most of the information in a multidimensional scaling (MDS) analysis.

Because of the many word clusters in this display, and the overlap among them, we get mainly a broad sense of the larger patterns among the words, a kind of impressionistic look at how words are related. We can make this still freer with the covers shown in Figure 3.9.

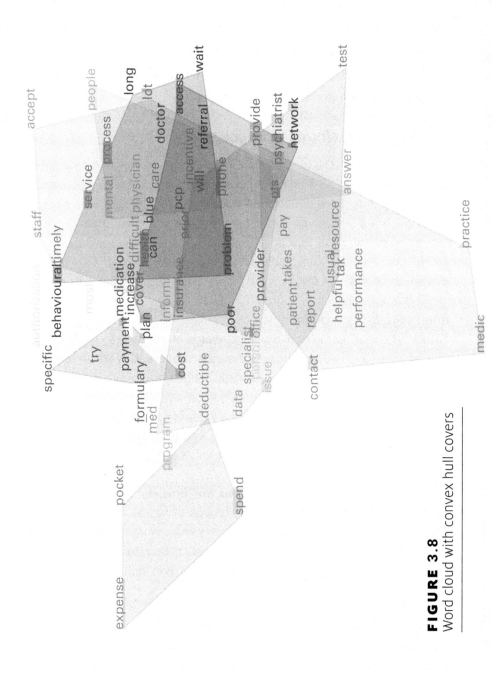

FIGURE 3.8
Word cloud with convex hull covers

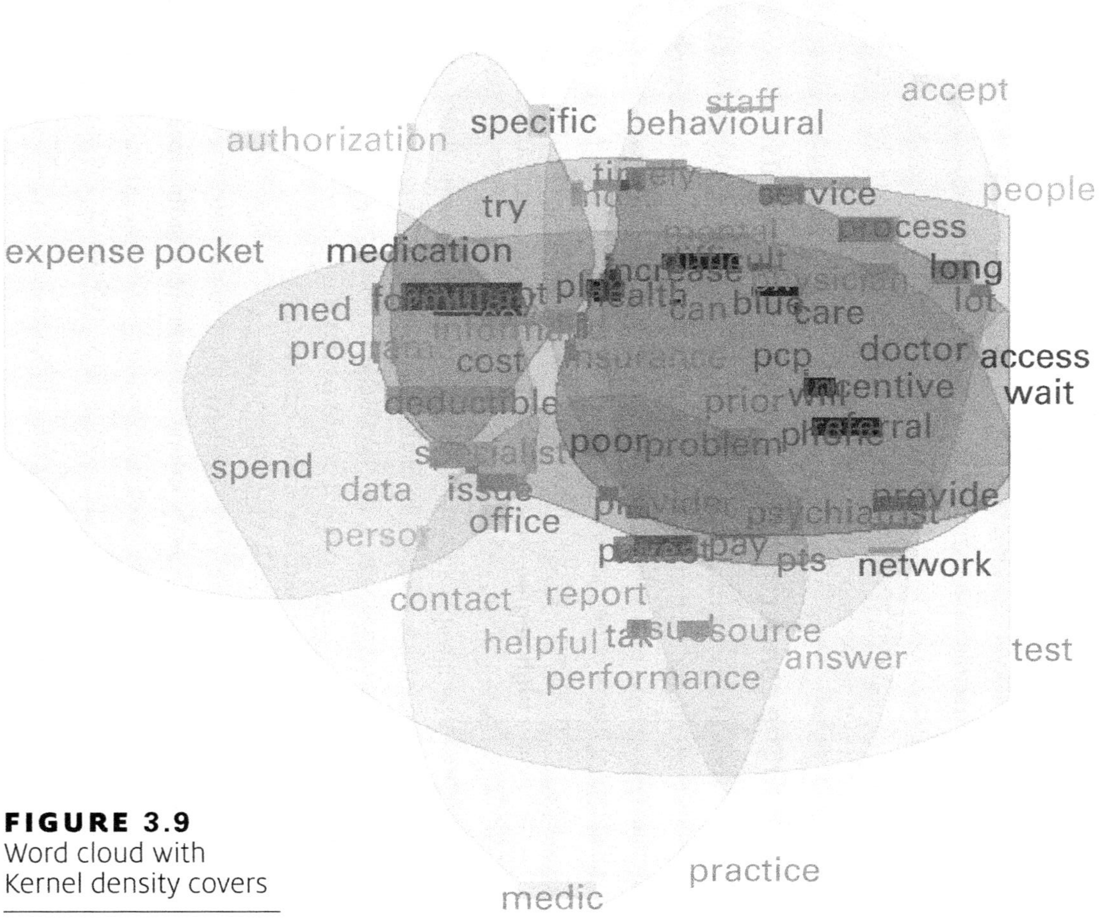

FIGURE 3.9
Word cloud with
Kernel density covers

These use what are called the **kernel density** method. Fortunately we have no need to understand why this name was chosen – and instead can focus on what it does. These covers tend to be rounded and to spread out over more words.

There is another type of cover, called an **alpha hull**. It is supposed to be tighter still than the convex hull, but in our example these two came out nearly identical. Again, whichever display you finally choose, word clouds – with careful review – show important information about patterns in the data.

With all these displays, please recall that the default multicolour scheme would produce a clearer sense of differences than the greyscale format used throughout this book. Even without colour, though, we get a sense of where boundaries and connections are found.

Seeing the connections: graph layouts of words

Information in this diagram is similar to that in the word cloud. This looks somewhat different in that the words have edges, or connections to other words. This type of display borrows from network analysis, which finds the salient items or people in a group.

Edges are shown by lines drawn between words. Words with a lot of edges have a **high degree**, meaning that they show up in connection with many other words in the document.

This has the possible advantage of looking like a network. It definitely conveys some of the complexity of the relationships among words. That also could be a disadvantage, as the tangle of lines may obscure some important details. That is, while it is interesting to see how all the words are connected, there are too many connections to get anything but a general impression. In the Figure 3.10, we can see many connections radiating out from **patient**, which we have highlighted with a heavy arrow. There also is a large tangle of connections around **authorization** and **plan,** slightly above centre.

One interesting feature of this map is how **reduce** (to the upper left) has a close association with **report** which in turn is linked to **quality**. This alone is telling.

Heat maps of words

One last display remains for us to discuss. This is the **heat map** of words. There was a time when heat maps were considered the height of sophisticated graphics, and so a good number of people have had a chance to

FIGURE 3.10   Graph layout of words

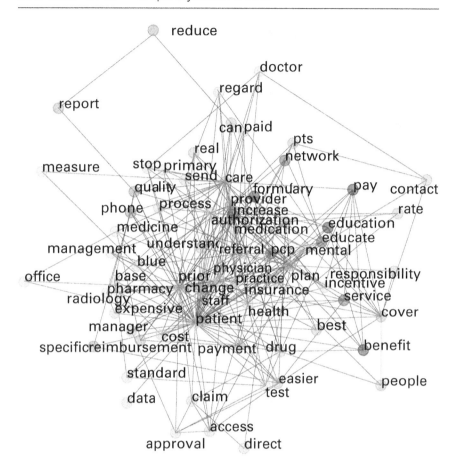

see them. You may not find them particularly approachable, though. As a general rule, the use of colour to represent intensity does not convey information accurately. (This was discovered by a researcher named Cleveland over 30 years ago and has been validated many times since.) Heat maps use intensity of colour. Let's take a look at one, which has the added feature of putting two copies of the clustering tree on the sides of the diagram. As a reminder, the clustering trees that appear in miniature show groupings of words, and longer lines bridging words mean less similarity among the words.

Just as with the chart of distances among cities, every word appears vs every other word, so this shows the same information twice. Darker shades mean words go together more frequently. The darkest 'hot spots'

FIGURE 3.11   Heat map

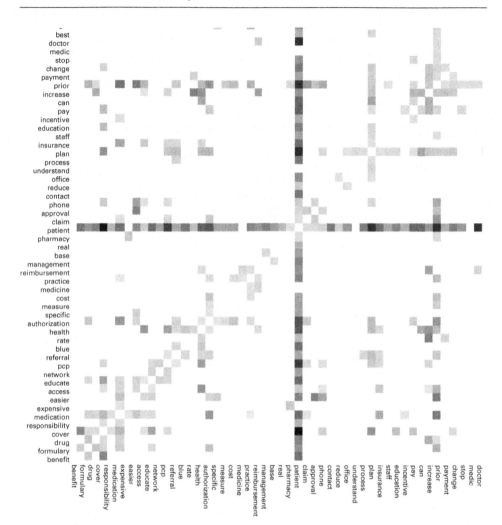

(which would glow a dramatic red in full colour) show the words that occur together often. All the darker spots are aligned with 'patient' (going both vertically and horizontally, showing the same information twice). **Care, provider** and **doctor** seem to go with patient most often, once we squint to see how words align.

Many will not find this chart a feast for the eyes, but heat maps have some currency, and so you may well encounter them. And of course, in some cases, they will indeed provide additional insights.

Applications, uses and cautions

The diagrams in this example all are slightly disguised versions of the text analytics used in a research study aimed at understanding use patterns, attitudes and opinions about companies providing insurance. Interviews were done among the administrators and managers who had to deal with the insurance plan providers. These diagrams did not serve as the centre of the analysis. Rather, that was found in the more quantitative measures used in the survey, including scaled questions about behaviours and intentions.

The word diagrams were used to add depth and richness to the exact measurements – and they did just that. We did not use all the diagrams, but rather carefully examined the variety at hand to pick the ones that best illustrated the key findings.

A survey is the most controlled environment for getting text answers, and is very likely to be the richest. All participants in this survey agreed to answer questions, and more importantly, were qualified to answer questions.

This is a salient advantage of any well-run survey over any exercise involving comments volunteered on the web. That is, in the survey, you have **screened** the participants so that you talk only to those who have had adequate experience with the topic. Gathering information from the wrong people obviously will produce useless information. With commentary from the web, it often is incorrect to assume that a given group reflects the people you really need to know about most.

For instance, information about beer drinking gathered on Facebook may be represented as the 'opinions of beer drinkers'. What you actually have, though, are the opinions of people who use Facebook and who choose to volunteer their opinions about their beer drinking there. The people most interested in certain beers may not even participate in Facebook – or if they do, they may not choose to write about their beer-drinking habits. It is easy to get dazzled by how many comments you can find on the web – but again, great masses of data that are wrong will not help you understand and take effective action, no matter how vast the quantities are.

Descriptive vs predictive

It is important to understand that all these graphical methods are **descriptive**. That means they show how words fit together, and which words are most frequent, but not the relationships of words to any outcome or behaviour.

> **Descriptive methods** show patterns and similarities but not effects on any outcome or behaviour. **Predictive methods** are required to show what effects are.

This is a key point and bears some additional explanation. A word could be both prevalent and connected to many other words, but not have any relationship with what individuals do, or even how they consider a subject. Common words may just be the basic language required to talk about a topic, and therefore may not carry other weight. Alternatively, the more prevalent words could indeed relate to some behaviour very strongly, but looking solely at these diagrams, we could not tell one way or the other.

To understand the extent to words are related to an outcome or behaviour, we need **predictive** methods. We will be talking about several of these in upcoming chapters, including regression, classification trees and Bayesian networks. So, as they used to say on television, don't touch that dial – there is a lot more to come.

Summary

We have reviewed several pictorial displays you can make from text. The **wordle** solely shows how often each word in the text appears. All the other displays we discussed start by clustering the words to find how similar they are. We determine similarity by how often words appear near each other. The most similar words are found many times within the space of a few words of each other. Similarity was determined statistically using a procedure called **clustering.**

Clustering leads to a diagram called the **tree diagram** or **dendrogram.** This in turn leads to a diagram that looks something like the wordle, but with extra analytical power. This is the **treemap** of words, and the way it extends clustering leads to more informative displays, highlighting both how frequently words appear and how they are related.

Other methods building on clustering include **word clouds, graph layouts of words** and **heat maps**. Graph layouts show a network-like display with many connections among the words. Word clouds can be enhanced with various **covers** that outline where groupings of words fall.

These graphical methods are **descriptive** methods, in that they cannot show the relationships any words might have with an outcome or a behaviour – this despite with their great power in revealing patterns. To understand how words relate to behaviours or outcomes, we will need to look into the **predictive methods** in coming chapters.

References

Berry, M (ed) (2003) *Survey of Text Mining: Clustering, classification, and retrieval*, Springer–Verlag, New York

Best, K and Altmannn, G (1996) Project Report, *Journal Quantitative Linguistics*, 3, pp 85–88

Cleveland, W S and McGill, R (1984) Graphical Perception: theory, experimentation, and application to the development of graphical methods, *Journal of the American Statistical Association*, 79, pp 531–54

Everitt, B, Landau, S, Leese, M and Stahl, D (2011) *Clustering Analysis*, John Wiley & Sons, Sussex, UK

Feldman, R and Sanger, J (2006) *The Text Mining Handbook*, Cambridge University Press, New York

Freedman, D A (2010) *Statistical Models and Causal Inference: A dialogue with the social sciences,* Cambridge University Press, Cambridge

Hartigan, J A (1975) *Clustering Algorithms*, John Wiley & Sons, New York

Johnson, B and Shneiderman, B (1991) Tree-maps: a space–filling approach to the visualization of hierarchical information structures, *VIS '91 Proceedings of the 2nd conference on Visualization*, IEEE Computer Society Press, Los Alamitos, CA

Indurkhya, N and Damerau, F (2010) *Handbook of Natural Language Processing,* 2nd edn, CRC Press, Boca Raton, FL

Miner, G, Elder, J, Hill, A, Nisbet, R, Delen, D and Fast, A (2012) *Practical Text Mining and Statistical Analysis for Non-structured Text Data Applications,* Academic Press, Waltham, MA

Murua, A, Stuetzle, W, Tantrum, J and Sieberts, S (2009) Model-based document classification and clustering, *International Journal of Tomography & Statistics*, 8, pp 1–24

Shawe-Taylor, J and Cristianini, N (2004) *Kernel Methods for Pattern Analysis*, Cambridge University Press, Cambridge

Srivastava, A and Sahami, M (2009) *Text Mining: Classification, clustering, and applications*, CRC Press, Boca Raton, FL

Wilkinson, L (2006) Revising the Pareto Chart, *The American Statistician*, 60, pp 332–34

Witten, I and Frank, E (2005) *Data Mining: Practical machine learning tools and techniques*, 2nd edn, Morgan Kaufmann, San Francisco

Zanasi, A (ed) (2007) *Text Mining and its Applications to Intelligence, CRM and Knowledge Management*, WIT Press, Southampton

PUTTING TEXT TOGETHER

04

Clustering documents using words

KEY QUESTIONS:

How do words relate across documents? How can I gather similar documents? What are the practical applications?

This chapter discusses ways of putting words and documents together. (A document is any group of words that we treat as a single block.) We will add new methods of clustering to those described in the last chapter, explaining how they work. We also discuss an activity highly related to clustering, classification. **Clustering** determines how to put documents into groups. **Classification** assigns documents to groups that have been defined. At times in this chapter, you may indeed need to hold on to your chair, as this is likely to be the only place in text analytics where you brush up against metaphysics, theories of existence, and Emmanuel Kant. We will visit then depart this lofty plane, concluding with specific applications of clustering and classification at work doing text analytics.

Where we have been and moving on to documents

In the last chapter, 'Words in pictures', we talked about clustering words. As a reminder, one kind of clustering (**hierarchical**) leads to a graphical representation of how words relate, called a **tree diagram** or **dendrogram**. In this diagram, the most similar words are grouped closest to each other. The tree structure also gives us some additional clues about how similar words are, based on the lengths of the branches that separate them from other words – with shorter branches meaning more similarity. You can see a tree diagram in Figure 3.3.

There are many other approaches to grouping in addition to hierarchical clustering. Each of these alternatives seeks better ways of capturing similarities. So far, no one method has emerged as working best in all – or even most – circumstances. Earlier, we also described another widely used method: **K-means**, or **iterative K-means.** We discuss a few other methods in this chapter, in connection with clustering documents.

From sliding windows to bags of words

The last chapter used an approach involving a **sliding window** or **n-gram sliding window to** determine how words were similar. This window is a certain number of words long (for instance, six words), and moves through the text. As it progresses, one word at a step, it counts how often words occur together in the window. This counting leads to a table or matrix showing the closeness of relationships among words – more occurrences together means more similarity. This approach treats the entire body of text as a single unit. It does not notice the spots where one person offering comments stops and another starts.

Looking at text this way, then, only the sequence of words matters, while syntax, grammar and separations among speakers do not. Indeed, treating words in this way is called a **sequential model**.

Another differing approach will count each row in the database as one **document** or block of text. However, it disregards sequence. This is the **word-vector** approach we discussed in Chapter 2. It also is called the **bag of words** method. In this, you could think metaphorically of each block of text as a physical bag holding actual words. After the extraneous words are removed, the words are shaken out of the bags and dropped into the correct slots in a table. In this table, the words are columns and the documents are the rows. This table or **matrix** could count how often words occur in each document or alternatively just note whether words are present or absent.

As we mentioned before, this matrix will consist mostly of empty spaces or zeroes, demarcating places where a given word is not present. Even though this table will seem quite sparse, if we use the right analytical methods, it can show us patterns of similarity among words and among documents. However, the bag-of-words approach has received a great deal of criticism for missing key points in the meaning of words. We will talk about some of these problems shortly.

Onward to clustering words

Once the words are safely stored in a spreadsheet-like space, we can analyse them for similarities. We will return to the same user satisfaction study of insurers that we used in Chapter 3, done among professionals who administer US insurance plans. As part of this survey, they typed in comments (online) about their concerns. Figure 4.1 shows a small corner of the table holding words (the columns) and documents (the rows). The entire table holds only the 85 most frequent words, all occurring in at least 1 per cent of the documents. As you can see, it indeed is mostly zeroes.

A table like this is the result of cleaning and regularizing words, which we discussed in Chapters 2 and 3. In Figure 4.1, you can see one word that has been regularized, 'avail', which in this context stands for 'available', 'availability', 'availabilities' (but most likely not the verb 'avail'). If we were to examine the rest of the table, we would see that all the usual procedures for regularizing words took place, including removing stray characters, eliminating stop words, correcting misspellings, making verbs the same tense, and removing endings of different forms of words (or stemming), and so on.

Now a question may arise. Why should we bother clustering if we already have the words nicely arranged in a table, and an excellent method

FIGURE 4.1   Table showing words and documents

	access	also	answer	area	author	avail	bcbs	behaviour	blue
1	0	0	0	0	0	0	0	0	0
2	0	0	0	0	0	0	0	0	0
3	0	0	0	0	0	0	0	0	0
4	0	0	0	0	0	0	0	0	0
5	0	0	0	0	0	0	0	0	0
6	0	0	0	0	0	0	0	0	0
7	0	0	0	0	0	0	0	0	0
8	0	0	0	0	0	1	0	0	0
9	0	0	0	0	0	0	0	0	0
10	0	0	0	0	0	0	0	0	0
11	0	0	0	0	0	0	0	0	0
12	0	0	0	0	1	0	0	0	0
13	0	0	0	0	0	0	0	0	0
14	0	0	0	0	1	0	0	0	0
15	0	0	0	0	0	0	0	0	0
16	0	0	0	0	0	0	0	0	0
17	0	0	0	0	0	0	1	0	0
18	0	0	0	0	0	0	0	0	0
19	0	0	0	0	0	0	0	0	0
20	0	0	0	0	0	0	0	0	0
21	0	0	0	0	0	0	0	0	0
22	0	0	0	0	0	0	0	1	0
23	0	0	0	0	0	0	0	0	0
25	0	0	0	0	0	0	0	0	0
25	0	0	0	0	0	0	0	0	0

for grouping variables in tables, **factor analysis**? That is, it seems sensible that clustering based on how close words are to each other could arise from using sliding windows. However, if we have text packaged in neat rows and columns, factor analysis is the most widely used method. (We talked about factor analysis in Chapter 2). What is the gain in using clustering? The answer is that each approach shows you different aspects of overall patterns. Factors give a numerical view, simplifying data down to the strongest and simplest forms of relationships. Factoring is in fact called a **data reduction** method. The clustering methods giving us a tree diagram (the **hierarchical** methods), show more nuanced patterns of similarities.

> **Factor analysis** is by far the most commonly used method for grouping variables. However, with words, **grouping using clustering** can produce more detailed and nuanced depictions of similarities and differences.

Of all the clustering methods, only the hierarchical methods produce a tree diagram. Other methods provide far different output. And importantly, few methods cluster variables. Most commonly, clustering methods group **rows** of data or, with text, **documents**. (As a reminder, words are considered **variables** because their presence **varies** from one document to the next.)

What we did

In the last chapter, we used **Ward's method**, a relatively sturdy type of **hierarchical clustering**. It tends to produce clusters that are about even in size. Seeking even groups is a good idea when dealing with words. The truth about clustering is that, while methods seek to find the right structure, they each have tendencies, or structures that they seemingly prefer. They even may 'find' these structures when others describe the data better.

Ward's method, then, has good predispositions for our purposes when we analyse text. Given how infrequently even the most common usable words occur, with many other hierarchical methods we run a salient risk of producing a lot of small, 'splinter' groupings that are hard to interpret and use.

This analysis

Clustering the documents in this analysis, to make results as comparable as possible with the clustering of words we did in the last chapter, we again used Ward's method, and we requested cluster memberships for 10 groups. (The program doing the analysis last time returned this many groups automatically.) But in spite of matching methods, the pictures we got are not the same.

Let's look at some differences in Figure 4.2. We will first describe some items that varied, and then (with some luck) clarify what happened. The top of the figure shows a section of the chart we had in Chapter 3 (in Figure 4.3). It zooms in on the most commonly used word, **patient**,

FIGURE 4.2   Differences in clustering for sequential vs bag-of-words approaches

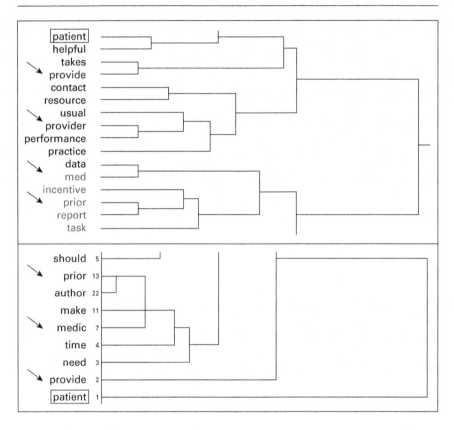

and the words most closely associated with it by the **sliding window** method. (**Patient** was in the middle of the diagram there.) The bottom figure comes from clustering words according to the **bag of words model**. Most notably, it shows **patient** on its own. (This analysis in fact identified it as the sole member of its own cluster.)

The words surrounding **patient** show more differences than similarities. We have put a box around the word itself, and have drawn arrows pointing to the words that are the same in one scheme as in the other. We have three matches, a low percentage of all the words shown. (Perhaps that is three and one-half matches, because the first program captured **provide** and **provider** as two separate words. It also left words more complete than did the second one. It most likely has a more sophisticated **lemmatization** routine that the second, allowing it to capture words as different parts of speech more accurately.) There are 15 words fairly close to patient in the first diagram and nine in the second.

Why are the results different?

If you are seeking perfection in earthly things, these results doubtless will seem frustrating. We have a real disagreement between these approaches about what is happening – and yet neither is wrong. In fact, both make sense, and one is not demonstrably better than the other. How can this be?

We need to consider first how patterns in the text were treated. The **sliding window** or sequential approach looks for physical proximity of words. The idea, then, is that if words appear near each other, this must reflect some underlying meaning. This seems sensible enough. However, clustering via the **word-vector model** also makes sense. This counts the patterns in words' occurrences across documents as mattering most. Words are more similar when they appear together in more documents.

In the second model, **patient** falls into its own group because its pattern of appearances differs strongly from those of all other words. **Patient** shows up most of all words often by a large margin. Taking a count of how often words occur, we find that it in fact shows up in 35 per cent of the documents and is mentioned up to five times per document. The next most frequent word, the stemmed form **provid** (which stands in for 'provide(s)', 'provided', 'provider(s)' and 'providing') appears in 23 per cent of the documents. After this, frequencies tail off sharply. The next most common words, **need** and **time,** appear in only 14 per cent of documents. The 85 most frequent words **on average** occur in about **3 per cent** of the documents.

In the lower diagram in Figure 4.2, we see that how often words occur clearly colours the groupings. The small number that appears next to each word shows its rank in frequency of occurrence. Still, we can recognize that it is not the sole factor. We see some near neighbours to these highly frequent words that do not appear nearly as often, such as **author** (which stands in for 'authorize' in its various tenses and 'authorization'), which is twenty-second in frequency of appearance.

We also see interesting differences if we look at the other word we highlighted in Chapter 3, **problem.** In the top part of Figure 4.3, which comes from the analysis in Chapter 3, **problem** is closely associated with

FIGURE 4.3   More differences in associations

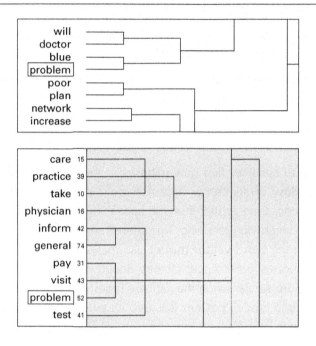

doctors, networks, increases and **blue** (as in Blue Cross, a large insurance provider). Ignoring a couple of non-meaningful words, the general pattern of associations seems highly logical.

At the bottom of Figure 4.3, we see **problem** is associated with **physician** (one linkage the two results have in common), but also with **pay, visit, test, practice** and **care** (and also with two non-meaningful words). This too makes eminent sense. So we have two patterns reflected by two different methods and perhaps no clear reason to choose one over the other.

Back to the elusive concept of similarity

When we discussed clustering in Chapter 3, we talked about how difficult it is to define similarity. Here we see a practical example of that problem. Two approaches to the same body of comments defined similarity in different ways and different pictures emerged.

This problem arises from the fact that, when we represent text, we are actively seeking to make those representations far more compact than the text itself. We might even say that one underlying purpose of text analytics is to extract information from text in a concise and condensed form. But this process of reduction means that we inevitably will lose some of the information that the original text held.

What precisely contributed to these differences may still seem perplexing. To get a better sense of what happened, we might think of the information we extracted from text as being like the shadow of a three-dimensional object, compared with the object itself. For instance, in Figure 4.4, we have two shadows which might look like entirely different things, but which in fact represent the same fellow (likely to be familiar to all of us) from two different angles. Only by referring back to a fuller representation, as we see on the right of Figure 4.4, is it clear that they both represent exactly the same object.

Clearly both shadows are accurate representations of the same figure. Yet because important information is missing, we most likely cannot tell that we are seeing two aspects of the same object. Information has been lost in both shadows, and this loss makes comparisons difficult.

With text, unfortunately we now have no way of quantifying how much information we are losing when we reduce the text, nor which information most needs to be kept. Text has connections and meanings that we miss

FIGURE 4.4   Two different looking depictions that actually show the same object

SOURCE: The Thinker, Rodin, part uploaded 2006 by David Monniaux, from Pixabay.
http://pixabay.com/en/the-thinker-rodin-rodin-museum-489753
http://commons.wikimedia.org/wiki/File:Rodin_The_Thinker_p1070090.jpg.
Assembled and modified by the author.

when we get text ready for processing. This is so even when we make text into factors, where we get a very clear answer about how much of the total variance (or pattern in the **variables**) we are retaining compared with the basic variable when allowing different numbers of factors in the solution. The transition from text to variables is where the problem lies. We have no clear metric to tell us how much we are losing in that step. Lacking this, we cannot tell which approach to clustering words works better by an objective mathematical means.

Clustering and classifying documents

Our brief visit with The Thinker may be a good bridge to this section. As murky as the ideas behind clustering words may seem, even more fog surrounds the clustering and classification of **documents**. So, hold on – we need to talk about some new vocabulary and new concepts, and even mention philosophy. Then we will get to some practical applications.

For a time, **clustering** and **classification** were central activities in text analytics. Again, **clustering** is the process of grouping similar documents together. **Classification** assigns documents to groups that have been formed. The computational problems can become ferocious – and continue to be examined at great length. We will get a glimpse of these. And document classification can be very a serious endeavour indeed, as it plays an important role in such areas a fraud detection and medical research.

Into the clouds with theory

Even treating words as single units, as we did in the last sections, we saw that clustering can get different results depending on the way we approach the problem. We also can investigate the meaning of entire documents by looking just at the words they contain, and we will show that this can provide useful results shortly in this chapter.

However, in attempting to get at the sense of documents, many have pointed out that this single-word methodology is lacking. How words are connected and the context in which words appear also must matter. Just consider these three sentences, all of which contain the words **low down payments**.

- **Low down payments** draw attention;
- He gave the **low down** on **payments**;
- **Payments** are **low down** in his list of concerns.

If we were just to extract the words and put them separately into a spread-sheet, we might misinterpret these sentences as being similar. Clearly this is not so. This arises for two principal reasons – as noted by many sources. First, words are **ambiguous**, in they may not have a clear defini-tion, and in addition often are **polysemous**, or capable of having many meanings. We typically can sense automatically which meanings to apply, but a machine often may not be so clever. Unless we instruct a computer very carefully, it may lose the sense that the document meant to impart while it busily pulls words apart and puts them into storage.

And here we arrive at ontologies

This may be the worst thicket we encounter. We do not need to get totally entangled, but at least to understand what people are talking about. You even can find vendors offering to sell you **ontologies**, so it is worth know-ing what you might get. Part of the problem with the term **ontology** is that it has more than one meaning, and these meanings blend into each other. For now, let us stick with the following definitions of **ontology**:

- It is a term in philosophy that means **a theory of existence**;
- It is a **body of knowledge** describing some specific field;
- Any of quite a few other things relating to knowledge, which are more or less clearly defined.

Around the edges of the first and second definition we may suddenly encounter such figures as Heidegger, Quine, and even as promised, Emmanuel Kant. Not to disappoint anybody, but careful reading of the pieces referencing these eminent philosophers strongly suggests that it is very nice to know the deep roots of the discussion, but we do not need to understand these to analyse text.

A few other points are worth noting. When you hear discussions about **ontologies** and text analytics, you most likely are hearing about a system of defined connections among words that makes meanings clearer. One simple example that might be illuminating concerns a couple of household pets, their designation as pets, and some of their eating habits. This example

IMAGE 4.1 Kant, almost certainly not discussing text analytics

SOURCE: Immanuel Kant, lecturing to Russian officers, uploaded 2006, authors listed as I Soyockina/V Gracov. http://en.wikipedia.org/wiki/Critique_of_Pure_Reason#mediaviewer/File:KantLecturing.jpg.

appears in Figure 4.5. The connections show us which items can appear with the others logically. Using this very simple ontology, the computer would not make the mistake of thinking that **Fido**, **pet dog**, eats **Wally**, **pet cat** (although this might be a very fond wish of his). it similarly would not make the mistake of thinking that **dog food** is a **pet**, or that **Fido** eats **mice** (at least when anybody has been looking).

FIGURE 4.5 A simple ontology

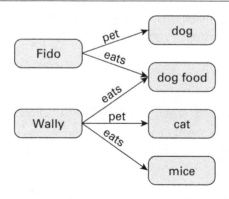

We also see that, based on the directions of the arrows, **dog food** and **mice** are things that the **pets eat**. (This scheme does not address the possibilities that the **mice** once were pets next door and probably gladly eat **dog food**. It covers only the main possibilities.)

This ontology, therefore, **shows the relationships that are permitted** and those that are not among these few words. Ontologies become more important in figuring out which documents are similar as the terminology becomes more technical and the documents become longer.

Almost there

We need to mention one more consideration. There are more vocabulary words, so hold tight. When ontologies are the hot topic of discussion, you may also hear references to **OWL.** This refers to **Web Ontology Language.** (Yes, the originators did notice that the letters in the acronym do not line up. They basically said, 'So what'.) This is a system for allowing computers to process the content in information instead of just presenting the information to us, the humans. **OWL** allows machines to interpret web content more fully than **XML** or other similar **markup languages.**

XML may seem familiar to you, and it is related to **HTML**, the standard web page format. **HTML** code describes, or **marks up**, web page content (such as text and graphic images) controlling the ways in which it is displayed and in which people can interact with it. **HTML tags** (or information embedded in HTML that we cannot see on the page) also are important in searching for documents.

XML means extended markup language, and indeed **XML** does more than **HTML.** Data in this format is known as self-describing, meaning that the structure of the data is contained inside the data. Because of this, when the data arrives, storage and display are both defined. You do not need to set up anything for a detailed picture to emerge.

This may seem quite abstract. As an example, some programs that draw networks containing data (like the Bayesian networks we discuss in Chapter 8) store the network in **XML** format. When one program makes the network, an entirely different program capable of reading the **XML** format can open it with the network and all its elements exactly in place and all the data ready to use. Years ago, knowledgeable computer-scientist types started saying that **XML** would be the future of all data on the web. When that shining day comes, you will be ready to meet it.

IMAGE 4.2   Unfortunately, not our owl

This section should leave you prepared for a good fraction of the mysterious-sounding language you may encounter. We hope this will give you some protection from getting completely snowed under in befuddling jargon. Few things contribute more to uncertainty and error than getting deluged with unknown verbiage. With that, we will move on to document clustering.

Clustering documents

We return to the example we used in Chapter 2, dealing with a survey about a social media site. This will enable us to compare clustering based on three ways of capturing words: the words alone, factors based on the words, and words that have been encoded. Then we will talk about some ways in which classification can be used.

To cluster documents, we used a clustering method called **TwoStep Cluster.** This is available in the statistics program SPSS. **TwoStep** is a good choice for dealing with word counts in documents because these tend to be very low, and you should get the best performance with a routine that clusters **nominal variables** and that can handle a lot of data easily. There are just a few that can do both.

A pause to review types of data

In case you are a bit rusty on the distinctions among the types of data, these fall into three large classes:

- Nominal
- Ordinal; and
- Continuous.

Nominal data has values but these do not have **numerical information.** For instance, we might have an encoded variable, such as region of the country. Since statistics programs handle numbers much more easily than text, we might set up a coding scheme like this:

☞ Northeast = 1

☞ Midwest = 2

☞ South = 3

☞ West = 4.

With nominal data, these numbers are just placeholders. The coding does not mean that 'West' is four times as much as 'Northeast' (although people living in the West might agree with that). It simply is making things easier for the computer, which would much rather juggle numerical data and then later go back to look up and apply the names that we want to see in the output.

Ordinal data has values, going from low to high, but we cannot tell how much space exists between any two of the values. Rankings are a good example. You do not know if the distance between the first ranked item and the second ranked item is larger or smaller than the distance

IMAGE 4.3   You probably knew we would work one of these into this section

SOURCE: Backofenthermometer, uploaded 2012 by Gmhofmann. Own work. Licensed under CC BY-SA 3.0 via Wikimedia Commons. http://commons.wikimedia.org/wiki/File:Backofenthermometer. jpg#mediaviewer/File:Backofenthermometer.jpg.

between the second and the third – or between the ninth and tenth ranking. We know there is a hierarchy, but nothing else.

Continuous data has both values and a fixed scale. If you have 20 pounds of sausage you know exactly how much more you have than Ralph does with his paltry 15 pounds. That is precisely as much of a difference as Ralph has vs poor Seamus, who is barely surviving with 10 pounds. The quantity difference is measurable and exact.

Continuous data further is divided into **interval** and **ratio data**. Some authors say that these two are different enough that we should talk about having **four** data types.

Interval data has a set scale but we cannot compare the quantities as multiples of each other. For instance, a temperature of 40 is not twice as hot as a temperature of 20. Nor is 10 twice as cold as 20 (although it might feel that way). We have a fixed scale, as we can see on the handy thermometer, but no way to see multiplicative relationships.

Ratio data gives the most complete information, in that it has both a fixed scale and we can get a multiplicative relationship out of it. Going back to Ralph and Seamus briefly, Ralph's 15 pounds of sausage indeed is 1.5 times as much as Seamus' poor allotment of 10 pounds. Therein lies the ratio: we can legitimately say that the ratio of sausage for Ralph vs Seamus is 1.5: 1. We cannot do this with temperature, an interval measurement.

Back to clustering

With all the many clustering methods available for different problems, our choices are restricted when it comes to dealing with words. As a reminder, the data files representing words are largely filled with ones and zeroes (which show that words are present or absent). This is sometimes called **binary data** (yet another data name to remember), and this is **nominal** since it just represents whether or not an item is there. Even if the software counts occurrences of words, in most documents we evaluate there will be very few values outside zero and one.

The widely used **K-means** approaches that we mentioned earlier can handle a lot of data, but do not process nominal variables well. The **hierarchical** methods can be pushed into handling nominal-level data, as we have seen, but with larger data sets, they tend to get bogged down and may stall entirely. Advances in computers' speed and memory capacities have enabled us to handle progressively larger problems with these methods, but they still are not well-suited for massive data sets.

> The most widely used clustering methods, the **hierarchical** and **K-means** types, typically do not work well with large amounts of text as it is stored in spreadsheet-like format. Other, somewhat less-known methods, such as **TwoStep clustering**, have worked better.

TwoStep clustering addresses these issues by handling nominal, ordinal and continuous data – and in being **scalable** to very large problems. **Scalable** is another term you may hear, and it simply means that the procedure breaks down less readily when confronted with enormous heaps of data.

TwoStep also communicates more with the user than do many other clustering routines, displaying a great many pictures of the data. Whether you find these helpful or not depends on your preferred style of seeing information. We will skip these images, though, using our own charts to illustrate the explanations as closely as possible.

In addition, TwoStep will do its best to select a solution with the best number of groups, unlike many other clustering routines. 'Do its best' in the last sentence reflects an important caveat. Experience has shown that the program's recommendations often are not terribly useful. That is, they may match some mathematical criterion for what is 'best', but they prove not to be interesting or applicable.

For instance, in our example, when clustering words, TwoStep selected a two-group solution as the 'best'. Dividing the world into two sections typically does not produce useful information. There is at least some more variety than that in almost all things human – and we found this to be so

IMAGE 4.4   Big or small, computers should not be the final arbiter.
You always need to check what they are saying

SOURCE: Supercomputer – the Beginnings, uploaded 2010, Jitze Couperus, Source Flickr.
http://en.wikipedia.org/wiki/CDC_6600#mediaviewer/File:CDC_6600.jc.jpg.

in this example. Differences in patterns of word use within the two groups that the method recommended did not reveal anything of interest. Adding just one more group showed a more detailed and useful picture.

This is one truism of the computer age: machines follow their rules very precisely, and usually return reliable results, but we still need to check all areas requiring judgment. With anything whatsoever requiring interpretation, you need to do some checking and thinking. Fortunately, as you consider several alternatives, the machine will gladly do the heavy lifting repeatedly. But do consider alternatives.

In this exercise, for instance, we also tried four groups and five groups in addition to the three-group solution we chose. The solutions with more groups created them by subdividing a group that was not interesting in the three-group solution. So we stayed with three groups as most informative.

Clustering based on words

As a reminder, this example uses the social networking site satisfaction survey that we encoded and on which we ran factor analysis after extracting words (in Chapter 2). With words, factors and codes, we now can contrast three approaches. As we will see, the words actually provided the most useful solution. This may seem surprising. Let's see how this happened as we follow the discussion of results.

A method of eliminating some solutions quickly

The first test of any clustering exercise lies in the sizes of the groups it produces. If clustering produces a very large group (half of the sample of more) and two or more small groups, as in the illustration to the right, that solution typically has little practical use. The large group tends to look a great deal like the total sample, and so examining it does not reveal anything new. The smaller groups can be too small to use in any meaningful way.

Why seeking groups of the right sizes matters

Underlying the notions about group size in the last paragraph is an idea that has made modern approaches to the marketplace far more efficient and successful than earlier efforts. This is the idea of **segmentation**, or of dividing your customers and prospects into groups that you can understand, that behave and think differently, that you can reach efficiently – and that are big enough to merit special effort in pursuing.

FIGURE 4.6   Really not a good solution

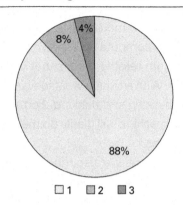

Odd as it may seem, before the 1950s, this idea was never articulated formally, and seemed to get little use. Organizations simply approached their markets as if they were large, amorphous masses, or alternatively as clumps of individuals that varied in mysterious ways.

The first of these early ways of thinking led to products and services that were supposedly developed 'for everybody'. In fact, there has not been a successful product or service 'for everybody' in decades – if such a thing has ever existed. All the most successful endeavours focus on a specific **segment**, understanding its needs, thoughts and opinions – and then develop services or products that fill those needs and views.

The second early view, seeing the market as filled with faceless people that varied in mysterious and myriad ways, led to a strategy of **product proliferation**. This attempted to make a great many different things in the hopes that somebody out there would find something to like in the many choices. This was obviously a highly inefficient, wasteful approach. Its vestiges still can annoy us even today.

Knowing the needs, opinions and thoughts of well-defined groups has supplanted both of these older approaches in most industries. Knowing what people say in their own words, and seeing if any patterns in differences emerge based on this, can become a valuable addition to this understanding.

IMAGE 4.5   A consequence of the electronics industry's lingering fondness for product proliferation: none of these batteries will fit your device

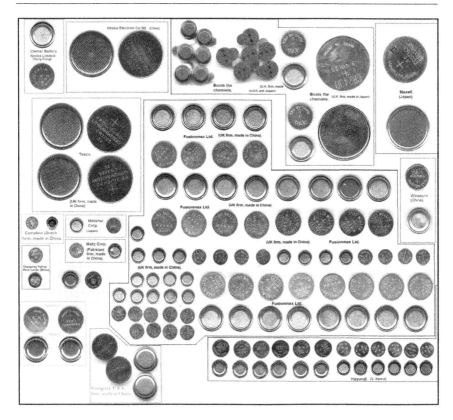

SOURCE: Button cells and 9v cells (3), uploaded 2010 by Wipsenade. Licensed under CC BY 3.0 via Wikimedia Commons. http://commons.wikimedia.org/wiki/File:Button_cells_and_9v_cells_(3).png#mediaviewer/File:Button_cells_and_9v_cells_(3).png. Modified by the author.

Clustering with words and factors: the size of the groups

As we mentioned earlier, when we clustered documents based on words, the TwoStep procedure recommended a two-group solution that we rejected very quickly. We then asked for three, four and five groups in the next three analyses. Three groups showed clear patterns of differences, while with four and five groups the procedure simply subdivided the one group that seemed least interesting (based on examining the words that differed in frequency of occurrence among the groups).

The three-cluster solution based on words also showed a division into well-sized-groups, as you can see in Figure 4.7a. However, when we tried to cluster based on the factors extracted from these words, results were not satisfactory. We ended with a very large group and two small ones with three groups. One large group and several small groups persisted as we went to four or five groups.

We therefore tried another method to cluster the factors, **K-means**. This approach in theory should work well here because factors are true continuous variables, being weighted composites of many other variables. (If this seems unclear, please look back to Chapter 2.) However, K-means did even worse than TwoStep, as 4.7b also shows. We also tried Ward's method from the hierarchical set, with even less luck.

FIGURE 4.7a   Cluster sizes based on words and on factors

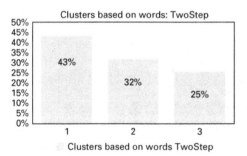
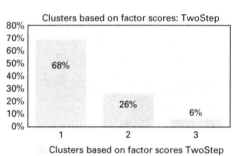

FIGURE 4.7b   Comparing cluster sizes from factor scores based on K-means and fuzzy clustering

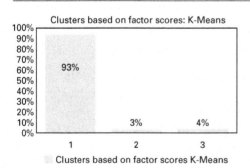
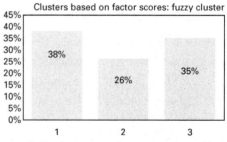

We therefore turned to another statistics program, **NCSS**. We do not endorse software, but still, NCSS must stand as the greatest bargain among all choices of large-scale statistics programs. It is comprehensive, easy to run, and has a fantastically good help system that actually explains the procedures. In any event, this program offers several other types of clustering, and among those we chose so-called **fuzzy clustering**.

This particular implementation of **fuzzy clustering** can handle any type of data. It works differently from most clustering methods – in fuzzy clustering each person or document is given a **likelihood** to belong to each cluster, rather than being assigned to just one group.

Using these likelihoods, it is simple to go back and put the person or document into the cluster where she/he/it has the most likelihood of belonging. That is what we did. This method's one drawback is that it takes more time than methods like TwoStep and K-means to get results.

In Figure 4.7b, we see the group sizes from the K-means approach and the fuzzy cluster approach. Even though these methods are distantly related, fuzzy clustering alone produced reasonably sized groups.

Diagnosing the two most plausible solutions

Here, then, we have two solutions that warrant further investigation: the TwoStep solution using words and the fuzzy clustering solution based on factors. The next logical area of investigation is examining the differences in the variables that formed each set of clusters – that is, the words for the first solution, and factors for the second solution.

Figure 4.8 shows how these two solutions differ. For the figure, we selected the variables with the strongest meaningful differences. (Words like 'would', which carry no clear meaning, were not included.) Immediately striking is how many more words we see under the word-based solution (to the left) than factors under the factor-based solution. However, we used the 85 most prevalent words in the first solution and had only 18 factors drawn from the words to use in the second solution. So we had both more ingoing variables and more emerging as differentiators in the word-based analysis.

A closer look shows that the factors have a different scaling than the words. The scale in factors always is shifted so that the overall average is zero and so that about two-thirds of the scores fall between +1 and -1. This process is called **standardization.** This is done so that items with different scales can be put into factors and their contributions will be weighed

FIGURE 4.8 Comparing what's different in word-based clusters (left) and in factor-based clusters (right)

	Clusters based on words			Overall Average
	1	2	3	
use	0.36	0.12	0.60	0.35
site	0.20	0.20	0.41	0.25
profession	0.06	0.44	0.33	0.25
This_site	0.11	0.10	0.58	0.23
network	0.03	0.39	0.29	0.21
peopl	0.06	0.13	0.40	0.17
connect	0.01	0.27	0.29	0.16
job	0.03	0.12	0.41	0.16
don	0.15	0.00	0.33	0.15
busi	0.06	0.15	0.25	0.14
like	0.09	0.06	0.27	0.13
good	0.03	0.24	0.11	0.12
great	0.01	0.25	0.11	0.11
way	0.00	0.17	0.16	0.10
know	0.05	0.01	0.26	0.09
find	0.04	0.06	0.21	0.09
social	0.07	0.04	0.18	0.09
contact	0.03	0.09	0.16	0.08
friend	0.06	0.05	0.15	0.08
work	0.03	0.06	0.19	0.08
much	0.09	0.01	0.14	0.08
get	0.05	0.03	0.18	0.08
look	0.01	0.03	0.20	0.07
can	0.03	0.04	0.23	0.08
recommend	0.06	0.01	0.14	0.06
see	0.02	0.01	0.19	0.06
time	0.04	0.01	0.15	0.06
Per cent of total	43%	32%	25%	

	Clusters based on factors			Overall Average
	1	2	3	
Scores for want know email	−0.04	−0.05	0.08	0.00
Scores for don't use much	−0.36	1.01	−0.37	0.00
Scores for seems post site	0.14	0.00	−0.15	0.00
Scores for way connect	−0.06	−0.07	0.11	0.00
Scores for help find job	−0.09	0.02	0.08	0.00
Scores for great tool network	−0.07	−0.08	0.14	0.00
Scores for business purpose	−0.11	0.05	0.08	0.00
Per cent of total	38%	26%	35%	

evenly. (Otherwise a variable measured on a 10-point scale, for instance, would have much more weight in the factor than one measured on a five-point scale, and the five-point scale much more weight than a three-point scale, and so on.)

The values in the table for words, to the left, all are percentages. We expressed these as decimals to avoid having a couple of hundred percentage signs to stare at in the table. (The maximum is one and the minimum is zero.) At first blush it appears that the differences among the percentages in the words are much bigger than most of the differences among score for the factors. However, because of the way the factors are scaled, about 0.2 points passes a test of statistical significance.

In the tables we have highlighted higher scores (reading across the three groups) by making the numbers **bold** and with a dark background. We also highlighted the lower scores by making them *italic* with a lighter background.

Careful scrutiny shows that these solutions do not reflect the same groupings of documents. Here we are talking about differences in the nature of the groups and not the inconsistency in the numbering of the groups. Two different clustering procedures can find nearly identical groups, but number them differently for reasons known only to the software.

A key contrast is found in association with the negative word '**don't**'. In the factor-based solution, the score for '**don't use much**' is extremely high in group 2. This is the **only** high score for that group. Looking over to group 3 in the word-based solution, where the words '**use**', '**don('t)**' and '**much**' score high, many other words also score high. That is, these many high scores show that a good number of concepts were linked with 'don't use much' in the word-based clusters but not in the factor-based clusters.

Now we have two ways of clustering the documents and two different results. Again, given the nature of clustering, this is not terribly surprising. However, we need to answer the large question: Which one should we use?

Solving the problem of which solution to pick

The question of which solution is 'better' would remain unanswerable if we did not have other information. Here we are fortunate because these comments come from a survey where a question about **willingness to recommend** also was included. Let's see how these solutions compare in terms of this key question. Figure 4.9 shows us that with the word-based

FIGURE 4.9   Clustering based on words more clearly differentiates based on willingness to recommend

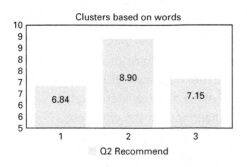
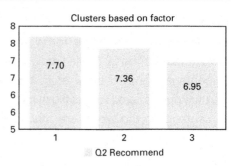

approach, we have a clear winner based on differentiation among the 'willingness to recommend' scores.

We can see in this figure that group 2 in the word-based clustering has a much stronger score in this area than the other two. Their score (8.9) would be considered a strong endorsement, based on experience with many such scores over the years. The lower scores are only lukewarm, not indicative of severe problems overall, but definitely signalling that these groups see ample room for improvement in performance.

The clusters based on factors do not show this clear a pattern of differences. The highest score is less than a point from the lowest, and none is particularly strong or weak.

Interpretation and possible actions

Going back to the words most often mentioned by each group in Figure 4.8, we see **great, good, network, connect,** and **profession** all mentioned most often by the enthusiastic group 2. Clearly they like the way this site allows them to connect in a professional way, or with others in their profession.

Knowing that group 3 is less likely to recommend the site, we can see many of their comments not as praise, but rather as areas where they would like to see performance improve, or at best as only adequate.

Therefore, the comments of this last group have particular diagnostic value, and suggest ways that new dialogues could be opened to improve experiences on this site. Also of note is that the first group, some 43 per cent, finds little worth saying, and yet has the lowest satisfaction scores.

This indicates a need for new ways to boost interest and engagement among a cohort that accounts for nearly half of members. Clearly work is yet to be done, and analysing text comments has delineated key needs.

About those coded responses

The coded responses we developed in Chapter 2 did not get mentioned in the last section because, contrary to expectations, using them as the basis for clustering did not produce good results. We tried all four varieties of clustering that we mentioned in the last section, and a few more that we will not introduce at this fairly late point in the chapter. All had highly similar poor results. Group sizes based on two of these attempts appear in Figure 4.10. The first shows the results based on all 300+ codes and sub-codes in the encoded text, which captured different ideas in the text at a very fine level of detail. The TwoStep results shown in the left part of the figure (again one very large groups and two small ones), actually were better than all the alternative clustering approaches tried.

A suspicion came to mind that this non-useful pattern might be due to the codes being too granular. That is, the 300+ codes might capture such fine distinctions in meaning that clustering them might be like trying to separate dust particles into meaningful groups.

We therefore also added the codes together into broader categories, or **netted** them. These **nets** did even worse than the codes alone in leading to usefully sized groups. Seeing that, we decided that using the words themselves did best of all approaches to processing text in this particular clustering exercise. This was a surprising outcome – but based on the large number of trials we made to find the best results, definitely so.

FIGURE 4.10   The disappointing cluster groupings based on coded words

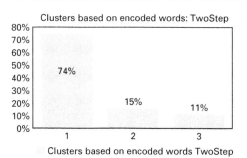

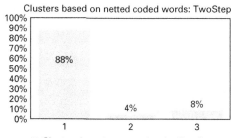

Reasons words alone may have worked best

Difficulty in clustering using factors may seem unintuitive, but it is not unforeseen based both on published research and experience. Two thorough studies done about 20 years ago showed that factors did not perform as well as regular variables in generating useful clusters. Those studies looked at a popular method for developing segments based on factoring the variables first, then doing the clustering ('popular' of course being a relative term). We should add that by regular variables, we do not mean data that has been completely unprocessed. Good data management includes removing obviously incorrect or extraneous items and eliminating or reducing extreme responses, or **outliers**.

This problem with factors may come about because they **smooth** data, always having an even, regular shape. If you look at a diagram of factor scores, they always follow a nice, normal distribution. There are few exceptionally high and very few exceptionally low scores. Those would fall into the small areas near the outer edges of the illustration to the right. There are increasingly more scores you approach the central point in a nice, smoothly rising and falling curve. A glance at the illustration shows this likely familiar shape. Normally distributed shapes like factors, in addition to scaring many people away from statistics for good, do not have any natural-looking dividing points. Where would you cut that figure into sections and for what reason?

FIGURE 4.11   All completely normal

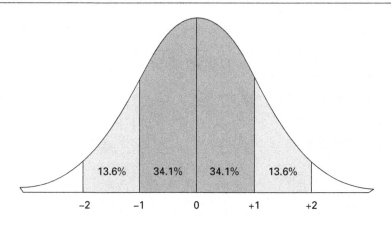

Raw, unsmoothed data, on the other hand, has a kind of irregular character, that some have called lumpy or gritty. This makes it relatively easy to find natural dividing points.

In the spirit of having at least one appealing diagram in each chapter, we offer this comparison. Raw data is something like the grapes to the left in Image 4.6, easy to split apart into natural groupings and with more than one way to get those groupings. Groups of factors form something more like that watermelon-like object to the right. You can cut them in many ways with no way being the best.

This is not to say that factors never work effectively in clustering. At times they do well and may even match the results with raw, unsmoothed data. However, your author has never seen them do better than the raw data, in more than 25 years. That is something to consider as you group documents based on words.

We speculated earlier that the **encoded responses** may have been too fine-grained to gather into groups. As we mentioned then, they might have been something like a pile of dust, too granular or fine to divide effectively. Still, because they gathered thematic ideas, their performance was unexpectedly poor with this data set. Coded data might do much better with another body of text. The only way to find out what works best is experimenting with the different ways of gathering words.

IMAGE 4.6   Raw, unsmoothed data (left) and factors (right) compared with more appealing things

SOURCE: Watermelon, http://pixabay.com/en/watermelon-fruit-green-skin-23487.
Grapes, http://commons.wikimedia.org/wiki/File:More_grapes.jpg.

Document classification

Classifying documents has great importance in many fields. For instance, medical researchers rely heavily on document classification to find the right research among the ever-exploding volume of papers published on the web. They might want to do an important task such as separating articles that discuss effects from bacterial infections more than effects from viruses. With the onrush of research papers appearing daily, automating this kind of classifying makes finding the right articles much easier.

Used in fraud detection, document classification locates certain phrases, patterns of usage, or inconsistencies that indicate fraudulent activity has

IMAGE 4.7   Some frauds are easier to detect

SOURCE: Hamlin's Wizard Oil, 1890, uploaded 2010. US Library of Congress, from a print by Hughes Lithographers, Chicago. http://www.flickr.com/photos/trialsanderrors/3449228921/

taken place. This can be critical when reviewing the reports sent in by insurance field agents, for instance. The differences between a fraudulent and non-fraudulent claim can be very subtle, and so may escape the agent filing the report. Obviously, the computerized systems doing this scanning have very sophisticated rules, or even complex **ontologies**, in place.

These systems require extensive **training** by experts who identify key characteristics of each type of document (for instance, fraudulent vs legitimate ones). A **scoring model** then gets developed, which matches new documents against the criteria that the experts have identified. Each document gets a **document score**, which gives it a likelihood of belonging in a certain group, such as being a fraudulent claim.

If you have this type of complex need, you most likely have an expert system in place. If not, this definitely is not the type of thing you want to construct without advice from a specialist.

Before we go on to practical applications you can use, we need to make another pause to fill our ever-expanding sack of vocabulary words. Scoring models fall under the heading of **supervised learning.** (This process of developing a scoring model is sometimes called **training a classifier.**) An activity is **supervised** learning when it has a specific outcome or pattern that is trying to reach. **Document classification** is **supervised** learning because we have predefined categories into which we want the documents to be assigned. We need to make a model that will accurately put the documents into these categories. (The **predictive modelling methods** we discuss in Chapters 6, 7, and 8 – regression, classification trees and Bayes Nets – all are **supervised learning** methods.

Supervised learning methods have a target outcome or pattern they are trying to reach. Document classification is a supervised method. So are predictive methods like regression and classification trees. **Unsupervised methods** try to find a pattern rather than match one. Clustering and factor analysis are unsupervised methods.

Clustering falls under the heading of **unsupervised learning**. We are seeking to discover patterns of relationships, rather than fit the variable into a known structure. There is no target or outcome we are trying to predict. **Factor analysis**, which we discussed in Chapter 2, also falls under the heading of unsupervised learning.

An application of document classification

You can create document classification schemes that will help you develop insights and shape actions. We saw the beginnings of one earlier in the chapter. Customers who made the most specific mentions of the features and possible benefits of the social networking site also were not highly satisfied. This seems like something that could be captured with a formal classification model. And that is precisely what we did.

This classification model was made using a method called **discriminant analysis** (which we will describe only briefly here). The model revealed that 77 per cent of members of the most negative group could be identified correctly based just on their patterns of word use. (Due to its complexity, we will not show that model here.)

This high correct identification level means that articulated concerns are consistent within this group and that these concerns differ from those of the other groups. We understand that the highly negative are a sizeable and coherent constituency, which should provide impetus to develop programs for investigating and addressing deficiencies in the areas they mentioned.

Discriminant analysis is a close relative of regression, but with a different set of goals. **Discriminant analysis** is designed to find which variables differentiate among groups, and how different these groups are from each other. (We will talk about the uses of regression in Chapter 6).

Discriminant analysis also develops **scoring models** that allow us to assign new people or documents to groups that have been formed by another procedure such as clustering. These models are very readily applied. It is one of the most established and well-tested of all methods used to develop classification models.

Another possible application of classification: uncovering customers at risk

Another particularly useful application of document classification is finding early warnings of customer churn. Key phrases in the comments made by customers who left or who reduced use of your product (or service) can be used to locate other customers who are at risk. Similarly, comments by customers who are least satisfied can be aligned with those of customers giving only lukewarm ratings, showing which members in the latter group are most vulnerable based on what they say spontaneously.

More specifically, it may be obvious to many of you that customers who rate a company four or less on a 10-point scale on a satisfaction survey are particularly prone to leaving. However, there may be other customers who give somewhat higher ratings who also are vulnerable. To find them by analysing text, you would look for the differences in comments that groups giving different ratings provided. While the customers giving the worst ratings are most at risk, the next most vulnerable would be customers in the next most negative group who made key comments that looked very much like those of the at-risk group. This communality of comments shows links in concerns linking the two groups. You could then work both on the most at-risk customers and develop programs to reach out to those in the 'somewhat higher rating but at-risk' group.

Developing a classification model that you can use

You can employ a wide range of methods to develop a classification model. In addition to **discriminant analysis**, many **predictive modelling** methods have been applied. We cannot get into depth about these without getting ahead of ourselves – predictive methods follow starting in Chapter 6. Two methods we discuss, **classification trees** and **Bayesian networks**, can be used to classify documents.

Other methods you may see mentioned include **logistic regression** and **support vector machines**. **Logistic regression** works something like discriminant analysis. It may have a slight edge in classifying documents that do not strongly belong in any group, but its classification models are not as easy to apply as those from discriminant analysis. As for **support vector machines**, your author has never encountered a non-data-scientist/statistician who could understand what they were doing, and few enough in the analytical community who could, for that matter. But you did hear about them here.

In this example, we will briefly preview what **classification trees** can do. Their name suggests strongly that they will do well at classifying documents or other items into groups, and that is indeed the case. We will describe the outputs they provide that are useful for classification, and will go into the details of their workings and structure in Chapter 7. We used a program called **KnowledgeSeeker** to perform the tree analysis.

These trees make a good example because they create a set of straightforward **if-then rules** that define small subgroups based on the combinations of words that appear in their documents. The subgroups differ significantly in our likelihood of finding a highly negative rater in each one. That is, in some groups using specific combinations of words, we are highly likely to find a negative rater, in some groups using other specific combinations of words we are moderately likely to find one, and in some groups we are unlikely to find one on the same basis.

How this works will become clearer as we look below at a few rules that a classification tree analysis developed. Using our same social networking survey data set, we divided responses to a scaled **willingness to recommend** question into three groups. These correspond to the groups used in the so-called **Net Promoter Score or NPS.** That is, the most positive group, sometimes called the promoters, give ratings of 9 or 10. The people in the middle give scores of 6, 7, or 8. Finally, the lowest group, giving ratings 5 and under, is sometimes called the detractors.

These cut-off points have little empirical justification – for instance, nobody has yet demonstrated that a person giving a rating of 8 generally differs from a person giving a rating of 9, but this NPS schema treats them as if they rest on opposite sides of a stark divide.

Still, NPS is relatively well known, and so will be used in this analysis. We will investigate the most strongly at-risk group, those giving scores of 5 or less, and see what most strongly characterized them in this analysis.

Rules from classification trees need to be read in their entirety. If three terms appear in a rule, for instance, they all need to appear in the document. If two terms are identified as present and one absent, then that must be the exact pattern – and so on. The tree model has an advantage of being compact. (Tree models generally are quite concise, including relatively few variables.) These rules are based on only these stemmed words: **use, network, good, connect, great, professi** and **don** for don't, which we will spell out **don't.** Let's start.

IMAGE 4.8   Almost certainly will not recommend

SOURCE: Portrait of Samuel Johnson commissioned for Henry Thrale's Streatham Park gallery, 1772, uploaded 2007. http://commons.wikimedia.org/wiki/File:Samuel_Johnson_by_Joshua_Reynolds.jpg.

The group where we are most likely to find negative raters is defined by this simple rule:

IF   Don't = 1, 2, 3 or 4
AND   Professi = 0

THEN

Most negative group =   63.9 per cent
Middling group =   26.7 per cent
Best (promoters) group =   9.4 per cent

This rule means that there must be no mention of **professional** in all its variations in the document, and that the word **don't** must appear at least once. This is the only time that the word **don't** appears in any of the rules, so this is a key defining term.

A more complex rules describes those next most likely to be negative raters. It has six conditions:

IF   Use = 1, 2, 3, 4 or 5
AND   Network = 0
AND   Good = 0
AND   Connect = 0
AND   Great = 0
AND   Don't = 0
AND   Professi = 0

THEN

Most negative group =   39.1 per cent
Middling group =   36.1 per cent
Best (promoters) group =   24.8 per cent

This second rule in regular language would read: The word **use** must be mentioned more than once AND none of these five words can appear: **network, good, connect, great, don't** and **professional.**

Again only one word (this time, **use**) is present. This one word is combined with a pattern of many absences. More specifically, if people mentioned some **use** of the site but not any of the key differentiating words reflecting ratings or activities, then they were highly likely to be negative raters. (We know they are mentioning some **use** because the word **don't** is absent.) This suggests that this site is not doing well with more specialized applications – the uses these users must be mentioning do not show up among the ones that most differentiate the comments in all documents.

The gains or leverage chart for scoring documents: a more in-depth description

We can get a more detailed view than is possible using simple rules, via a chart called a **gains chart** or a **leverage chart**. This puts all the groups in descending order of likelihood of giving the most negative ratings. The group at the top has the highest likelihood, going down to the one at the bottom, which has the lowest likelihood. This chart also shows how large the groups are, as well as the percentage of the total sample and the percentage of the most negative raters each group holds – along with some index values that we will explain.

Let's take a look at the top part of the chart, and then talk about what the **cumulative** figures mean. Figure 4.12a shows the first three out of

FIGURE 4.12a   The top half of a gains chart based for the most negative group

	Individual group figures				Cumulative figures			
	Group as a per cent of the total sample	Per cent of all the most negative	Likelihood of being in most negative group	Lift or leverage (Index: 100 = average)	Groups cumulated as a per cent of the total sample	Cumulative per cent of all the most negative	Cumulative likelihood of belonging to most negative	Cumulative lift or leverage (Index: 100 = average)
Don't = 1, 2, 3, 4 AND Professi = 0	11.4%	26.8%	63.9%	234	11.4%	26.8%	63.9%	234
Use = 1, 2, 3, 4, 5 AND Network = 0 AND Good = 0 AND Connect = 0 AND Great = 0 AND Don't = 0 AND Professi = 0	11.7%	16.8%	39.1%	143	23.1%	43.6%	51.4%	188
Use = 0 AND Network = 0 AND Good = 0 AND Connect = 0 AND Great = 0 AND Don't = 0 AND Professi = 0	29.7%	35.0%	32.1%	118	52.9%	78.6%	40.5%	149

nine total rules, describing the groups having the highest likelihood of giving negative ratings.

Cumulative figures mean figures down to and including the last group you are reading. Cumulative figures shown for the second group, for instance, sum or average values from both the first and second group, while cumulative figures shown with the third group include figures from the first, second and third.

This is easy enough to see with the percentages in the groups. For instance, the first group has 11.4 per cent of the total sample in it, and the second has 11.7 per cent. This cumulates to 23.1 per cent. The third group has 29.1 per cent of the total sample, and when this is added to, or cumulated with, the first two groups, we get a cumulative value of 52.9 per cent.

The cumulative likelihoods (in the second column to the right of the vertical line) may be somewhat less apparent. We start with those in the top group who have a 63.9 per cent likelihood of giving the most negative ratings. We then average in those in the second group, who have a 39.1 per cent likelihood. The cumulative figure is 51.4 per cent. This is an average that is weighted by the size of each group.

Finally, let us take a look at the perhaps mysterious **lift** or **leverage**. This shows how much more likely you are to run across a person giving the most negative ratings in any given group than you are on average. The first group has an index of 234, meaning you are 2.34 times as likely to find a highly negative rater there as you would be on average. That is a great deal more likely.

The second group has an index of 143, meaning that in this group, you are 1.43 times as likely to run into a negative rater as you would be on average. The cumulative index for the first two groups is 188. That is, if you combine the first two groups, you will be 1.88 times as likely to encounter a highly negative rater as you would be on average.

To clarify this chart by looking at one group, let us spell out the figures for the third group, which appears at the bottom of the chart. Connected with this group we find the following information:

- This group is defined by the absence of all the key words in the model (**use, network, good, connect, great, don't** and **professional**), or they apparently had little to say;
- They make up 29.7 per cent of the total sample;
- They make up 35.0 per cent of those giving highly negative ratings;

- Members of this group have a 32.1 per cent likelihood of giving highly negative ratings;
- The lift index is 118, meaning that within this group, you are 1.18 times as likely to run into a negative rater as you would be on average;
- When this group added to the first two groups, or cumulated, this gives us 52.9 per cent of the total sample;
- When this group added to the first two groups, or cumulated, this gives us 83 per cent of those giving the most negative ratings;
- The cumulative likelihood of giving the most negative rating, averaged across the first three groups, is 40.5 per cent;
- And lastly, the cumulative or average lift index across the three groups of 149. This means that taking all three groups together, we are 1.49 times as likely to encounter a highly negative rater as we are on average.

The rest of the cast in order of appearance

For the sake of completeness we are including the bottom section of the gains chart in Figure 4.12b. This shows all the combinations of words that are associated with the individuals having the lowest likelihoods of giving negative ratings. Note that, in the group at the very bottom (individuals who could express no more of the key differentiating phrases than 'great') there is a vanishingly small likelihood the person will give a negative rating – some 6.4 per cent. We definitely would not do well throwing a ball into this group and hoping to hit a highly negative rater.

Now what we do with this

A natural question follows, that being: 'Is this good enough to use in any way?' Recalling that the goal was finding customers who might be at risk, the answer is **yes**. If we find somebody whose ratings are better than 5 and who has a pattern of responses like those in the first **two** groups, we can consider that person much more likely than average to be at risk. That is, based on what they said spontaneously, we would expect them to be in the highly negative group.

We are using the presence and absence of those key words that significantly differentiated among the groups to tag them as being like the most negative users. Their pattern of word use makes them look like the

FIGURE 4.12b The rest of the gains chart, showing the groups not likely to contain highly negative raters

	Group as a per cent of the total sample	Per cent of all the most negative	Likelihood of being in most negative group	Lift or leverage (Index: 100 = average)	Groups cumulated as a per cent of the total sample	Cumulative per cent of all the most negative	Cumulative likelihood of belonging to most negative	Cumulative lift or leverage (Index: 100 = average)
Network = 1, 2, 3								
AND Good = 0								
AND Connect = 0								
AND Great = 0								
AND Don't = 0								
AND Professi = 0	5.6%	4.4%	21.6%	79	58.4%	83.0%	38.7%	142
Site = 1, 2, 3, 4								
AND Professi = 1 2	6.5%	3.8%	15.9%	58	64.9%	86.8%	36.5%	134
Good = 1, 2								
AND Connect = 0								
AND Great = 0								
AND Don't = 0								
AND Professi = 0	5.8%	3.0%	14.2%	52	70.7%	89.8%	34.6%	127
Connect = 1, 2, 3, 4								
AND Great = 0								
AND Don't = 0								
AND Professi = 0	6.2%	3.0%	13.4%	49	76.9%	92.8%	32.9%	121
Site = 0, 1, 2, 3, 4, 5								
AND Professi = 1, 2	16.0%	5.5%	9.4%	34	92.9%	98.3%	28.9%	106
Great = 1, 2								
AND Don't = 0								
AND Professi = 0	7.1%	1.7%	6.4%	23	100.0%	100.0%	27.3%	100

most negative raters, but their ratings are slightly higher. This gives us cause to suspect the ratings. These people could well be at risk.

We can conclude that scoring these documents based on the single words used in comments definitely did help us characterize those users most at risk. Further, this even guided us to some highly likely to be at risk, who yet who did not give the lowest ratings.

An important caution about clustering

As we saw in this chapter and the last, clustering does not produce a definitive solution. If we try six different methods, we almost surely will get six different answers. A worse secret about clustering is that some methods are not 100 per cent reliable. That is, if you run some variety of clustering twice, it may not return exactly the same answer. The K-means types of methods are notorious in this regard. This happens because they start at some random point for each group's average scores, and keep pushing that point around as they try out more members for inclusion in the group. As different members fit into the group, they contribute their own scores to the group's average, and so it moves. Starting twice from different places picked at random, and adding members to the group based on those starting points, can indeed end up with two different results.

Over the years, your author has learned to become a little more relaxed about this imprecision. The differences tend to be small, and tend to happen among documents or people who do not fit very well into any group. You could say the far edges of the groups, where individuals or documents do not clearly belong anywhere, move around a little. This is not optimal, but it is not grievously bad either.

Still, if you have not seen it happen, it can be disconcerting to run the same procedure exactly the same way twice and not get exactly the same outcomes. Learning to value usefulness more than absolute precision helps deal with this problem.

Summary

Clustering documents means grouping ones that are similar. **Classifying documents** means assigning documents to groups that have already been defined. The topic of clustering and classifying documents is vast and sprawling, as you have doubtless noticed by having read this far. And thank you for taking this sometimes tortuous journey.

A seemingly simple idea, grouping documents that are similar, touches on a staggering range of concepts. These range from **ontologies**, or systems of defined meanings and relationships among words, to nearly metaphysical discussions. You do not need to dig too deeply into the literature before you find authors touching on the world of philosophers, ranging from Quine and Heidegger to our good friend Emmanuel Kant.

In the more computational realms, we run up against groups trying to make language intelligible to machines so that computers can do some information processing before they deliver the results that we poor humans need to use. Here we touched briefly on markup languages, like **XML**, that package and store information simultaneously, and came upon **OWL**s. **OWL**s, as a reminder, are Web Ontology Languages, and these promise to make locating and using text on the web much more efficient, one day.

Once we emerged from this thicket, we got down to the business of grouping documents and applying classifications. Although computers are advancing in understanding phrases and themes in documents, the tools widely available to us deal with words in just three forms: the words themselves, words gathered into factors, and encoded words. The complex

IMAGE 4.9   Still not our OWL

SOURCE: Great horned and Snowdon owls, 1892, uploaded 2010, by Inuew.
http://commons.wikimedia.org/wiki/File:PSM_V41_D334_Great_horned_and_snowdon_owls.jpg.

systems that do things like sniff out fraudulent documents still are the domain of experts, who set them up and maintain them.

However, you can produce useful results using text, without getting into the deep structure of language. We showed that clustering words led to insights that could direct actions to address possible problem areas. We also showed that classifying documents added to the information in ratings that customers provided in a satisfaction survey. Our analysis revealed a group that was very likely at risk in spite of their lukewarm evaluations.

Along the way we gave a refresher on the types of data, useful if you want to know which clustering methods you can use successfully. With that as a preamble to our example, we tried several clustering algorithms, underlining the principle that a single pass through unstructured data rarely, if ever, gets you the most useful answer. We also saw that clustering the occurences of words can at times give more useful results than clustering based on two methods used to extract concepts, factor analysis and encoding words. The relatively poor performance of the encoded words was a surprising result. We talked about possible reasons for this and the fact that having some difficulty clustering factors should not come as startling news.

We brushed briefly on the many classification methods, and gave a demonstration of classification using classification trees, which produce the most compact and immediately intelligible **classification rules**. These are a set of simple '**if-then**' statements. We showed how the rules look and the way they can help us create a table called a **gains analysis** or **leverage analysis**. This table gave us highly detailed information on the groups formed by the classification trees, including incidences of the people we were interested in investigating within those groups (the negative raters), the sizes of groups, and a host of other information.

A **gains analysis** is a valuable supplement to document clustering. It provides a detailed roadmap allowing you to understand the characteristics that most and least define the group you are investigating or seeking to find. (We will see more about classification tree methods in Chapter 7.)

In conducting these analysis, we used **SPSS,** a mainstay full-featured software package, to do clustering and for some of the diagnosing of the solutions we obtained. We also used another very substantial full-featured software package, **NCSS**, which does several kinds of clustering that SPSS does not. We ran the trees with a package called **KnowledgeSeeker**, which we discuss more fully in Chapter 7.

We even had a brief visit from **Dr Samuel Johnson**, who stood in for the person very unlikely to recommend anything. Overall, we covered a great deal of material.

You may have noticed that clustering and classification only became truly useful when they were linked with data obtained by asking people other questions. In the example, we linked the text to a question we asked about willingness to recommend the site we were analysing. This 'willingness to recommend' measure is taken very seriously by many organizations – and indeed among all the different scaled questions we might ask, this has been one of those most closely aligned with actual behaviour.

Answers to this question together with text from verbatim comments together gave us more insight, and better equipped us to take action, than either type of information did alone. This represents the best use of text analytics. At least so far, and from your author's perspective. When linked with other data, text analytics expands and enriches our understanding so we can address needs and problems among customers and prospects more effectively.

And yet, for all that, a large group of organizations is busily working on using text alone as a guidepost, without reference to questions about ratings or behaviours. This brings us to a main topic of the next chapter, **sentiment analysis**. Read on and encounter a view differing from those of many promoting this activity as an answer to a wide range of problems.

References

Berners-Lee, T, Hendler, J and Lassila, O (2001) The semantic web: a new form of web content that is meaningful to computers will unleash a revolution of new possibilities, *Scientific American*, 284 (**5**), pp 34–43

Bosak, J and Bray, T (1999) XML and the second-generation web, *Scientific American*, 269 (**5**) pp 89–93.

Buitelaar, P and Cimiano, P (eds) (2008) Ontology learning and population: bridging the gap between text and knowledge, *Frontiers in Artificial Intelligence and Applications*, IOS Press, Amsterdam, Netherlands

Everitt, B S and Dunn, G (1992) *Applied Multivariate Data Analysis*, Oxford University Press, New York

Green, P E, Tull, D S and Albaum, G (1978) *Research for Marketing Decisions*, Prentice-Hall, Englewood Cliffs, NJ

Hartigan, J (1975) *Clustering Algorithms*, John Wiley, New York

James, M (1985) *Classification Algorithms*, John Wiley, New York

Kass, G (1980) An exploratory technique for investigating large quantities of categorical data, *Applied Statistics*, **29** (2), pp 119–27

Kaufman, L and Rousseeuw, P J (1990) *Finding Groups in Data*, John Wiley, New York

Mather, P (1976) *Computational Methods of Multivariate Analysis in Physical Geography*, John Wiley, New York

Myers, J H and Tauber, E (1977) *Market Structure Analysis*, American Marketing Association, Chicago, IL

Punji, G and Stewart, D R (1983) Cluster analysis in marketing research: review and suggestions for application, *Journal of Marketing Research*, **XX** (May), pp 134–48

Schaffer, C M and Green, P E (1996) An empirical comparison of variable standardization methods in cluster analysis, *Multivariate Behavior Research*, **31** (2), pp 149–67

Schaffer, C M and Green, P E (1998) Cluster-based market segmentation: some further comparisons of alternative approaches, *Journal of the Market Research Society*, **40** (2), pp 155–63

Sheth, J P and Ramakrishnan, C (2003) Semantic (web) technology in action: ontology driven information systems for search, integration and analysis, *IEEE Data Engineering Bulletin*, 26 (**4**), pp 40–46

Smith, W R (1956) Product differentiation and market segmentation as alternative marketing strategies, *Journal of Marketing* (July), pp 3–8

Spath, H (1985) *Cluster Dissection and Analysis*, Halsted Press, New York

Stewart, D W (1981) The application and misapplication of factor analysis in marketing research, *Journal of Marketing Research*, **XVIII**, (February), pp 51–62

Struhl, S (2013) *Market Segmentation*, 2nd edn, American Marketing Association Press, Chicago, IL

Sundberg, R (1976) An iterative method for solution of the likelihood equations for incomplete data from exponential families, *Communications in Statistics – Simulation and Computation*, **5** (1), pp 55–64

Tull, D S and Hawkins, D I (1980) *Marketing Research*, 2nd edn, Macmillan, Englewood Cliffs, NJ

Wilkie, W L (1971) Market segmentation research: a conceptual analysis, Paper No 324, Institute for Research in the Behavioral, Economic and Management Sciences (Purdue University)

Wong, W, Liu, W and Bennamoun, M (2012) Ontology learning from text: a look back and into the future, *ACM Computing Surveys (CSUR)*, 44 (**4**), pp 20–36

IN THE MOOD FOR SENTIMENT (AND COUNTING)

KEY QUESTIONS

What can I learn from just counting words? How does sentiment analysis work, how do I use it best and what are possible pitfalls to avoid?

Chapter 5 examines the difficult process of assigning positive or negative meanings to words and phrases. We will explore sentiments analysis, including its definitions, its many uses and misuses. We start with counting words, showing how this and the common forms of sentiment analysis are close relatives.

Basics of sentiment and counting

Sentiment has been with mankind since time immemorial. Sentiment as something you can analyse in text is much more recent. Some of the first mentions come about 1995. This of course is ancient history in this field, and indeed **sentiment analysis** has changed since the first efforts.

Sentiment analysis means one of many ways to measure whether documents are positive or negative in tone. As 'many ways' implies, what goes into this form of analysis varies considerably, depending on who is talking. Discussion of sentiment does not become as thorny and impenetrable as some areas in document classification, but people do appear to be describing a number of different things using the same name.

We will make a brief trip through two areas closely related to many varieties of sentiment analysis, counting words and centrality of words, before we get to sentiment. As we progress, you will come to see why such dissimilar-seeming topics actually belong together in this chapter.

Counting words

Only in text analytics does counting getting included among forms of analysis. This stretching of our ideas about what falls under the heading 'analytics' arises in part because it is so difficult to estimate numerical patterns in text. This in turn is partly due to the difficulties that we described in earlier chapters in just getting text into a form that you can analyse. That said, simply counting words can give you some preliminary insights into what a body of text, including a document or group of documents, might have as main areas of interest.

Simple counts can reveal patterns

Returning to the text from our social media site survey, you can see a count of words in Figure 5.1. The usual cleaning operations have taken place, including correcting spelling, removing extraneous characters, removing stop words, regularizing verb tenses, stemming, and so on. These are the words that remain.

The leading words, **site, professional, network, people** and **busy,** far outstrip all other words in number of occurrences. The dashed line shows

FIGURE 5.1   Count of words and expected number of
occurrences

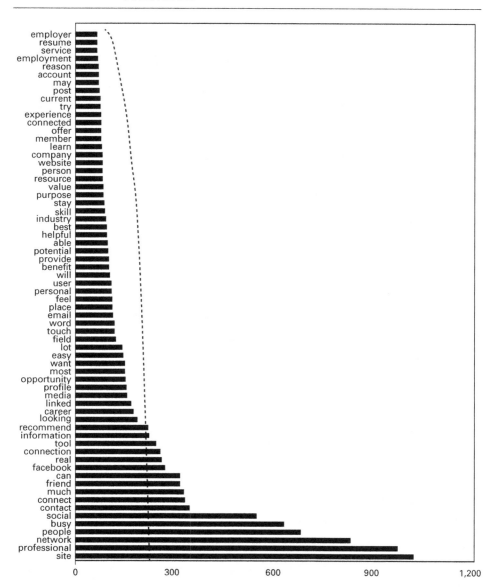

how often we would expect words to appear just based on chance – that
is, in a random group of words not about any topic. If we have just a
chance assortment, some words still occur more often haphazardly.
Looking at the line, we see the set of words we highlighted goes far
beyond expectations.

Most words actually occur less often than we would expect, shown by their corresponding bars falling to the left of the dotted line. This means that comments focus very heavily on the leading concerns. (This site is not Facebook, so all the comments about Facebook are comparative.)

Betweenness and counting

Centrality or **betweenness centrality** is a more sophisticated type of counting. It counts connections, and comes from the world of network analysis, where it often gets used to find individuals who have many relationships to two or more groups of people. These people with high **centrality** or **betweenness** are seen as influential in bridging the communications of different groups.

In text analysis, words with higher **betweenness centrality** appear with the most other words representing different concepts. These words with high betweenness words might have multiple meanings in addition to connecting with many different ideas.

In the word diagrams we discussed in Chapter 3, the graph layout of words (Figure 3.10) shows centrality clearly. The words with the most connections have the highest degree of centrality.

In spite of the greater sophistication involved in counting connections than in simple counting, the most frequent words emerged as having the highest centrality. This seems to happen as a matter of course. For this reason, we are discussing counting and centrality together.

Closely associated words

Determining which words occur most often near a word that you have flagged also requires no more than counting. Still, this can give you a sense of the closely related concerns. Going back to the study of professionals who deal with insurance plans for doctors, we flagged two words, **patient** and **problem**. These appear in Figure 5.3.

We can see at a glance that **patients** are central to these professional's work lives, seeing just the large number of words that occur in connection with them. By contrast, the word **problem** relates to a relatively small number of areas including: **attendant, complex, multiple, order, solve**, and (perhaps no surprise) **patient**.

FIGURE 5.2   Betweenness centrality of words

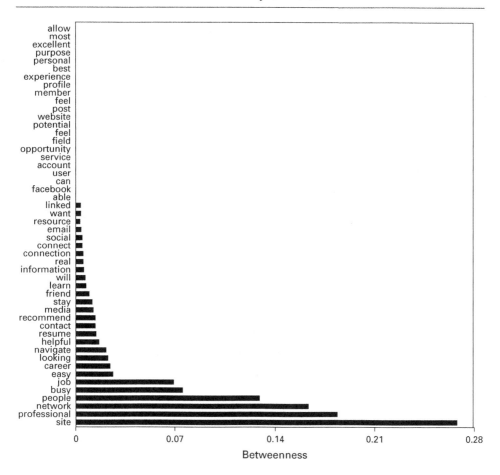

Locations of words and themes

Where words occur in a longer document can show emerging themes or shifts in concerns. We used a program that treated all the documents as a single block (**Advisor**, mentioned in the last chapter), but more or less tricked it into showing how words were associated with different overall ratings across many documents. We did this by sorting the documents based on the overall ratings associated with them, with those corresponding to the lowest ratings coming first in a file, and those associated with the highest ratings last. This chart that came from this analysis appears in Figure 5.4. Words located more to the left were associated more with lower ratings.

FIGURE 5.3   Words commonly associated with two key words in the insurance example

Flagged Word	Associated Words
patient	achieve actual address aggravate allow annual answer appropriate approval approve authorization avoided base believe benefit best can cant capitated capitation care centre change check child clearance clearer clinic common communication complex compliant complicate confuse contact contract coordination cost counsel cover cross customer data decision deductible deserve diabetes diagnose difference direct disconnect discourage discuss doctor drug dumping easy educate educating education effort facilitate failed fall fee goal grid guideline happy health held helpful haemoglobin honest hoop hound hypertension idea imaging impediment include increase info inform information informed insurance insurer interfering judge jump kill limbo lower make manage management manager may med medical medication medicine mental metric much navigate network notify ongoing order panel patient pay payment pcp people performance phone physician plan point policies prescribe prescription primary prior promote provider punish quick range rate real referral regard reimbursement require responsibility responsible restriction rid same school send sense serve service shop sicker signed simpler simplify specialist specific spend standard statement stop studies suggestion suspect system talk test therapy transparent treat trench try unneeded Walmart
problem	attendant complex multiple order patient solve

Each dot on the chart represents five occurrences of a word. Perhaps one of the more surprising features of this chart is how evenly distributed (from left to right) most of the words appear to be. This means that regardless of overall ratings given to the insurance provider, concerns generally involved the same key words. The heavy concentration of dots following the word **patient** shows that these professional discuss patients most of all, and they come into the commentary regardless of the overall ratings given.

There appears to be some moderate clumping of words near the left, associated with lower ratings, for several words. These include **plan, data, payment and deductible**. These words are highlighted in the rectangle in the diagram. This indicates some dissatisfaction in these areas.

There is no discernible clumping near the highest ratings to the right, which strongly suggests that this provider is not performing outstandingly well in any area. A few words seem to clump in moderately high range, including **expenses, pocket, office** and **referrals**. We would not be going

FIGURE 5.4   Occurrences of words as a way of better understanding ratings

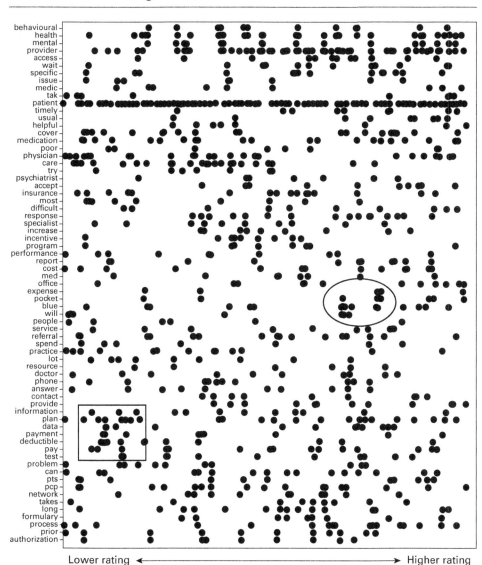

Lower rating ←————————————————————————→ Higher rating

too far afield to assume that these comments have to do with the needed **referrals** to specialists and with **out-of-pocket office expenses**. This provider apparently does better taking care of the little expenses than they do with the major payments. This makes eminent sense, based on experience with insurance companies.

Understanding sentiment

Sentiment analysis aims to understand the positive and negative tone in documents. It typically involves an attempt to get at this tonality without asking for any direct ratings, or indeed asking directly about anything. As it is most commonly done, this type of analysis is closely related to counting. That is, documents get compared to a list or **lexicon** in which specific words (and perhaps phrases) have positive or negative scores. Then the occurrences of these words gets counted. The balance of positive and negative words determines the **sentiment score** for the document. A sentiment score can be applied to any text, including text found anywhere on the web. Because it can be attached to text from individuals who have not been vetted, and so whose actual habits and usage patterns and are unknown, in these applications it needs to be applied with particular caution, as we will discuss.

> **Sentiment analysis** tries to find the positive or negative tone in documents. It typically works by comparing the words in the documents to words tagged as positive and negative in external lists or **lexicons**. The balance of positive and negative words determines the **sentiment scores**.

A freely available set of lists developed by Liu often gets used in defining sentiment. You can find it and download it at **http://www.cs.uic.edu/~liub/FBS/sentiment-analysis.html**. These comprise a negative list having about 4,800 words and a positive list with about 2,000. Liu is a serious and thorough scholar of language as used by computers, so his lists are widely accepted. You can see the first parts of these lists in Figure 5.5. (Liu notes that these words include some deliberate misspellings, in an attempt to capture the natural language used by people providing opinions.)

However, the important term here is 'widely accepted'. Sentiment is defined by the users of sentiment, rather than having a specific set of mathematical properties, as we would find in, for instance, statistical significance or statistical power. You can readily modify sentiment lexicons yourself (they are just simple text files).

FIGURE 5.5 Several positive and negative sentiment words as defined by Liu

Positive	Negative
a+	2-faced
abound	2-faces
abounds	abnormal
abundance	abolish
abundant	abominable
accessable	abominably
accessible	abominate
acclaim	abomination
acclaimed	abort
acclamation	aborted
accolade	aborts
accolades	abrade
accommodative	abrasive
accomodative	abrupt

Some programs even have a number of alternative sentiment dictionaries. The SPSS Text Analysis for Surveys program that we discussed in Chapter 2 has separate dictionaries for uses as specific as customer satisfaction or new product introduction.

Plausible as these dictionaries may seem, they are crafted based on what **seems** to make sense, rather than any proven relationship to opinions or behaviours. Each dictionary was put together by some person or group of people who judged that the words included have a certain emotional tone. But what specifically does an assigned emotional tone have to do with the ways in which people act or decide?

Indeed, this is the leading question for any sentiment analysis: does the sentiment you are measuring in any way relate to some quantifiable phenomenon in the outside world?

We may of course, want to use sentiment analysis without regard to behaviour. For instance, monitoring sentiment might provide an early warning of some incipient problem. How seriously you take sentiment, though, also lies in how well you know the audience providing the commentary. We find the most serious need for caution in analysing populations where you really do not know who is providing the comments.

Here come the cautions about sentiment

Uses and misuses of sentiment

Sentiment gets a fair amount of attention in the news. Much of the analysis discussed here is done completely incorrectly.

For instance, *USA Today*, a newspaper which has printed its share of **factoids**, ran sentiment scores every day before the 2012 US presidential election for each of the candidates. This was supposed to reflect public opinion. Calling this flawed is mild language. Marc Smith, an expert in the social organization of online communities, and the co-creator of the open-source network analysis tool, NodeXL, put it more bluntly. 'That is irresponsible,' he said. 'That is remarkably poor data. That is borderline criminal, I would argue.' He added that this was not public opinion, but just a measure of which side shouted the loudest.

> **Factoids** are incorrect or inaccurate statements presented in the press that seem likely to be true. When reading about **sentiment**, or indeed **any topic related to text data** in the press, you must be constantly on guard against **factoids**.

These articles had another serious problem as well. With opinions gathered from any social media platform, you typically do not know whether the people posting have any idea what they are talking about. And indeed you often have no idea who is posting.

Missing the sample frame with social media

In Chapter 1, we talked about the problem of incorrect **sample frames**, and the terrific mistakes in predictions that can be made by using the wrong frames. This is important enough to go over again. It should be particularly handy for those of you who do not yet have that chapter completely memorized.

Any location from which you draw text, including any site on the web, is a **sample frame**. The **frame** defines the nature of the population, and so defines the responses that you will be measuring. This is very much like the frame around a picture, as we discussed in Chapter 1. Again, this comparison is important enough to reiterate, although we are freshening it up with a new picture.

If you have the correct frame, as on the left in Figure 5.6, you will see the picture that you intend to see. If you get the frame wrong, as on the right, you get to see something else. You may not even be able to discern the actual nature of the picture, as is the case there. It may indeed leave you staring at a blank wall, even if an interestingly textured one.

It does not matter how large the frame is if it is not the right one. In Chapter 1, we talked about the 1936 election, in which a sample of **2.4 million**, but a sample drawn from the wrong sampling frame, miscalled the election terribly. Not only did this mammoth survey predict the wrong winner, but the results were wrong by a margin of 19 per cent. This has been called the largest error ever in a major public opinion poll.

The problem of using the wrong sample frame was not widely understood back in 1936. George Gallup (creator of the Gallup poll) did know

FIGURE 5.6   The frame is correct and the frame is incorrect, revisited

SOURCE: The storm tossed vessel, circa 1889, Henri, Rousseau.
http://www.wikiart.org/en/henri-rousseau/the-storm-tossed-vessel#supersized-
artistPaintings-191415. Frame photographed by the author. Image assembled by the author.

about this, and conducted a more modest (but still large) survey with the right frame. He correctly forecast that in January of the next year, we would not be seeing President Alf Landon. (The winner was a slightly better known person, one Franklin Delano Roosevelt, who won by a margin of 62 per cent to 38 per cent.)

The main source of the problem, as we mentioned, was that the survey got answers from **2.4 million of the wrong people**. It did not matter that this was a huge group, representing about 6 per cent of the entire voting population at the time. This sample was too affluent and too literate to reflect the US voting public at the time. Basing a prediction on them led to incredibly wrong results.

A more pernicious issue still: unknown frames are hit or miss

Not understanding the sample frame, or not knowing who is offering the comments you are collecting, you may get the answer right one time, and then wrong the next time – for unknown and unknowable reasons. You may be left scrambling for explanations, and may never come up with anything that fixes the problems you ran into after your first (and undeserved) success.

A telling example comes from Google. With great fanfare, they announced in 2009 that they had found a way to anticipate flu trends reported by the US Centers for Disease Control, simply based on Google searches about flu. As they put it: 'We can accurately estimate the current level of weekly influenza activity in each region of the United States, with a reporting lag of about one day.'

At first, they seemed to have hit upon an answer. But then came the Swine Flu epidemic of 2009. They missed it. In fact, as Lazar *et al* reported, they were wrong for 100 out of 108 weeks starting in August 2011.

How can this be so? It happened for several reasons, one of the most important being that most people are highly ignorant about the symptoms, processes and sequelae of 'the flu' – and that includes those making searches deemed to be related to the subject.

Another problem lies in the phrase 'deemed to be related'. Even assuming people knew what to search for, would searches about the flu include all those related to body aches and pains, running noses, sore throats, elevated temperatures, and so on? Who could possibly answer this question? (Apparently not Google.)

IMAGE 5.1   A more solid indicator that the flu is around

SOURCE: Street car conductor in Seattle not allowing passengers aboard without a mask, 1918, uploaded 2006, author unknown.
http://commons.wikimedia.org/wiki/File:165-WW-269B-11-trolley-l.jpg.

Hit or miss performance must follow from not understanding the nature of your sample, even in the best of all possible worlds. But this world, unfortunately, does not meet that ideal standard. The web is now populated by what has been described as 'armies of bots' or fake personas, that can be purchased to tweet or post repeatedly about a subject, a brand, or a celebrity. The author of one article claimed to have created 20 such bots easily with 'minimal programming skills' (and just as an experiment of course). The professionals can generate thousands for the purpose of making something or somebody appear prominent. This article identified over 10 per cent of one celebrity's 'followers' as robotic fakes.

Showing the great vulnerability of the web to robotic posting (and voting), comedian Steven Colbert won an online contest to have a new bridge in Hungary named after himself. With the new name about to be chosen in an online election, he asked his viewers to vote for the 'Steven Colbert Hid [Bridge]'. Some constructed bots to do so.

He won a landslide victory, reportedly receiving some 17 million votes. However, the rules were then revealed to have some hidden conditions (the winner had to speak fluent Hungarian and be dead – a seeming contradiction, but never mind). Now the bridge has the much more appropriate-sounding designation of Megyeri Hid.

Still, this did not happen before the power of false postings was revealed. This is another factor to consider carefully when you venture near any public forum discussing a topic surrounded by controversy – or which features a call for endorsements.

IMAGE 5.2   If you think that the name Steven Colbert Bridge got 17 million legitimate votes online, we have another one in Brooklyn to sell you

SOURCE: Megyeri Bridge, no upload date, File: Civertanmegyeri4.jpg. http://en.wikipedia.org/wiki/Megyeri_Bridge.

Extensions of sentiment analysis

A number of authors are now recognizing that sentiment scores alone are not adequate. Some point to the fact that a single number cannot adequately capture the nuances or meanings in most text. Others say that it is important to understand what the words refer to in a document. For instance, we would run into problems assigning a simple score if encountering a review that says:

'Wow, the new SoggyOs Cereal is great! Compared to this my Sorghum Sweeties taste bad and my Kardboard Krunchies taste terrible!'

Solely toting up the negative and positive words we would say that this review was negative, as we have one positive word ('great') and two negatives ('bad' and 'terrible'). We would be wrong. In fact, understanding the exact referents or antecedents of words in a document poses terrific computational challenges. Numerous sophisticated solutions have been proposed, and vast amounts continue to be written about the best way get machines to do better.

This difficulty highlights an important theme that runs throughout this book. It is precisely because we lack other critical data that pure sentiment analysis is hard to do correctly. Even assuming we do know for certain who is giving an opinion, in analysing words by themselves, we lack anything against which to anchor the opinion, such as a rating given by the person or a certain behaviour, such as a level of purchasing. Adding this type of knowledge has been what gives text analytics its greatest level of usefulness.

Suggestions to overcome weaknesses in sentiment scores

Many different approaches use still more sophisticated processing and apply more detailed systems of word associations. Other systems try to add some sort of information outside just comments. At least one of these aims to improve sentiment scores by determining the demographics of people offering their opinions. This is troubling when we consider personal privacy. How do they get those demographics? Alternatively, if they are talking about the demographics of those who freely offer that information, do those people reflect your users and prospects?

Beyond this, demographics do not define interests, world views or use patterns. If you doubt this, just look at your neighbours. For instance, consider that fellow down the block who thinks that the height of fun is putting on his fake Viking helmet (the one with gold horns) and riding on that motorcycle that seems to have permanently lost its muffler. (If that is you, we meant somebody else entirely, and the last sentence was just a terrible printer's error.)

IMAGE 5.3   A good time had by all

SOURCE: Glenn Curtiss on his V-8 motorcycle, Ormond Beach, Florida 1907. http://en.wikipedia.org/
wiki/Motorcycle_land-speed_record#mediaviewer/File:Glenn_Curtiss_on_his_V-8_motorcycle,_
Ormond_Beach,_Florida_1907.jpg.

IMAGE 5.4   It used to be easier to know who was truly influential

SOURCE: King George in 1923. http://commons.wikimedia.org/wiki/File:Kinggeorgev1923.jpg. This is a
press photograph from the George Grantham Bain collection, which was purchased by the Library of
Congress in 1948.

The fact is that people are quite different even given very similar demographics. Of course, it is good to discount the comments of an 11 year-old about your beer, but that excessively verbal 44 year-old may not be at all typical of your users.

Similar concerns hold for identifying people with a great deal of **betweenness centrality**, or people who get involved in a great many online conversations. These people are thought to be opinion leaders, and that contacting and 'engaging' them therefore will reap you vastly expanded revenues. This seems to make sense, but the question still remains about how much the number of comments somebody offers reflects her/his influence. Some individuals of course are highly respected in their circles, and many people pay attention to what they say. But whether this influences behaviour noticeably in relation to **your** fine product or service remains an open question.

Sentiment as a Type III error

Before we get to actually doing sentiment analysis, maybe we all could use a respite from the many needed caveats. When you do not know where the text comes from, and still obsess about semantics, shades of meanings and degrees of connections, that is technically called making a **Type III error**.

There really is such a thing, and it follows our old friends from Chapter 1, **Types I and II errors**. To have this all in one place, directly below they are described in not completely technical terms:

- **Type I error:** going on a wild goose chase, or pronouncing something to be so when it is not.
  - Statisticians are very much on guard against this. **Statistical significance** is the measure.
- **Type II error:** missing something when you should have seen it.
  - Not such a concern in statistics, but it should be. Its measure is **statistical power**.
- **Type III error:** getting a very precise answer to the wrong question.
  - No official measure, but we should always be particularly vigilant about this.

Much to your author's amazement, other types of error, all the way up to Type X (that truly is Type 10), already have been staked out and defined.

We must conclude that if people are good at anything, it is making many different mistakes.

However, there is room for one more, and so we now humbly propose what may be the most prevalent of all, **Type XI error**: **getting a very imprecise answer to the wrong question.**

How do I do sentiment analysis?

If you want to try sentiment analysis for yourself, most text analytics programs offer some form of it. However, unless you are using the largest and most automated programs, you may encounter highly picky behaviour about accepting text as you would like to offer it. Otherwise, programs may choke unexpectedly on some other phase of the analysis, such as reading lexicons or writing output. You or the people working with you likely will end up spending some time reading manuals, looking at tutorials, visiting online forums, and perhaps even talking to technical support (if it exists).

You need to decide whether the ratio of effort to results is worthwhile. Figure 5.7 shows the output from a sentiment analysis done with Statistica Text Miner. This comes from the text comments offered in the survey about the social media platform that we have been discussing. It is **all** of the output.

Some programs now include sentiment analysis as a kind of free bonus. For instance, the SPSS Text Analytics for Surveys program that we discussed in Chapter 2 assigns emotional valences as a part of its coding process. Certain phrases get tagged as negative or positive, so we have codes such as 'business (positive mentions)', for instance, or 'navigation

FIGURE 5.7   Sentiment score output from the social media survey

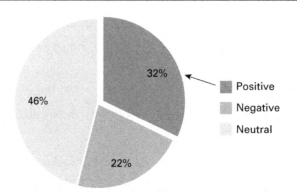

(negative mentions)'. This added identification of tonality was done as a matter of course with one of the special lexicons included in the program.

Uses, with the usual prescriptions, caveats and cautions

You can make good use of sentiment analysis in the right settings and with the right goals. If you have, for instance, an online community or warranty forms including comments, an ongoing customer (tracking) survey, or a customer call centre where messages are transcribed, sentiment analysis can provide a quick way to take a pulse and watch for problems. In these applications, it does not matter much that all dictionaries defining positive and negative moods are somewhat arbitrary – if you stay with the same dictionary. That is, if you are tracking responses on a consistent basis, you can then see early signs that call for a more formal investigation.

Sticking with the same dictionary is definitely one important practice in situations like these, in spite of the nagging temptation to tinker with it, aiming to make improvements. Fiddling with the means of tracking opinions of course wipes out comparability over time, and while on reflection this sounds like an incredibly foolish idea, it has happened regularly since the inception of following opinions.

IMAGE 5.5   The old dictionary can keep on working

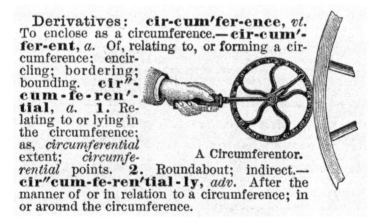

Your author has lost count of the crestfallen clients who insisted on alterations in traditional opinion tracking studies, in spite of all cautions, only to reap the inevitable outcome of non-comparable data. It is sad that advice about this so rarely sticks. Anyhow, you did hear it here.

Another valuable way to use sentiment analysis is in monitoring for any negative notions, true or false, that might be brewing in the strange channels of cyberspace. In Chapter 1, we talked about Proctor and Gamble deciding to change the logo they had used for over 100 years due to rumours that the image had satanic associations. Earlier, Gerber's Baby Food had to devote considerable time and resources to fend off another false rumour about additives in its baby food. These both happened before 1990, and since there was no internet back then, rumours were all people had to damage a company pointlessly.

Now slander, calumny and canard can spread with amazing speed (as can the occasional sad truth). For instance, when an anonymous video of rats scampering around a NY Taco Bell surfaced in 2007, the company's sales and stock price both dropped. Even the best monitoring program cannot fend off marauding rodents, but you definitely do not want to be the last to know if some horrible story about you is going viral.

To add to the excitement (if that is the right word), a company's own employees can get into the act. This happened to Domino's in 2009, when two workers posted a video of themselves doing unhygienic things that we wish we had never seen.

IMAGE 5.6   I'll have mine with extra cheese and some disinfectant

Social media excoriated Domino's, but questions still remain about whether such negative publicity does any lasting damage. Stemming the harm requires a response that is reasonably thorough, even if not reasonably speedy (as was the case with this incident). For instance, Domino's stock price did decline briefly after the video went online, but in the five years following, it steadily rose to about 10 times its 2009 level.

Still, monitoring the tone of social media commentary and being ready to respond seems only prudent. However, it also seems prudent to consider using a service for this if your only interest is in covering all the possibilities.

Summary

We started with **counting words,** showing how even this simple activity can reveal themes and concerns in a body of text. Counting is related to a more complex form of analysis, seeking the **betweenness or centrality** of words, and results are similar. Looking at where words occur in a body of text also is an activity related to counting, and can have additional value if you sort the comments based on some other information, such as the overall ratings given by each person providing a comment. As we showed, this allows you to see which words have stronger associations with higher and lower ratings.

Sentiment analysis aims to find the emotional values in text without asking those offering the comments any direct questions. Although it can grow very complex, looking for subtle linguistic patterns to discern meanings, most sentiment analysis largely involves counting words. In this, the text in documents gets compared with a list of positive and negative words, a kind of dictionary or **lexicon**, and the relative frequencies of each type of word gets determined. If a document has more words on the negative list than on the positive, it gets a negative score, and if more positive, a positive score.

All sentiment scores are in some measure subjective. They do not have mathematically defined properties like tests of statistical significance. You can get different sentiment scores depending on which dictionary you use. You also can modify many dictionaries easily, as they often are simple text files holding lists of words.

Sentiment gets a fair amount of attention in the press. Much of what is written about sentiment there and elsewhere consists of **factoids**. When dealing with sentiment, and text in general, it is critical to understand what factoids are. These are items that may seem true, but that are inaccurate or false, and get repeated often. You need to read critically, ask for evidence, and read that carefully also.

The bottom line about sentiment is that it definitely can be useful if you have a source of text that you control, such as an online community, warranty forms including comments, an ongoing customer (tracking) survey, or a phone centre where you get transcribed customer conversations. In any of these settings, sentiment can provide a preliminary, early measure that can alert you to problems or concerns that need a more thorough investigation.

On social media platforms, you run into the insuperable problems of not knowing if people have any idea what they are talking about, and indeed of really knowing which populations are providing the observations. The person who makes the most comments – or just the most noise – about your product or service may not even faintly represent the people who have the most use for it.

Every location from which you get text commentary is a **sample frame**. The frame defines who provides the text you collect and therefore the nature of the commentary that you encounter. Choosing the right frame is critical, as mistakes here can lead you to horrendously wrong predictions. It is very much like framing a picture. If the frame is right, you see what you mean to, and if it is far enough off, you could end up staring at a blank wall. Again, it does not matter how many people you have in your frame if they are the wrong people. We actually found that out as long ago as 1936, when a colossal sample of 2.4 million led to the reportedly largest error ever in a major public opinion poll.

Still, it is only prudent to know whether something pernicious to you is starting to circulate anywhere on the web. Once stories start, they can move quickly. Thorough responses can undo much or all of the damage, as was shown by the case of Domino's Pizza. Still, having a response that is both thorough **and** quick must work even better.

Various sources have pointed out weaknesses in simple sentiment scores. However, proposals seem lacking when suggesting we can improve on the scores from social media by somehow adding the demographics of the people making the comments. Even assuming such data can be found legitimately, demographics do not define our opinions, world view or behaviour. To confirm that, just take a look at your neighbours.

Another proposal suggests finding people with a great deal of **centrality** or **betweenness**, meaning that they are connected to many conversations. This seems sensible, but you must ask yourself if the people talking most on a given site are really representative of **your** customers' and prospects' needs.

Systems for measuring sentiment can involve incredible computational complexity. Still, if you spend a great deal of time obsessing about linguistics or social connections, but still do not know which population is providing your text commentary, then you have fallen into **Type III error**. This type of error may be the second greatest pitfall of the computer age, namely, getting **a very precise answer to the wrong question**. In your author's opinion, more prevalent still is what we now respectfully propose as Type XI error (Types IV through X already being spoken for, amazingly enough). Type XI error is getting an imprecise answer to the wrong question.

The motivations for wanting a lot out of sentiment are easy to understand. It would be wonderful just to have data flow in and answers flow out in easy, steady streams. However fond that hope, if you really want to know what people think and what they want, you still need to ask, and to know how to ask in the right ways. Many of you have doubtless noticed that throughout this book, we refer to a survey done by a major social networking site. They of course do a great deal of passive monitoring, but when they really want to improve something, they put that aside and engage in talking directly to their customers and prospects.

References

Asur, S and Huberman, B (2010) Predicting the future with social media, HP Research Labs, eprint arXiv: 1003.5699 [online] http://www.hpl.hp.com/research/scl/papers/socialmedia/socialmedia.pdf [accessed 12 February 2015]

Baldridge, J (2014) *Practical Sentiment Analysis Tutorial*, Presented at the Sentiment Analysis Symposium, 2014 [online] http://www.slideshare.net/PeoplePattern/practical-sentiment-analysis-33376773?qid=c181aa4a-aa15-4de9-9a56-5cd78b60c802&v=default&b=&from_search=1 [accessed 12 February 2015]

Bilton, N (2014) Friends, and influence, for sale online, *The New York Times*, Bits, blogs, 20 April 2014 [online] http://bits.blogs.nytimes.com/2014/04/20/friends-and-influence-for-sale-online [accessed 12 February 2105]

Clifford, S (2009) Video prank at Domino's taints brand, *The New York Times*, 15 April 2009 [online] http://www.nytimes.com/2009/04/16/business/media/16dominos.html?_r=0 [accessed 12 February 2105]

Daniel, L G and Onwuegbuzie, A J (2000) Towards an extended typology of research errors, presented at the Annual Meeting of the Mid-South Educational Research Association (28th), Bowling Green, KY [online] http://eric.ed.gov/?id=ED449166 [accessed 12 February 2105]

finance.yahoo.com [accessed 12 February 2015] Domino's historical stock prices [online] http://finance.yahoo.com/q/hp?s=DPZ

Ginsberg, J, Mohebbi, M H, Patel, R S, Brammer, L, Smolinski, M S and Brilliant, L (2009) Detecting influenza epidemics using search engine query data, *Nature*, **457**, pp 1012–14

Harris, S (1998) Absurd rumours, real harm: urban legends are fiction, but the fact is, they hurt consumers, businesses, *Baltimore Sun*, 13 September 1998 [online] http://articles.baltimoresun.com/1998-09-13/news/1998256043_1_urban-legends-tommy-hilfiger-liz-claiborne [accessed 12 February 2015]

Ingersoll, G, Morton, T and Farris, L (2013) *Taming Text*, Manning Publications, Shelter Island, NY, pp 276–81

Kessler, S (2014) The problem with sentiment analysis: sorting social media chatter into 'positive' and 'negative' buckets is so 2009, FastCompany, 5 November 2014 [online] http://www.fastcompany.com/3037915/the-problem-with-sentiment-analysis [accessed 12 February 2014]

Lacy, K [accessed 12 February 2014] Does negative social media and PR really hurt brands?, blog, *Kyle Lacy*, 4 February 2011 [online] http://kylelacy.com/does-negative-social-media-and-pr-really-hurt-a-brand/

Lazer, D, Kennedy, R, King, G and Vespignani, A (2014) Big data: the parable of google flu: traps in big data analysis, *Science*, 14 March 2014 (343), pp 1203–05

Maynard, D [accessed 12 February 2014] *Practical Sentiment Analysis*, presented at the 2012 San Francisco Sentiment Analysis Symposium, 29 October 2012 [online] http://www.slideshare.net/dianamaynard/practical-sentiment-analysis

Pang, B and Lee, L (2008) Opinion mining and sentiment analysis, *Foundations and Trends in Information Retrieval*, **2** (1–2), pp 1–135

Waxer, C (2011) Help for social media mayhem, *CNN Money*, 24 August 2011 [online] http://money.cnn.com/2011/08/24/smallbusiness/social_media_business/ [accessed 12 February 2014]

Wikipedia [accessed 12 February 2014] Myergi Bridge description [online]
    http://en.wikipedia.org/wiki/Megyeri_Bridge

Zhang, J, Zhang, R, Zhang, Y and Yan, G (2013) On the impact of social
    botnets for spam distribution and digital-influence manipulation,
    2013 IEEE Conference on Communications and Network Security (CNS),
    pp 46–54

PREDICTIVE MODELS 1

06

Having words with regressions

KEY QUESTIONS

What more can we do with text than describe or depict it?
And how does regression do that?

C hapter 6 delves into the subject that held many of us in awe, or terror, in a class in statistics: regression – but this time in connection with analysing text. We aim first to show that it is not that bad after all, conceptually. The great familiarity of **regression,** compared with other types of advanced analytics, means that this may be the most acceptable form of predictive modelling for some clients. Regression, though, actually has more rules and expectations about data than the other predictive methods we will investigate in detail, classification trees and Bayesian networks. We will discuss a few of the basic requirements for regression so that you follow what is happening in the demonstrations of practical applications. We also highlight and explain the output from two heavyweight statistical programs, Statistica and SPSS.

Understanding predictive models

The methods we reviewed so far, including clustering, factor analysis and putting words into pictures all have an important quality in common. They show patterns and similarities, but do not show the ways in which a variable or variables will influence an outcome. That is, they are **descriptive**, rather than **predictive**. We discussed the distinctions between these two types of models in the last chapter. Still, for those of you who skipped directly to this section, or who feel a little unhabituated to the differences, here is a brief review.

Descriptive models show patterns and relationships. They give you valuable information about overall patterns, predominant features and relationships. They do not show what influences results and do not generate models that can be used for forecasting or prediction.

Predictive models, on the other hand, are designed to give you guidance about what influences or explains some result. For instance, you might want to know what motivates people to buy something, to donate to a charity, or to stay on a website. You also might want to know what makes people say they are more satisfied or more likely to recommend your fine product.

One way to think about the difference is shown in Figure 6.1. Descriptive models are like the landscape at the top, an overview that can provide a great deal of useful information. Predictive models are like the map, giving you directions that will get you to a destination. Both types of models obviously are useful. Descriptive methods can be described as more **exploratory**. Predictive models often **follow** more descriptive ones, building on them to create a better pathway to an intended outcome.

FIGURE 6.1   One way to think of descriptive vs predictive models

The Brandywine Valley Scenic Byway on Route 52 looking toward Route 100 at Winterthur between Greenville and Centreville, Delaware, uploaded 2010, Rick Darke for the US Dept of Transportation website. http://commons.wikimedia.org/wiki/File:Chateau_country.jpeg. Declared Public Domain at above website of Federal Highway Administration. See also http://www.fhwa.dot.gov/byways/photos/60774.

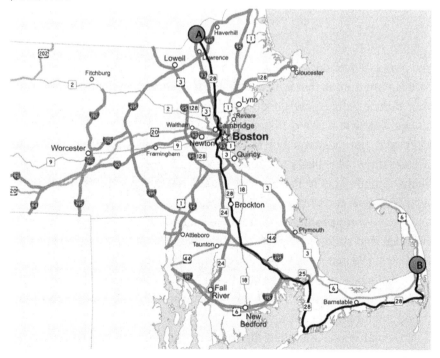

Map of major highways in Massachusetts with Massachusetts Route 28 highlighted, 15 November 2009, own work by uploader 'Sswonk' based on public data from Office of Geographic and Environmental Information (MassGIS). http://commons.wikimedia.org/wiki/File:Massachusetts_Route_28.png.

Starting from the basics with regression

Regression has had a terrific history in predictive modelling. It has developed in many directions over the years. To interpret and use this powerful method, though, we need some basic knowledge. Let's start at the beginning. (If you are an old hand at regression, you might perhaps want to skip to 'lines and regression'. Otherwise, here we go.)

To get a regression model, we need at least these elements: one variable that we want to forecast or predict and another variable that we will use to predict it. The variable we want to forecast is called the **dependent variable** or **target variable**. The variable we are using to forecast or predict it is called the **independent variable** or the **predictor variable**.

> Regressions have a **target variable** that we are trying to forecast or predict using the other variables. The target is called the **dependent** and the other variables the **independents**. We really cannot predict anything, but rather can make **forecasts**. Think of weather forecasts rather than magical answers when dealing with so-called **predictive modelling.**

You may well wonder why the last paragraph said 'forecast or predict'. The unfortunate truth is that we cannot actually **predict** anything. If we could, your author would now be on his private island – writing this book of course, but on that island. Instead, we can **forecast.** Just think of a weather forecast to get the distinction between a forecast and a prediction. That is, we can say what is **likely** to happen, and we may even be able to say **how likely** something is to happen. We cannot say what actually **will** happen with complete certainty.

Still, the term **predictive models** has gained a tremendous amount of currency, and although it is not accurate, we will not fight the flow, and so will use it. We just need to recall that these methods do not have magical or even oracular properties, and go from there. A colleague is fond of saying that the goal of analytics is reducing uncertainty. That is less lofty than telling the future, but still an admirable objective.

Now that we have settled that, we can get back to – well – predictive models. We construct one of these either because we cannot directly measure the target variable we want to predict, or because we want to know which variables influence a target variable and just how much influence these variables have.

Predictions and glue

Let's take a specific example. Suppose we need to heat up a pot of glue until it is warm enough to work its best. We would like to have a reliable to way to know, for future reference, how much natural gas we need to warm the pot to the right temperature. We have a valve on the natural gas burner that ranges from zero to 10. We turn the dial on the gas from zero to one and measure the glue's temperature with our rusty old thermometer. Then we raise the dial a notch at a time.

The result appears in the chart in Figure 6.2. The plot that accompanies it shows the same information in graphical form. We also have included

IMAGE 6.1   Finding the melting point

SOURCE: Pressure cooker on induction burner, uploaded 2013.
http://www.flickr.com/photos/dinnerseries/8556666861.

a straight line that represents an average of the relationship between the two variables, the independent (gas valve reading) and the target (temperature).

The plot in Figure 6.2 follows the well-established tradition of putting the **independent variable** along the horizontal or **x-axis** and the **target variable** along the vertical or **y-axis**. Looking at this this plot, we can see that the straight line very nearly captures the relationship between the two variables. We can create a formula or **equation** that explains how much temperature rises on average with each turn of the dial. It looks like this:

$$\text{Temperature} = (5 \times \text{dial reading} + 75) \text{ or}$$
$$y = 5x + 75$$

That simply says that if the dial is zero, temperature is still 75, and if we increase the dial by one unit, on average we increase temperature by 5 units or degrees. In a regression, the term at the end (75) is called the **constant**. As you can see, it is a starting point for the line, the value when the independent variable is zero.

Now suppose we would like to buy a bigger burner that goes up to 20, and would like to **forecast** (or **predict**) how much that would heat the glue at its highest setting. We can use the same formula as our best estimate, and would get the following value: (5 x 20 + 75) or 175.

FIGURE 6.2   Plotting the values of an independent and target variable

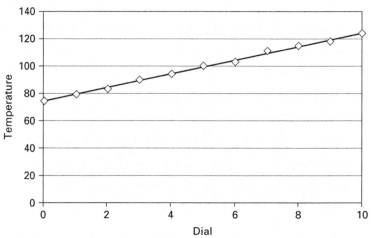

Dial	Temp
0	75
1	80
2	84
3	91
4	95
5	101
6	104
7	112
8	116
9	119
10	125

Lines and regressions

You might have noticed in the example that the relationship, as measured with our old thermometer, does not fall perfectly on a straight line. It is close but not exact. Regression can tell us precisely how close we are to a perfect straight-line relationship. We could in fact say that the business of regressions is finding and quantifying straight-line relationships. (There are some very advanced variants of regression that deal with curved lines, but you are not likely to see those outside the sciences.)

R-squared is the most commonly used measure of how well the regression performs – and one that is likely to be familiar to many of you. It summarizes how well the points fit a straight line. This can vary from zero to one, with one meaning a perfect fit to a straight line, and zero meaning that you cannot fit a straight line, no matter what you try.

The 'R' that is squared is the correlation coefficient. In statistics, **correlation** only means a simple summary measure of how well two variables fit a straight line. Correlation can range from a high of +1, where the two variables rise and fall in a perfect straight line relationship, down to −1, where the two variables have a perfect inverse relationship (one falls precisely as the other one rises). Outside the statistical world, correlation is taken to mean many things, often as a sort of shorthand for any relation between two quantities. We need to recall the more precise meaning when talking about regressions.

Correlation is a simple summary measure of how closely two variables fall compared to a perfect straight-line relationship. Correlation is known as **R** in statistics. **R-squared** is the most widely used measure showing how well a regression model performs and also shows how well values fit a straight line.

You may wonder why we need regressions and R-squared values if we have correlations, that already summarize how close points fall to a perfect straight-line relationship. Regression will tell us the **strength** of the relationship as well. In our glue example, each unit on the dial raised the temperature by 5 degrees. That was captured in the regression equation, $y = 5x + 75$. The correlation would be the same whether each notch on the dial raised the temperature by 3 degrees or 10 degrees or 50 degrees. The regression adds valuable information about the **strengths** of effects. Also, and as importantly, the R-squared applies if we have more than one predictor variable. Correlation is strictly for a pair of variables.

Not all the world falls into a line

Many regular, predictable relationships do not fall in a straight line, or are not **linear.** Figure 6.3 shows three examples. The first is a standard growth curve. You might see this pattern in nature when a colony of mould grows in a Petri dish. It takes a while for growth to become noticeable. Then growth takes off and stays at a fairly steady rate. In time, growth reaches a saturation level. It slows and then stops.

We also often see this curve with the adoption of products. A small brand has a great deal of trouble making itself visible, but once it reaches a certain threshold, growth comes much more rapidly. Finally, the brand reaches a point where it has saturated its market and further growth becomes very difficult.

Even though a straight line does not fit the pattern well, the correlation could still be deceptively strong, even as high as 0.9, misleadingly suggesting that the relationship is a straight line. In the last two examples in Figure 6.3, the correlation actually is **zero**. If we paid attention only to this statistic, we might be fooled into thinking that there was no relationship at all. We can in fact quantify these latter two relationships, but not in a way that linear regression can easily capture.

In our glue example, by the way, the correlation was an impressive 0.99. Perhaps we should polish the thermometer and keep it after all.

FIGURE 6.3   Regular relationships that are not linear

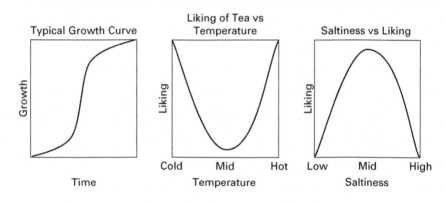

As long as we have only two variables to consider, and as long as we do not let the procedure get fooled by curved lines, regression can tell us a great deal. Here are five characteristics of a numerical relationship that a two-variable regression can reveal: (1) whether a relationship exists, (2) its strength, (3) its size, (4) its direction, and (5) something about its pattern.

Rules of the road for regression

When you are trying to analyse text, you will almost invariably have more than two variables in the mix. Once more variables get added, you have more to consider. The rules or assumptions of regression start to matter a great deal. When you bend or break these rules, you can encounter problems.

Conditions in a controlled experiment are ideal for regression analysis. Experiments fit every expectation or assumption of regression analysis. But what are these expectations?

1 *The model is correct*

That is, we have all the ingredients we need to make a good forecast. We do not have anything extra and we have not missed anything important. In an experiment, we aim to measure only those things that matter.

In that setting, it often is simple to understand the factors that are important. For instance, if we were doing an experiment to figure out how much water and fertilizer gives us the best yield of a crop, we would not measure the colours of the bags of fertilizer, or the ages of the people doing the watering.

Those last two are obviously nonsensical, but when we start to consider what people say and how this relates to their underlying attitudes and their behaviour, figuring out what to measure is not at all easy.

2 *The variables are not related to each other*

This has two components. The first of these is that the variables are not highly correlated. The problem of strong correlations among the variables has the perhaps familiar name **collinearity** or **multicollinearity**. We mention this because it is a term you may hear people throwing around quite casually. There are formal tests to see if this is happening. However, you can have variables that are too closely related and that do not set off an alarm in these tests.

That particular problem is more subtle and relates to the first point, namely, that you need to have just the right ingredients in the mix.

3 *There are no extreme cases in the mix*
If you have just one case (or one person) with a really extreme value, it can destroy the results of your regression model. Let's take a look at how this happens in Figure 6.4. It shows incomes vs house values in a neighbourhood. The chart to the right shows what happens to the regression when we include the hedge fund manager who bought all the desirable shorefront property. The regression sacrifices all the other relationships in an attempt to fit this one extreme point. The formal name for a value far outside the norm is an **outlier**.

The coefficient in the regression changes from 7.55 to 0.58. All the less extreme values get squeezed into the lower right corner. The R-squared value also goes to a stratospheric value (0.99), yet clearly does not reflect how income relates to house size in nearly all cases. In short, you need to be very careful about such extreme values when running any regression.

4 *The dependent variable can take a nearly infinite number of values*
This does not happen often with the data we encounter, unless we are predicting something like how much people will spend, or 'share of wallet' (percentage of total spending), or perhaps how many microseconds people will stay on a website. Often, instead we are attempting to forecast qualities such as how much people say they like something, or how interested they are in giving a recommendation, or answers to other scaled rating questions.

When we try to predict scaled responses, we are actually bending a regression rule. Scaled variables can take only a relatively few values, for instance, whole numbers between one and seven. This method often works in spite of this. Still, when we ask regression to have a dependent that takes few values, it becomes more difficult to diagnose how well the regression model is performing, for a variety of technical reasons. You can relax about this, as we will not discuss those reasons here.

5 *All the variables fall in straight lines or are 'yes/no' variables*
This generally gets ignored in the regression analyses we encounter. All the variables ideally should fall into nice straight lines, with the single exception that variables can be 'yes/no' or

FIGURE 6.4 Income vs house size without any outliers (left) and with an outlier (right)

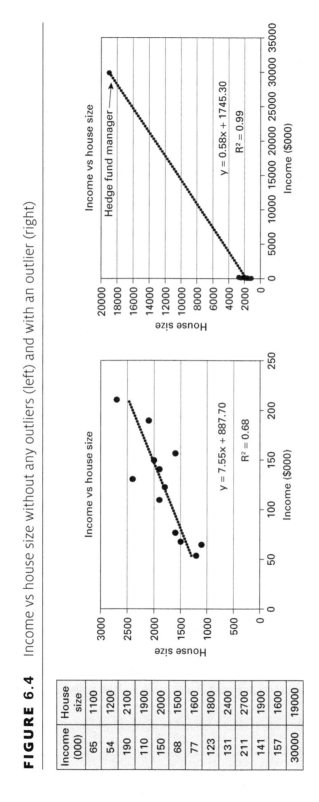

Income (000)	House size
65	1100
54	1200
190	2100
110	1900
150	2000
68	1500
77	1600
123	1800
131	2400
211	2700
141	1900
157	1600
30000	19000

Income vs house size

$y = 7.55x + 887.70$

$R^2 = 0.68$

Income ($000)

Income vs house size

Hedge fund manager

$y = 0.58x + 1745.30$

$R^2 = 0.99$

Income ($000)

0/1 type variables. This latter type of variable is sometimes called a **dummy variable**. When we analyse text in a regression, in many cases it will be represented in a 1/0 variable, with the code of one meaning that text item was present, and zero meaning that item was absent. Text also may be represented as a part of a **factor**, derived from factor analysis (we discussed factor analysis in Chapter 2). The second example uses text in factors.

> **Yes/no** or 1/0 style variables show whether something is present or absent. **Text** often gets encoded into a series of 1/0 variables. These also are called **dummy variables**.

Divergent roads: regression aims and regression uses

Regression is commonly used to investigate which variables have the strongest effects on a target variable and how variables' effects compare. (This is sometimes called regression-based 'drivers analysis'.) In an experiment, looking for strengths of effects is a legitimate line of inquiry. However, in less-controlled circumstances, this use of regression breaks down in many instances.

As we will see in our first example, regression may distort the strengths of variables to get a more accurate-looking prediction. That is, it will do the best to match the value of the target variable with whatever we throw at it as predictors – and if that means squeezing, expanding or even reversing some effects to get a better estimation, it will do so.

> The presence of other variables in a regression model often has more influence on effects reported by the regression than any underlying relationship between a predictor variable and the target variable.

This may seem very strange, and stranger still because regression gets used so often to determine the strengths of effects. We must be very wary of getting misled.

In fact, if we do an analysis and miss enough of the basic underlying expectations of regression, we cannot discern how important variables are. Fortunately, we can run regressions in a way that will at least tip us off to this problem, as we will discuss below. We then can be prepared if a client demands a regression-based analysis and the importances we report do not make complete sense.

Getting words into a regression

Let us all take a deep breath here, get away from the rules, and go on to what you do with text so that it works in a regression. We will need to do all initial cleaning we discussed in Chapters 2 and 4, removing extraneous punctuation, correcting misspellings, and stemming the words. Text then must be encoded or reduced from its messy form.

If you have a great many codes, you will need to stick with the most prevalent ones. Regression models can work with a great many variables, but you need to limit yourself. Even if you somehow manage to include hundreds in a model, that many variables will have no practical meaning. Just consider that if you have 100 variables in a regression model, the average importance of each variable is only 1 per cent. Since you invariably will find several variables that are much more important than the others, most variables will contribute nearly nothing to the model.

However, as we will see, regression models are likely to run into problems well before the total count of variables grows huge. The first example will show exactly how you detect when this happens.

Aside from encoding, another way of reducing the count of variables is through factor analysis. We will pick up the factor analysis example from Chapter 2, using those factors and responses to some scaled questions to predict an overall outcome. As a reminder, factor analysis combines the words that had some similarities in use into groups or factors. Words having different weights or influences in those factors. The way words are grouped will show something about the underlying ideas captured in the factor.

Practical examples

One more step we must take: what to expect from the output

Statistics programs differ in what they choose to show you in the output. We will show you output from the program SPSS. This is both venerable and truly heavyweight, dating back to the days of computer cards and basement mainframe computer labs in the 1960s – and now including many hundreds of procedures. There are two broad classes of SPSS programs: regular SPSS, which has many add-ons, and SPSS Data Modeller. Both are not inexpensive, and the Data Modeller is in the enterprise range, or well into five figures. The examples use regular SPSS.

One basic ingredient of all output is the formula or **equation** that regression creates. In this, each variable is multiplied by some value, called a **coefficient**, and there also is a constant. In algebraic format we have it as:

y = mx +b, where:

- y = the dependent (or target, the vertically plotted variable);
- x = the independent (or horizontally plotted variable);
- b = the constant or intercept (the point at which the line we draw crosses the y-axis, or where x = 0); and
- m = the change in units of y per change in a unit of x or the **slope** of the line.

Although this may seem deliberately confusing, statistical notation is different, as follows:

$$y = \beta_0 + \beta_1 x$$

We now have two kinds of 'B' (β) terms to keep track of, one for the constant or intercept (β_0) and one for the coefficient (β_1). Also, in this formulation, the constant comes first.

What does the actual regression output show?

We will start with just one independent variable and the constant that we mentioned earlier. The target or dependent variable is 'likelihood to recommend', the predictor satisfaction. Both variables are measured on a 0 to 10 scale.

FIGURE 6.5   Coefficients in a regression

Model		Unstandardized Coefficients		Standardized Coefficients		
		B	Std. Error	Beta	t	Sig.
1	(Constant)	1.474	.054		27.280	.000
	Q3 Satisfaction	.750	.006	.653	125.183	0.000

You can see this output in Figure 6.5. There is a fair amount of terminology here, but you may hear some of this bandied about, so it is worth a brief review.

The unstandardized coefficient or **B** gives the direct measures of effects. This shows that, if we want to forecast or predict the dependent variable, 'willingness to recommend', we should multiply the value of Q3 (satisfaction) by 0.750 and then add the constant, 1.474 to that.

- If the independent variable is 6, for instance, we multiply that by 0.750 to get 4.5, then add 1.474, which leads to 5.974. In fact, testing different values in this equation reveals that these variables are predicted to be very close at most points. The most divergence occurs when satisfaction is zero when 'willingness to recommend' is predicted to be 1.47.

You may have noticed that regression has no problems making a forecast which is an answer nobody could have given. That is because regression expects all variables to be continuous, or able to take on any value. Scaled answers which can be only whole numbers typically will lead to predictions between the actual responses.

The **constant** is the estimate of the point on the y-axis at which the line crosses (or what y would be when x is zero). As mentioned, when the independent is zero, the best estimate from the regression for the value of the dependent is 1.47.

The **standardized coefficient** or **Beta** is present so that we can compare the effects of variables that have different scales. In our full example following, we have variables using a 0 to 10 scale, and text using a 1/0 (yes/no) coding (the text item is present or absent). These differences in scales are called different **metrics**. When we have more than one independent variable, and they have different metrics, the unstandardized coefficients may be hard to interpret. We will see this as we follow the example.

FIGURE 6.6   Model summary showing the R-squared

Model	R	R Square	Adjusted R Square	Std. Error of the Estimate
1	.785	.616	.616	1.508

Another piece of critical information is the R-squared. Figure 6.6 shows how it looks in SPSS (with some of the footnotes and extra verbiage cut).

The **R** is the simple correlation and the **R-squared** is our measure of how well the model performed. More formally, this means that the predictor variables explained or predicted 61.6 per cent of the variance (or pattern in scoring) in the target variable. The **adjusted R-squared** is somewhat lower in certain cases with several predictors, and is seen as a more realistic view of the strength of the model when it differs from the regular R-squared. The number to the left under 'model' keeps track of where you are if you use the **stepwise** form of regression we discuss below. The standard error of the estimate is another measure of precision and can be helpful if you are comparing a number of regressions – here lower is better.

The first example: coded text in a regression

This involves a large customer satisfaction survey in which participants could write in a short comment (90 characters or fewer) explaining their main reason behind their overall rating. The verbatim responses were encoded into 20 yes/no (1/0) type variables and went into a regression along with their responses to scaled questions about performance. The overall rating and the scaled question used a zero to 10 scale.

For the sake of comparison, two other regressions were run: one using just the coded verbatim responses as independent variables and one using just the scaled questions. The scaled questions all have names that start with the letter 'Q', and the coded verbatims all have names that start with 'nom' (for nominal).

Our method: stepwise regression, one way to watch for regression problems

We used a method called **stepwise regression**. This checks the variables, finds the one that is the strongest predictor, and enters it into a first model. With that variable in place, it then goes back to find the variable that predicts the next most strongly – and so on.

The default in most regression programs is simply to dump everything you have listed into a model, significant or not. This is not a good idea with text, as many text codes will not have a strong relationship with the target variable. Many non-significant variables can cloud effects reported by the regression and even detract from the overall performance of the model.

Stepwise regression will continue until it finds no more variables that pass a test of statistical significance. That is, using the standard cutoff, we want to be 95 per cent certain that adding the variable is not adding nothing. (As you may recall, statistical significance is about being really sure that you are **not** doing nothing – that is, that you are avoiding making a pronouncement if there is nothing to pronounce.)

Significance is shown by the t-value. Anything greater than 1.96 is significant. In Figure 6.7 below, where we show the first three steps, you can see some very strongly significant effects.

In these first three steps (the three sections labelled Models 1, 2 and 3), we see our first problematic result. The first variable entered into the model has a Beta coefficient of 0.653 in the first step (highlighted with the oval), but by the third step this has dropped to 0.381 (highlighted by the rectangle). Clearly, the underlying relationship between satisfaction and the target (willingness to recommend) should remain the same, but it has

FIGURE 6.7   Stepwise regression reveals a problem

	Coefficients					
		Unstandardized Coefficients		Standardized Coefficients		
Model		B	Std.Error	Beta	t	Sig.
1	(Constant)	1.474	.054		27.280	0.000
	Q3 Satisfaction	.750	.006	.653	125.183	0.000
2	(Constant)	1.864	.051		36.304	0.000
	Q3 Satisfaction	.728	.006	.634	128.939	0.000
	nom8 Hoping to see more/get more	-2.186	.042	-.259	-52.576	0.000
3	(Constant)	1.502	.051		29.634	0.000
	Q3 Satisfaction	.437	.010	.381	45.836	0.000
	nom8 Hoping to see more/get more	-2.091	.040	-.247	-51.814	0.000
	Q12 Went the extra mile	.335	.009	.310	37.312	0.000

not. The combination of three variables, two scaled variables and one nominal, somehow is distorting at least one coefficient.

Note the differences in size between the B coefficients and the Betas. The Beta values try to put all variables on the same footing regardless of their scale of measurement. This does a lot to pull the 1/0 variable's effect into line with the effects of the variables on the 0 to 10 scale. Still, as we mentioned, this is just pulling it into line with the distorted coefficients of the scaled variables.

When we skip to step 20 (the regression has entered another 17 variables), we see another problem emerging. This appears at the bottom of Figure 6.8 below.

The last variable to enter, nom19, 'Fixed/resolved problems well', has a negative sign, even though it is clearly a positive comment. (Nom20 'Fixed issues quickly/right away' also is suspect, but we cannot say certainly that its coefficient is backwards. Repair service could conceivably be quick but still leave the customer unhappy because of the way in which the service was delivered – and if so it would still detract from overall scores.)

The regression went on to take seven more steps entering variables past this point, but once an effect is reversed from what we would expect

FIGURE 6.8   The regression reaches a stopping point

Coefficients

Model		Unstandardized Coefficients		Standardized Coefficients		
		B	Std. Error	Beta	t	Sig.
20	(Constant)	2.790	.060		46.487	0.000
	Q3 Satisfaction	.299	.010	.261	30.954	.000
	nom8 Hoping to see more/get more	−2.506	037	−.296	−67.683	0.000
	Q12 Went the extra mile	.187	.010	.173	18.208	.000
	nom11 Nobody owns problems/takes charge	−2.796	.070	−.173	−40.153	0.000
	nom16 Behind the market/lagging	−2.582	.072	−.155	−35.867	.000
	Q6 Wait time short	.085	.005	.095	18.911	.000
	nom17 Dropped order/lost order	−1.866	.060	−.152	−31.007	.000
	nom4 Nothing special/same as others	−1.600	.069	−.102	−23.029	.000
	nom6 Want more products/services	−2.290	.131	−.076	−17.466	.000
	nom5 Mediocre/fair	−1.908	.133	−.061	−14.332	.000
	nom14 Not responsive	−1.675	.122	−.060	−13.783	.000
	nom3 Average provider	−1.461	.136	−.046	−10.756	.000
	nom9 Thin product offering/limited products	−1.925	.185	−.045	−10.420	.000
	nom20 Fixed issues quickly/right away.	−2.505	.281	−.038	−8.914	.000
	nom15 Comptetitors doing more/better	−1.973	.259	−.033	−7.609	.000
	Q8 Took ownership	.057	.013	.049	4.500	.000
	nom18 Did not fulfil/missed deadline	−2.102	.309	−.029	−6.795	.000
	nom13 Slow/slow moving	−3.091	.676	−.020	−4.575	.000
	Q7 Listened	.045	.011	.037	4.085	.000
	nom19 Fixed/resolved problems well	−439	.110	−.017	−3.980	.000

logically, everything after that must be considered highly suspect. We would be most prudent to stop the model right before this step (at model 19).

We can stop the regression from including every variable that statistical testing might have allowed for the basic reason that no test can infallibly show us what makes sense. Statistical significance values are highly useful in preventing us from pursuing ideas that have no real chance of being meaningful. They place a fairly stringent lower boundary on what to accept as a real finding, but your understanding needs to be the final arbiter.

We can see from the chart in Figure 6.9 how much the extra variables going to step 27 add. This should give us more confidence that stopping the model was a good decision. The chart shows the R-squared after each variable has been added. This so-called 'model summary' reveals that if we do not continue past step 19, we lose hardly anything in predictive strength versus including more variables. The R-squared value increases by a minuscule 0.001 adding these last steps. We probably could eliminate all variables past step 12 or 13 if we wanted a simpler model that still had a fair number of predictors.

By the way, going back to Figure 6.8, we see that the first variable's coefficient has shrunk still further in step 20. The regression is now estimating its effect as being even smaller than the effect of the second variable into the model. This clearly does not make a great deal of sense. The first variable should be the strongest in stepwise regression, as variables are entered in order of strength. We also saw earlier that the two scaled measures (satisfaction and willingness to recommend) are very closely related, and so would be expected to have a stronger relation than either one would have with an encoded verbatim comment.

In spite of these problems with the coefficients, the estimates that the model provides will be accurate. The R-squared value of 0.616 at step 19 (highlighted) is good.

In addition, this R-squared value is better than the model with just scaled questions, which reached an R-squared of 0.484 with 9 predictors. With coded text alone, the model reached an R-squared of 0.414, with 16 predictors.

Clearly, adding the coded text improved predictive accuracy and added insights compared with the analysis including just the scaled questions. This highlights the way in which text can extend and enrich analytics based solely on numeric variables.

FIGURE 6.9   Changes in R-squared as variables are added to the model

Model Summary

Model	R	R Square	Adjusted R Square	Std. Error of the Estimate
1	0.653	.427	.427	1.843
2	0.702	.493	.493	1.733
3	0.724	.525	.524	1.678
4	0.740	.547	.547	1.638
5	0.752	.565	.565	1.605
6	0.760	.578	.578	1.582
7	0.767	.589	.589	1.561
8	0.772	.596	.596	1.546
9	0.775	.601	.601	1.538
10	0.778	.605	.604	1.531
11	0.779	.608	.607	1.525
12	0.781	.609	.609	1.521
13	0.782	.611	.611	1.518
14	0.783	.613	.613	1.515
15	0.784	.614	.614	1.513
16	0.784	.615	.615	1.511
17	0.785	.616	.615	1.510
18	0.785	.616	.616	1.509
19	0.785	.616	.616	1.508
20	0.785	.617	.616	1.508
21	0.785	.617	.617	1.507
22	0.786	.617	.617	1.507
23	0.786	.617	.617	1.506
24	0.786	.618	.617	1.506
25	0.786	.618	.617	1.506
26	0.786	.618	.617	1.506
27	0.786	.618	.617	1.505

Example 2: using text converted into factors

This next example also uses text that has been regularized, cleaned, and converted into stemmed words. The program doing this is Statistica data miner. Statistica is another very large statistical program and the data miner is its 'enterprise' version, so it comes with an enterprise price.

Other less expensive programs can do this type of clean-up, including the free programs Weka and RapidMiner, although (as is usual with free software), they are likely to require considerable trial and error before you get a result. Statistica has the advantages of working with a relatively small learning curve, and of moving directly from the cleaned and stemmed text to factor analysis.

This example uses the factor analysed text that appeared in Chapter 2. The factors are based on verbatim responses from a survey about a social networking site. As we saw, they differ conceptually from the factors we find in grouping responses to scaled questions. That type of factor is thought to represent underlying ideas or themes that the questions refer back to – larger hidden or latent variables that we have only measured in part. The factors that we get from text are the words that tend to occur together most frequently across **documents** or individual comments. These might refer to a common theme, but instead might be words that are mentioned together without sharing much meaning. These factors also may group too few words to do more than suggest an idea.

We used Statistica to develop the factors. As you may recall from Chapter 2, Statistica stores words using the **word vector** model, that is,

FIGURE 6.10   Words stored in word vector format

Term-document frequency matrix

	1 abl	2 also	3 benefit	4 best	5 busi	6 can	7 career	8 colleagu	9 connect	10 contact	11 could	12 don	13 easi	14 email	15 employ
1															
2								1							
3									1						
4				1					1						
5													1		
6							1		1						
7				1						1					
8		1													
9															
10															
11															
12															
13															
14															
15		1							1				1		
16									1						
17					1	1		1	2						
18						1									
19									1	2					
20															
21						1									
22									1						
23			1												
24															
25									1			1			

FIGURE 6.11 The first seven factors extracted

	Component						
	1	2	3	4	5	6	7
don't	.685						
much	.655						
use	.575						
really	.461						
media		.895					
social		.884					
touch			.805				
keep			.729				
colleague							
email				.645			
get				.415			
recommend					.748		
would					.650		
friend					.431		
job						.766	
search						.718	
industries							.659
place							.422

in a spreadsheet-like matrix that is mostly empty spaces. The empty spaces actually are zero values which show that the word is absent in a given row of data or **document.** Figure 6.10 shows a few of the words and a few of the cases that Statistica extracted – and the prevalence of vacant spots.

Factor analysis, as we described in Chapter 2, does not produce a hard and fast answer. We rather looked at some diagnostics and how words were falling into groups to find what we evaluated as a best solution. This contained some 18 factors, the first seven of which appear in Figure 6.11. We used SPSS to generate this output. We added highlights to make the groupings more visible.

Regression results

Running the regression, we used the same stepwise method as in the last example, trying to enter the 18 factors and the responses to nine scaled questions about satisfaction with various areas of performance. The first variable to enter the model was a scaled question about satisfaction with ability to put views forth (Q2), as Figure 6.12 shows. By the third step, the same problem as emerged in the last regression emerged here – the coefficient of Q2 has shrunk from .640 down to .319. This again indicates a problem in the regression model – most likely the presence of variables that are highly conceptually similar.

The model added another 12 variables, including a number of factors (again, made from groups of words that occurred with each other in the documents). Figure 6.13 shows the final set of 15 variables.

The meanings behind some of the factors' coefficients are not clear – 'recommend friend' (FAC9 1) is negative, and possibly could reflect people not wanting to recommend the site to a friend. The negatives could have been expressed in too many alternative ways to have been captured or, depending on the **stop word** dictionary, the word **not** could have been among the stop words eliminated from analysis.

The factors added a modest amount to the overall prediction levels reached in a regression with just scaled measures, raising the R-squared to 0.59 from 0.53. This is about 10 per cent better (a 0.06 increment vs a baseline level of 0.53). Unfortunately, the factor analysed text does not provide meanings that are as clear the encoded text in the first example. While it still provides more insight and more guidance than the response to the scaled questions alone, the extra thought and labour involved in encoding text did appear to repay the effort.

FIGURE 6.12   The first three variables in the regression model

Coefficients

Model		Unstandardized Coefficients		Standardized Coefficients	t	Sig.
		B	Std. Error	Beta		
1	(Constant)	2.682	.180		14.894	.000
	Q2 Put views forth	.662	.023	.640	29.226	.000
2	(Constant)	2.120	.174		12.188	.000
	Q2 Put views forth	.450	.027	.435	16.868	.000
	Q19 Read comments of other members	.307	.023	.339	13.149	.000
3	(Constant)	1.971	.169		11.631	.000
	Q2 Put views forth	.330	.029	.319	11.324	.000
	Q19 Read comments of other members	.227	.024	.251	9.329	.000
	Q12 Easy to navigate	.241	.027	.256	8.958	.000

FIGURE 6.13   The final set of predictors including scaled measures and factors

Coefficients

Model	B	Std. Error	Beta	t	Sig.
		Unstandardized Coefficients	Standardized Coefficients		
15					
(Constant)	2.431	.170		14.340	.000
Q2 Put views forth	.216	.029	.209	7.382	.000
Q19 Read comments of other members	.142	.025	.157	5.741	.000
Q12 Easy to navigate	.161	.026	.171	6.086	.000
FAC2 1 Scores for don't use much	−.390	.052	−.144	−7.497	.000
Q11 Updates about others useful	.105	.024	.144	4.356	.000
FAC12 1 Scores for great tool network	.260	.044	.111	5.899	.000
FAC9 1 Scores for recommend friend	−.253	.048	−.098	−5.313	.000
FAC15 1 Scores for provide best career opportunity	.198	.046	.079	4.268	.000
FAC3 1 Scores for keep in touch w colleagues	.164	.045	.068	3.665	.000
FAC10 1 Scores for way connect	.150	.047	.060	3.195	.001
FAC13 1 Scores for havent yet benefit	−.216	.059	−.068	−3.651	.000
FAC1 1 Scores for want know email	−.163	.051	−.060	−3.198	.001
Q21 Follow influential people	.063	.025	.071	2.558	.011
FAC18 1 Scores for little value	−.106	.048	−.041	−2.218	.027
Q8 Trust them about privacy	.046	.023	.049	1.981	.048

Summary

Regression stands as one of the most familiar **predictive** methods. It is very powerful and has a venerable history. Still, we should think of it as a means of forecasting – that is, of showing what is likely to happen, rather than as having the oracular properties that the word 'predictive' seems to imply.

Regression does exceptionally well in highly controlled situations, like scientific experiments. Unfortunately, tackling highly unstructured data such as text falls about as far as is possible from an experiment in the continuum of analytical activities. That can give rise to problems. Regression has a number of expectations or assumptions about what data will be like, and coded text does not fit most of them.

Regression can deliver accurate estimates of the value of a target variable even if we bend or break many of its rules. It aims to forecast the values of the target variable exactly, and will do so with whatever we throw its way. If we violate enough of its basic principles, though, it may distort the strengths of variables we include in a model to give the most precise estimates of the target variable.

Including variables that do not truly belong in the model and omitting variables that should be in the model can both cause problems in interpreting the strengths of variables in a regression. Tests exist that can alert us if variables in a regression model are too closely related, and in particular, if we have a problem of close correlations among variables, perhaps familiar as **collinearity**.

However, variables may not trip off these tests and still be related too closely to fit together in a model. Unfortunately, there is no definite way to know that a variable which should be in a model is missing.

IMAGE 6.2   Straight lines can be highly illuminating

SOURCE: Chicago, Illinois, in the waiting room of the Union Station, 1943, Jack Delano.
http://commons.wikimedia.org/wiki/File:Chicago_Union_Station_1943.jpg.

As our examples showed, the simple presence of other variables in a regression model can have more influence on the reported strengths of effects than any underlying relationship between a predictor variable and a target. Keeping this in mind will help you avoid getting misled by regression results.

With all those cautions in mind, in a regression, text can provide useful additional insights beyond those coming from using scaled questions alone. Certain clients may find the other predictive methods we discuss difficult to follow, and if so, a regression may be the best alternative. Predicted (or rather, forecast) values for the target variable often are highly accurate even if the strengths of variables seem somewhat suspect.

You can still get a good idea of the most important topics mentioned in text commentary, especially if you watch how the final model comes together. Using a stepwise method will give you a much better sense of what fits in a model than the default method in many statistics programs, simply including every variable you list, whether it belongs or not.

For audiences more open to less familiar methods, Bayesian networks can provide compelling models and give accurate readings of variables' effects even when regression-based approaches do not. We discuss those and classification tree models in the next two chapters.

References

Achen, C H (1973) *Interpreting and Using Regression*, Sage Publications, Beverly Hills

Darlington, R B (1968) Multiple regression in psychological research and practice, *Psychological Bulletin*, **69**, pp 161–82

Denby, L and Pregibon, D (1987) An example of the use of graphics in regression, *The American Statistician*, **41**, pp 33–38

Gorsuch, R L (1973) Data analysis of correlated independent variables, *Multivariate Behavioral Research*, **8**, pp 89–107

Lorenz, F O (1987) Teaching about influence in simple regression, *Teaching Sociology*, **15**, 173–77

Mansfield, E R and Conerly, M D (1987) Diagnostic value of residual and partial residual plots, *The American Statistician*, **41**, 107–16

Mauro, R (1990) Understanding l.o.v.e. (left out variables error): a method for estimating the effects of omitted variables, *Psychological Bulletin*, **108**, 314–29

Mosteller, F and Tukey, J (1977) *Data Analysis and Regression: A second course in statistics*, Pearson, Upper Saddle River, NJ

Stevens, J P (1984) Outliers and influential data points in regression analysis, *Psychological Bulletin*, **95**, 334–44

Wolf, G and Cartwright, B (1974) Rules for coding dummy variables in multiple regression, *Psychological Bulletin*, **81**, 173–79

Wilkinson, L, Blank, G and Gruber, C (1995) *Desktop Data Analysis with Systat*, SPSS Inc, Chicago, IL

PREDICTIVE MODELS 2

07

Classifications that grow on trees

KEY QUESTION

What are classification trees, and how can they predict outcomes by analysing text?

This chapter describes the 'classification tree' methods, in particular CHAID, and what makes them so well suited to finding predictive relationships using text as the predicting variables. Several handy illustrations will take the mystery out of this method and show how well it applies.

Classification trees: understanding an amazing analytical method

Now that we have absorbed a great many facts about regression, it is time for something completely different. As a reminder, regression is a means of seeing how one or many variables lead to or influence an outcome. Over the years this has become an incredibly powerful and well-studied predictive method. Classification trees have a different take on the world.

As a reminder, regression has certain expectations. Chief among them:

- The variable that we want to predict has a lot of values that fall in a specific order, from lowest to highest – that is, it is a **continuous** variable;
- We can add up effects to lead to a result, something like adding ingredients to get a cake;
- A straight line is a good approximation for how various factors relate to an outcome;
- We have the right ingredients to create the result we want, neither too many nor too few;
- Everything we care to measure also has values that fall into an order from lowest to highest;
- We do not have much, if any, missing data.

These ideas bear repeating because they differ sharply from the assumptions underlying classification trees. (If any of these concepts about regression seem unclear, please refer back to the last chapter.)

In this chapter we will be discussing the classification tree method called **CHAID.** There are a host of other, closely related methods with different names, most notably **CART** (also called **C&RT** and **CRT**). We will talk about how CHAID and CART (and the others) compare and contrast after we review the applications.

Seeing how trees work, step by step

Splitting and re-splitting

CHAID and related methods split the data into groups, seeking to find some group (or groups) with more of some desired characteristic. For instance, seeking buyers of a product, we might use a variable such as number of children at home to find those who buy more (say those with five or more children at home) than those who buy less (those with fewer than five children at home). Classification trees were designed to zero in on differences of this kind.

Once they split the data, these methods then return to the smaller groups formed and split those again and again. Each split produces still smaller groups, and some of those groups will have a great deal of the desired characteristic. This may sound abstract, so let's take a look at how this actually works.

The example will be concrete, dealing with behaviour and demographics. It starts with a survey, in which everybody answers questions about what they typically eat for breakfast. Some 20 per cent have the good taste to consume the client's breakfast substance, **SoggyOs**.

We also have information about the demographic characteristics of the people participating in the survey, such as the type of place in which they live, their stated household incomes, their education levels and the presence and ages of children – and so on. The survey has recorded some 46 demographic characteristics for each participant. Figure 7.1 depicts the survey population.

The classification tree procedure (CHAID) will examine all the demographic characteristics, seeking the one that can be best used to split the sample

FIGURE 7.1   Survey participants and the incidence of SoggyOs eaters

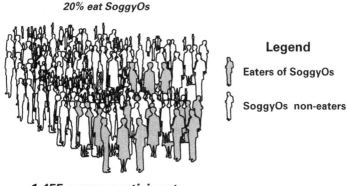

20% eat SoggyOs

Legend

Eaters of SoggyOs

SoggyOs non-eaters

1,455 survey participants
(men, women, and very small humanoids)

776 participants

into smaller groups that differ as much as possible in terms of their likelihoods to eat SoggyOs. The CHAID software in question can split the sample into anywhere between two and 15 groups.

Examining all the demographic factors, CHAID finds the strongest difference is in contrasting those who **live in suburban areas** in one group vs those **living in either cities or rural areas** in a second group. Some 22 per cent of those in the suburbs eat SoggyOs vs 17 per cent in the other two areas combined. That is, the suburban group is 1.3 times as likely as the other to be users of our favourite breakfast substance. We see this division in Figure 7.2.

The procedure did something quite advanced here, which may not be immediately apparent. It found that we needed to combine the study participants in **two geographies into one group** so that we get the strongest contrast in incidences. For the CHAID procedure to select this variable as the strongest differentiator, it needed to examine splitting the population based on this variable in four different ways. (Another way of dividing would have been combining people in cities and suburbs into one group vs those in rural areas, another combining people in the suburbs and rural areas vs those in cities, and the last simply splitting the three geographies into three groups.)

Sifting through four ways of grouping people to determine which is best may not seem that impressive, but recall that the procedure simultaneously looked at all 45 other demographic characteristics – and at all the ways in which those could be used to divide the population. CHAID in fact uses a form of artificial intelligence to choose the best way to divide groups.

FIGURE 7.2   The sample gets split into two contrasting groups

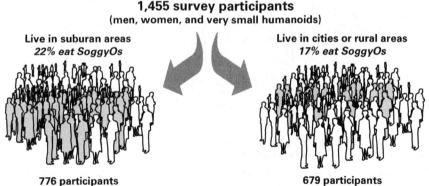

1,455 survey participants
(men, women, and very small humanoids)

Live in suburan areas
22% eat SoggyOs

Live in cities or rural areas
17% eat SoggyOs

776 participants   679 participants

What the program does next adds more value (and complexity) to the findings. It returns to the first group split from the total, the one with 776 participants. It then searches all the remaining demographic characteristics to find the one that will lead to a group with a still higher incidence of SoggyOs eaters.

Figure 7.3 shows what the procedure found. This is a three-way split of the group living in the suburbs.

We see a very strong contrast among these three smaller groups: some 28 per cent of suburbanites with 5+ children eat SoggyOs, which is nearly three times as high as the incidence among suburbanites with 1 to 3 children (only 10 per cent eat SoggyOs in this group).

Here we see an **interaction** between two demographic characteristics. An **interaction** between variables means that the effects of two (or more) together are different than the sums of each individual effect. More specifically, in this example the percentage eating SoggyOs among those

FIGURE 7.3   Re-splitting the first sub-sample into three more sharply contrasted groups

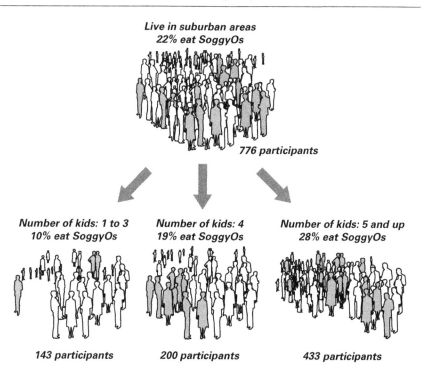

Live in suburban areas
22% eat SoggyOs

776 participants

Number of kids: 1 to 3   *Number of kids: 4*   *Number of kids: 5 and up*
10% eat SoggyOs   *19% eat SoggyOs*   *28% eat SoggyOs*

143 participants   *200 participants*   *433 participants*

FIGURE 7.4   A small classification tree

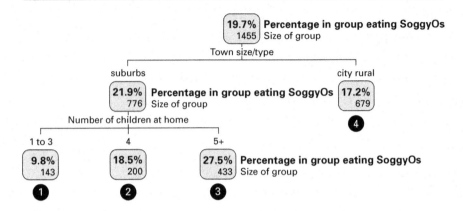

who live in the suburbs **and** who have 5+ children is higher than we would expect either among people who just live in the suburbs or among people who just have 5+ children. We must have **specific values of both variables** to see this high a percentage of SoggyOs eaters.

> **Interaction:** When the effect of two or more variables working together to produce an outcome is different from what we would expect based on the effects of the variables separately.

That is, the variables work together to lead to this unexpectedly strong outcome. This is one time when we can use the once popular buzzword **synergistic** and mean it.

CHAID is amazingly good at finding interactions. The word CHAID actually is an acronym standing for **Ch**i-**s**quared **a**utomatic **i**nteraction **d**etector. Classification trees may be unique in that interactions are unmistakable in their output. Interactions do not automatically appear in nearly all other statistical procedures. Also, most other procedures do not tell you if you are missing an important interaction.

Clearly, if you want to understand effects on some outcome, you should understand if two or more variables combine to act in an unexpected way. CHAID has unique problem-solving abilities simply in revealing and displaying these patterns.

What precisely does this have to do with a tree? The common display that CHAID produces looks somewhat tree-like. Let's look at the splits we just laid out again, this time in the standard format.

Perhaps not that apparent is the remarkable analysis the program performed in dividing the suburban group based on the number of children at home. This is a three-way division we just discussed.

We can see that the group with five or more children at home is the largest of the three (433 study participants), and that it still was not divided into smaller groups having different numbers of children. (Participants stated they had up to an awe-inspiring 14 children at home.)

This choice of grouping was based on complex statistical testing. All families with five or more children have the same statistical likelihood of eating SoggyOs. That is, those with 5 children have the same likelihood as those with 6, or those with 7 or those with 8 – and so on.

The classification tree program was instructed to separate people into groups only where it found statistically significant differences while it searched through all possible ways of dividing the sample to find the one that was the strongest. This group of 433 was large enough to divide further, but there were no differences based on numbers of children that could lead to a further division.

This contrast the program found (based on number of children at home) is very strong statistically. There is only a 0.00001 per cent chance that the three groups found have the same incidence of eating SoggyOs. This is very far beyond the lowest acceptable threshold (a 5 per cent chance of the groups being the same). If you feel in need of a refresher on statistical significance, please check back to Chapter 1.

The full analysis would continue past this point, continuing to grow the tree until we ran out of demographic characteristics that led to further significant differences, or until we decided the groups were too small to split further.

We will say a fond farewell to SoggyOs by noting again that a very high 27.5 per cent of all families with five or more children use this fine product. Perhaps we can trace this to the success of SoggyOs' economy gunny-sack size – or vice versa.

Optimal recoding

Classification trees' ability to split a variable in the best possible way, picking the breaking points and the number of groups, is a remarkable

IMAGE 7.1   A strictly fictional breakfast substance

SOURCE: Photo by author, composite image by author, processed by author, courtesy of shed in author's garden.

analytical strength. This is called **optimal recoding.** It has particular value when dealing with text or other **categorical** variables. As a reminder, a categorical variable is one where the numeric codes hold places for non-numerical values. In our example, town type/size was a categorical variable. The program held the values of 1, 2 and 3 for this variable, corresponding respectively to city, suburban and urban.

> **Optimal recoding:** Classification trees' ability to split the codes in a variable in the best possible way to predict an outcome variable. Codes are automatically arranged into groups and the best splitting.

Text works best when it has been **encoded** in a predictive analysis based on classification trees, as is true with many other forms of analysis. We discussed the process of, and rationale for, **coding text** in Chapter 2. As a reminder, coding gathers similar comments into groups.

Computers are getting much better at coding as, for instance, with the SPSS Text Analysis program we discussed in Chapter 2. Even with a program this sophisticated, though, this process typically requires at least some human intervention, with a person supervising and checking the **coding scheme**.

Optimal recoding works well with text because it sorts and combines the codes in a variable that they predict some outcome, like satisfaction levels, intent to buy or actual purchasing. This may abstract, so let's get to an example of this remarkable capability.

This example comes from a customer rating system run by a major financial institution, asking customers for both numeric (scaled) ratings and for comments about their experience on the telephone. There were over 270,000 responses. Customers were asked to submit a brief comment (character count restricted to 90 characters) to explain their overall ratings. Because the comments were short, each person's main concern could be captured in a single code and these could all be encoded into a single variable. There were 20 codes in all. As an example, some of the codes were as follows:

- Code 1: Satisfied/positive;
- Code 2: Get to live rep easier;
- Code 3: Time spent on hold;
- Code 4: Phone menu.

This encoded variable then was entered into a classification tree analysis. We will see the result below. The tree diagram is slightly more detailed than the simplified one in our earlier example. Figure 7.5 shows the elements displayed.

FIGURE 7.5   Elements displayed in the tree diagram

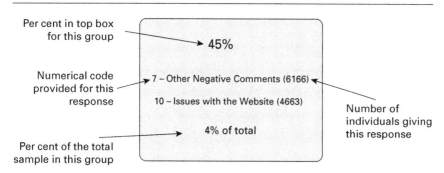

In the diagram, **per cent in top box** simply means the per cent giving the highest possible rating on a 7-point scale ('completely satisfied'). Below this, we show the encoded responses that correspond to this average level of top box responses with their code numbers, followed by the number of individuals giving each encoded response. Below, we show how large the group is as a per cent of the total sample.

In this example, some 6,166 gave the response coded '7' or 'other negative comments' and some 4,664 gave the response coded '10', or 'issues with the website'. Note that the tree program has put together these two codes out of all 20, meaning that the group of 6,166 and the group of 4,664 have statistically identical percentages of people giving a top box rating. Code 7 actually comprises many responses, none of which was viewed by those doing the coding as prevalent enough to warrant a separate code.

Finally, we can see that this grouping of 10,829 people represents some 4 per cent of the total (about 270,000 responses). While this may not be a dominant set of issues, we can see that they still affect a great many people.

Figure 7.6 shows the entire tree diagram. We see that the 20 codes (along with a placeholder for 'no response') have been put into seven groups, all of which differ statistically from each other in percentage of top box responses. We have a very broad range of values among these groups, from only 26 per cent in the 'top box' at the bottom left of the diagram to some 81 per cent in the 'top box' at the upper right corner of the diagram. The group with the worst average level of satisfaction is only **one-third** as likely to be completely satisfied as the most positive group.

We also can see that the largest group consists of those who did not answer (along with some foreign language responses that were not translated). This points out one additional strength of CHAID. **Missing values** can be handled just as any other response. You must ask the program to do this. If you do, these responses are put into the group of codes where they best boost contrasts in responses to the dependent variable.

In fact, some analysts use CHAID to **impute** or estimate what missing values might be. Since these missing responses can be grouped with the responses that have statistically identical levels of the target variable, this can be a very sensible way of estimating what those missing values could be.

FIGURE 7.6 Classification tree sorting coded responses by optimal recoding

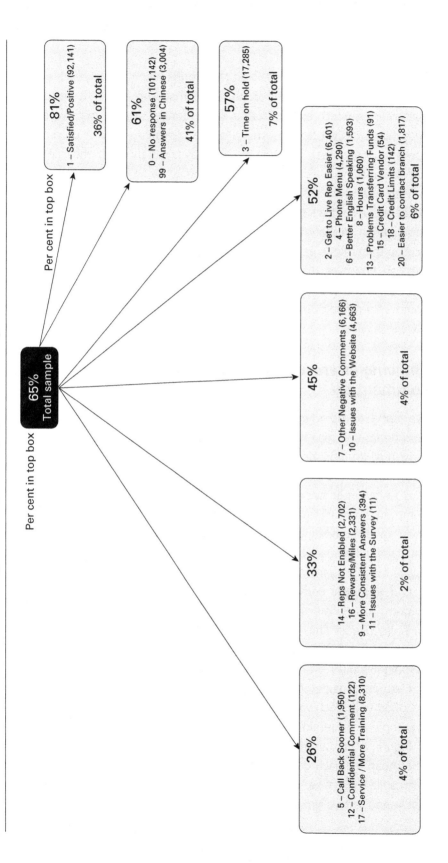

In Figure 7.6, we also can see that the groups with relatively low levels of satisfaction (the four to the bottom left) make up some 16 per cent of customers – which amounts to a good number. (Recall that we started with over 270,000 people.) The relatively dissatisfied make up a pool of some 44,000 in fact, so knowing and paying attention to their concerns turned out to have a strong positive payoff.

These verbatim responses helped a great deal with a survey that was deliberately kept as short as possible to ensure the highest levels of participation. Verbatim responses gave customers a chance to say what was on their minds beyond the 15 scaled questions that they were asked. We can now see that these comments added valuable insights about what led to higher and lower levels of satisfaction, as well as which comments reflected the most serious concerns, and how serious those concerns were.

Showing interactions analysing with more open-ended commentary

We need to do something different where people can offer longer comments that may hold several points. You cannot use a single variable to hold all the encoded comments in this situation, because that type of encoding works only if each person has just one main point to make. You might encounter longer statements if you are dealing with (for instance) commentary picked up from an online community. Other settings where comments can be longer are numerous, including, for instance, customer satisfaction feedback systems, customer reviews, warrantee cards, blogs, online bulletin boards and surveys.

Our example comes from another very large customer satisfaction system. This classification tree is somewhat different, because the target variable, overall satisfaction, is treated as a continuous variable with an average or mean on a 1-to-10 scale. Overall, average satisfaction is a respectable 8.05.

Here we considered a large set of possible predictor variables based on encoded text. Each variable holds one comment coded as yes/no (either that topic was mentioned or not).

Figure 7.7 shows the elements that appear in this classification tree. The mean for each group is the largest element in the diagram. Above each split in the tree, we also see the significance level of the difference between the two groups formed. In each spot, as in the one highlighted

FIGURE 7.7   Elements in the classification tree

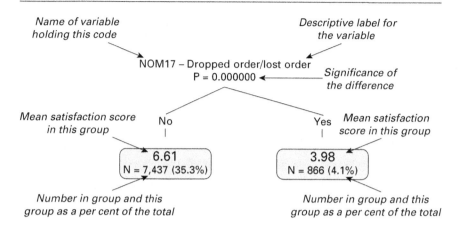

Name of variable holding this code

Descriptive label for the variable

NOM17 – Dropped order/lost order
P = 0.000000 ← Significance of the difference

Mean satisfaction score in this group   No

Yes   Mean satisfaction score in this group

6.61
N = 7,437 (35.3%)

3.98
N = 866 (4.1%)

Number in group and this group as a per cent of the total

Number in group and this group as a per cent of the total

in Figure 7.7, the split is very strongly significant, far beyond the 0.05 cutoff point. The six zeros shown mean that the value exceeds what the program prints out, being less than 0.00000 – or very, very small.

In this excerpt from the full classification tree (below), we have two groups that either mentioned the **order being dropped** or not. The larger group not saying the order was dropped has a far higher level of satisfaction (6.61 on average) than the group that did mention this (only 3.98 on average).

The larger group consists of some 7437 people or about 35 per cent of the sample. The smaller group is 866 people or about 4 per cent of the sample. This is a great many dropped orders. Clearly, just from this excerpt we can see that something must be done about this problem.

One other point about this diagram may need explanation. You can see both a short variable name (NOM17) at the top, and a longer descriptive label that says what the variable means. Statistics programs generally work most smoothly with shorter variable names, especially those programs where you may be typing in commands (or **syntax**) referring to the variables.

Mostly, though, short names are a hold-over from the time (not that long ago) when these programs only could accommodate a variable name that was 8 characters or less. This tradition in nomenclature has remained remarkably persistent in the data-analytical community.

The full classification tree in Figure 7.8 shows the **actions** and the **interactions** of the encoded comments. We can see how these variables

FIGURE 7.8   The entire classification tree diagram

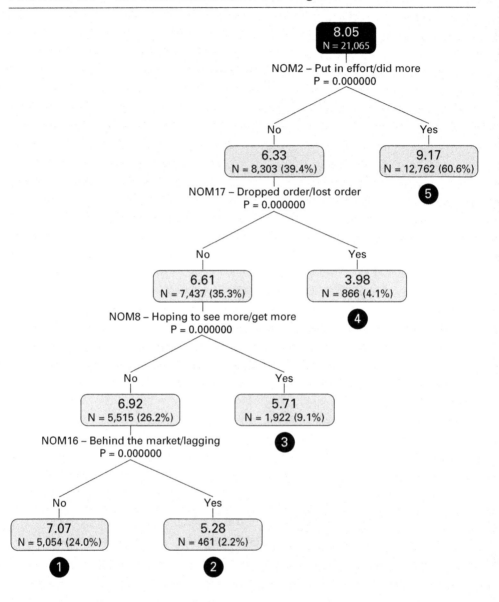

combine to lead to higher and lower levels of overall satisfaction. This tree has four **tiers** (or levels) below the target variable. It also has five **terminal nodes** at the ends of its branches. We have numbered these in the figure.

Interpreting the tree diagram

The first split shows the difference between those who mentioned this provider **doing something extra** and those who did not. Making an effort that the customer notices clearly pays off. Average satisfaction among those who made this comment was an outstanding 9.17 on the 10-point scale. Fortunately, this was 60.6 per cent of customers, as we can see from the figures in the rightmost box (or node). This is the node numbered '5'.

This average is so high that no comment beyond this corresponded to a higher satisfaction level. The classification tree program stopped growth at this point in this **branch** of the tree because there were no further significant predictors to be found.

In the other branch, the remaining 40 per cent, satisfaction levels average a dismal 6.33. This is likely to be a cause for concern. (We have only rules of thumb for comparing scaled ratings, even on the familiar 1-to-10 scale. Some relationship between actual behaviour and scaled opinion measures definitely exists, but its nature has eluded exact definition. Work with these scaled measures over many years has convinced your author that a ratings below 7 correspond to fairly serious problems.)

The next stop down in the tree diagram shows that there is more to this poor rating than is apparent at first glance. (This is the section of the tree that was highlighted in Figure 7.7.) The group we just discussed, where satisfaction averages 6.61, in fact comprises two smaller groups. There are those who said that **an order was dropped or missed** and those who did not.

The contrast here is very strong, just as it was in the top level or **tier** of the tree. Those mentioning a dropped order had an alarmingly low overall satisfaction level of only 3.98. This is a group that makes up some 4.1 per cent of the sample. As we mentioned earlier, something needs to be done about this deficiency.

Rules and trees

To express what the trees show to this point, we can use a set of **rules**. Classification trees do not generate equations like regression, just a set of simple 'if-then' statements.

Here are the rules describing the two groups at this point in the tree – normally, we would use the short variable names, but for clarity we are showing the longer descriptive labels:

Rule 1
IF 'Put in more effort/did more' = No
AND 'dropped/lost an order' = No,
THEN average satisfaction = 6.61

Rule 2
IF 'Put in more effort/did more' = No
AND 'dropped/lost an order' = Yes,
THEN average satisfaction = 3.98

Similarly, we would describe the last group at the bottom left with a longer 'if-then' rule. This one (Rule 3 below) requires three and statements, meaning that this group is defined by the combination of these three conditions. **All three** conditions must be in place for a person to be a member of this group. As we can see in the classification tree diagram, just one or two of these comments is not enough to define people who have this average level of satisfaction.

Rule 3
IF 'Put in more effort/did more' = No
AND 'dropped/lost an order' = No,
AND 'Hoping to see/get more'= No
AND 'Behind the market/lagging' = yes,
THEN average satisfaction = 7.07

> **Classification tree rules:** A set of simple **if-then statements** describing the combinations of predictor variables that lead to different values of the target variable. They typically describe just the ending boxes or **nodes** in the tree.

Typically, we use rules describing only the very ends of the tree, or the **terminal nodes**. These terminal nodes show the most detailed information about the group in question.

Rules like these are all we need to describe the output, or **create a model**. This model is what we would use with another data set. Suppose we had another set of customers who gave only a single verbatim response. We could use these rules to forecast which ones had the lowest satisfaction levels, by encoding their responses and applying the rules in the classification tree. Use of these simple conversational rules, and the consequent lack of equations, is a highly appealing feature of classification trees.

This tree would require only five rules, one for each terminal node. We also used only four predictor variables. This tree has done a tremendous amount to clarify the data with a very small model. Even with a database in the millions, no more than 12 or so rules may be needed to display the most meaningful patterns in the data. This is a tremendous strength of classification tree methods. With some audiences it may pose some difficulties. They may not believe that you can reveal so much about a data set with so few variables, and may even question why their favourite item did not make it into the set of predictors.

Growing trees: automated or guided?

We could have made this tree larger, or have grown it further, but elected to stop at this point because adding more splits provided no additional information useful in directing tactics. That is, we **guided** the growth of the tree.

You can either let classification tree programs run automatically or (for some of them) guide what the program does. Some programs run only automatically, which in this author's opinion is a strong disadvantage if you want to do anything more than optimal recoding on a single variable.

One main reason this automation can be a serious problem is that tree programs will automatically choose the one variable that looks 'best' at each spot in the tree, even if that variable would not lead to the best overall result when adding other variables later. That is, the procedure **does not look forward** to see what the implications of choosing this 'best' variable would have further down in the tree.

In fact we encounter this issue with nearly all methods that try to include multiple variables. It is worse with trees because choosing the wrong variable can lead to no further growth in the tree – recalling that trees typically do not contain many variables. (As we noted, there are only four in our example.) Sometimes the 'best' variable or even the next 'best' will cause the tree to stop growing because no further statistically significant variables can be found below it. However, some other statistically significant variable will lead to further growth, and to further valuable information about what influences an overall outcome.

Technically, trees are an example of a **greedy algorithm**. This is a method that makes a choice at each given point and then deals with whatever problems arise later.

IMAGE 7.2   Complete automation can lead to problems

SOURCE: *Modern Times*, 1936, Charles Chaplin.
https://www.flickr.com/photos/26516557@No3/2495878692.

We often find that many variables would pass the test of significance at any given spot in a tree diagram – that is, that any of many variables would lead to a significant difference at that point. Often the differences in significance between the 'best' variable and the next few best or even the next 20 or more are vanishingly small. The best predictor could be significant at something like the 10^{-16} level (that is 16 zeros after the decimal point, or to write this out just once, 0.0000000000000000). The next few on the list might be significant at better than the 10^{-14} level, so the differences in statistical significance are microscopic. Yet putting in different variables at any point can lead to very different trees below.

Recommendations on tree growing

Typically results are excellent if you let the program pick automatically first and then go back and check any spots that seem problematic – for instance, a place where a large group was left undivided. The best classification tree programs (from this author's point of view) let you look at a list of possible variables that could split the sample at each point in the tree (all of these variables pass your chosen test of statistical significance) – and then allow you to explore how the tree grows when you swap the program's first choice for another variable.

No matter which program you use, you will need to set the acceptable significance level, and the smallest group you will allow when the program does splitting. If you do not set a minimum, the program may even split off a single person into his or her own group. And of course, the minimum size you select will influence how the tree grows.

All these factors lead to the conclusion that we may never reach a **demonstrably optimal tree**. Small fluctuations in the data – for instance, dropping one person with questionable responses – might lead to very different-looking trees being selected as the best possible by a computer program.

Still, while this is a caution, it should not be a deterrent to using this remarkable method. The goal should always be to create a model that has **the most useful information** and that has **very good predictive power**. Squeezing the last possible drop out of a score showing the goodness of prediction should not be your aim. Scores are valuable things, but real world applicability is more important. Sacrificing a few points for a more useful model makes a great deal of sense.

About testing the goodness of classification tree models

Growing this tree, we kept a constant watch on the overall measure for correctly predicting scores, **explained variance**. The changes in this measure as we added more levels or tiers to the tree confirmed our decision to stop tree growth. Explained variance for the tree as a whole was 0.40 at point where we stopped – quite a good result for using only text commentary to explain overall scores. Explained variance did not improve by more than two points when adding more to the tree.

We discussed **explained variance** (or as statisticians sometimes call it, **variance explained**) in the chapter on regression. As a reminder, this is the traditional measure used to decide how well the regression performed. Explained variance ranges between zero and one.

We can think of this as a measure of how well the predictors capture the pattern of values in the target or dependent variable. A score of 0.40 means you are in the right neighbourhood much of the time. It does not mean you are precisely right 40 per cent of the time and wrong 60 per cent of the time, as we discussed in Chapter 2.

Explained variance is the measure of model fit or goodness for a tree that has a **continuous** target variable, like this last example. The tip off that we have a continuous variable as our target is seeing its score expressed as a decimal value.

> **Overall goodness of the overall model in a classification tree**: Explained variance is a key measure if the target variable is **continuous**. This is interpreted like explained variance in a regression. If the target variable is categorical, then the measure is **correct classification**, the per cent of times the correct category would be predicted, based on the model made from the predictor variables. At each point in the tree, comparisons are based on statistical significance levels.

Other trees can have **categorical variables** as a target. Such a target variable might be membership in any of four groups, for instance. The classification tree would determine which predictor variables corresponded to a higher likelihood of belonging to each of the four groups. With a categorical target variable, the tree will show the **per cent correct classification**. This score is indeed the per cent of the time that the model got it right, correctly predicting which group each person would belong to, based solely on knowing responses to the predictor variables.

At each point in the tree, possible predictor variables are compared based on statistical significance, as we mentioned earlier. The program will automatically pick the predictor with the strongest level of statistical significance.

CHAID and CART (and CRT, C&RT, QUEST, J48 and others)

Before we get to conclusions and recommendations, we need to clear up some terminology. As you have no doubt noticed, throughout, we have been talking here about a specific type of classification tree analysis called **CHAID**.

Reliably useful classification tree methods have existed only since the 1980s. Over the last few decades a healthy host of related methods have been developed, supplanting the notoriously inaccurate original method, AID. CHAID was the first method to solve the problem of comparing significance when using variables that have different numbers of categories – as it turns out, a fiendishly difficult problem. Since then, many alternatives to CHAID have been proposed. We will go out on a limb here and say that they all do basically the same things, but with different restrictions and rules. At one time, there were fierce partisans of various methods. Now that classification trees are no longer the latest word in predictive models, the rancorous language seems to have subsided.

Perhaps the disputes also have quieted because there now are so many variations of classification tree methods. We have encountered more than 40. The most widely used along with **CHAID** is called **CART** (also called **CRT** and **C&RT** because those who give out trademarks strangely decided **CART** was a word that could be trademarked). CART and its relatives, such as **QUEST,** do only two-way splits while CHAID can split much more finely. Some users still prefer CART, but for the purpose of performing optimal recoding on text, CHAID appears to be more efficient – all the groups you need can be formed at once, rather than in a series of two-way splits.

You may also encounter such programs as **AC2**, **J48**, **C4.5** (free) and **C5** (not free). There also are outgrowths of classification trees, such as **random forests** and **boosted decision stumps** (both useful methods in spite of the odd names). You can breathe easily here because we will not be discussing any of these aside from mentioning that they exist.

Summary: applications and cautions

We discussed the **CHAID** method, which can produce many-way splits. This is particularly efficient if you have one large categorical variable that holds many codes corresponding to different comments, as we did in our first example. The other type of classification tree method, exemplified in **CART** (or C&RT or CRT) produces only two-way splits and so makes optimal recoding somewhat more cumbersome.

As a reminder, you can create one variable holding all the codes only if each person had just **one** important idea in his or her comments. Otherwise, you must split the codes into a series of yes/no variables that show whether the person made the comment or did not. Each person can then have as many 'yes' codes as needed to correspond to what she or he said. If you do this kind of encoding, you will then get only two-way splits. With these, either CHAID or CART should produce identical results.

Classification trees remain preeminent for teasing out and seeing **interactions** – the ways in which variables' influence on a target variable is stronger or weaker than expected when they work in combination. When two variables work together to produce an effect that is stronger than we would expect based on the ways that each behaves separately, we can actually say for once that these effects are **synergistic** – and mean it.

Other analytical methods allow variables to interact as part of their normal operation, in particular the **Bayes Nets** we discuss next. But nowhere are these patterns as apparent as they are in a classification tree analysis. These methods are so effective at finding interactions that they make a good first step before other methods of analysis, such as regression-based models. The important interactions that classification trees find can be entered into the regression, improving results.

These methods do not produce equations like regressions. Classification tree models typically are small, with few variables and few **classification rules**. Rules are the simple **if-then statements** that describe how the variables work together to lead to an outcome. This simplicity, even with very large datasets, is a salient strength of these methods, because we often can explain everything important quickly and efficiently. Some audiences may find this hard to believe though, so this could require some advance explanation.

Classification tree methods do not produce a **truly definitive model**. Small fluctuations in the data or small changes the way you choose to set minimum acceptable group sizes, for instance, can lead to very different-looking trees. If you allow the software to do all the choosing in shaping the tree, you might get a result that is not best suited to your strategic or tactical needs. While some programs claim to find the best possible model automatically, you alone know what you really need. Therefore you are best served by a program that allows you to modify the model to fit your objectives.

Unfortunately, the world of classification tree vendors is murky, with the behaviour of many programs not discussed on the websites that offer them. Prices also are conspicuously absent in many instances. The examples in this chapter were all produced using Angoss Software's KnowledgeSeeker program. This is simply a statement of what was used, reflecting the author's preference for a program that allows manual testing of the tree – and not an endorsement. The other programs mentioned here also perform very well, with somewhat different sets of features and strengths.

If you are interested in classification trees as a method, it is best to understand that all programs doing this form of analysis have a learning curve. Even the easiest (a relative term) is likely to use some terminology that we did not have space to discuss here, and to have a number of controls and settings that will not seem immediately intuitive. Our advice is that you look at some of the web pages that list a number of programs, use some trial versions, and find one that best fits your needs, capabilities and budget.

Whether you do the work yourself or seek out expert consultation, classification tree analysis has truly unique strengths that make it a worthwhile addition to your analytical armamentarium. Applied to text, these methods definitely repay the effort needed to understand and use them.

References

Breiman, L, Friedman, J, Olshen, R and Stone, C (1984) *Classification and Regression Trees*, Chapman and Hall, New York

Brodley, C E and Utgoff, P E (1995) Multivariate decision trees, *Machine Learning*, **19**, pp 45–77

Buntine, W (1992) Learning classification trees, *Statistics and Computing*, **2**, pp 63–73

Clark, L A and Pregibon, D (1993) Tree-based models, in J M Chambers and T J Hastie, eds, *Statistical Models*, Chapman and Hall, New York, pp 377–419

Hazewinkel, M (ed) (1987) Greedy algorithm, *Encyclopedia of Mathematics, Supplement III*, Springer, Norwell, MA

Hochberg, Y and Tamhane, A C (1987) *Multiple Comparison Procedures*, Wiley, New York

Holte, R C (1993) Very simple classification rules perform well on most commonly used datasets, *Machine Learning*, **11**, pp 63–90

Kass, G V (1980) An exploratory technique for investigating large quantities of categorical data, *Applied Statistics*, **29**, pp 119–27

Lim, T S, Loh, W Y and Shih, Y S (2000) A comparison of prediction accuracy, complexity, and training time of thirty-three old and new classification algorithms, *Machine Learning*, **40**, 203–28

Morowitz, V (2001) Methods for forecasting from intentions data, in J Armstrong (ed), *Principles of Forecasting*, Springer, New York

Muller, W and Wysotzki, F (1994) Automatic construction of decision trees for classification, *Annals of Operations Research*, **52**, 231–47

Quinlan, J R (1989) Unknown attribute values in induction, *Proceedings of the Sixth International Machine Learning Workshop*, pp 164–68

Steinberg, D and Colla, P (1992) *CART: A Supplementary Module for SYSTAT*, SYSTAT Inc, Evanston, IL

White, A P and Liu, W Z (1994) Bias in information-based measures in decision tree induction, *Machine Learning*, **15**, pp 321–29

Witten I and Frank, E (2005) *Data Mining: Practical machine learning tools and techniques*, 2nd edn, Morgan Kaufmann, San Francisco

PREDICTIVE MODELS 3

08

All in the family with Bayes Nets

KEY QUESTION

What are Bayes Nets and what can they do predictively that other methods cannot?

In this chapter we will learn about the remarkable set of methods called Bayes Nets or Bayesian networks. We will show how they variables fit together into natural groupings, and trim groups of variables and generally make sense of largely unstructured data. With numerous illustrations Chapter 8 demonstrates the remarkable properties of these methods and how they apply to text.

What are Bayes Nets and how do they compare with other methods?

Now that we have assimilated a great deal about regressions and classification trees, here is something very different yet again: **Bayes Nets** (or Bayesian networks).

Bayes Nets have remarkable properties allowing them often to surpass other methods, and even to solve some problems that elude other methods entirely. They will repay learning a third way to think about data.

Where we have been

Let's start with **a brief review** of the methods we have discussed. First let's consider the properties of regressions. **Regressions** take the view that we can add the effects of variables to predict the values of some target variable (which could be, for instance, a scaled rating or the level of use of a product or service). And as we discussed in Chapter 6, the forms of regression that we typically use all work based on straight lines. Hence, the designation **linear additive models**.

Regressions are based on the patterns of **correlations** among variables. As a reminder, while **correlation** has been taken to mean many things, with regression it means a simple summary measure of how closely two variables fall into a straight-line relationship.

Some extensions to regression deal with curved lines for the target variable, but you are not likely to encounter these outside scientific settings. Even if the line is curved, regression seeks the best fit to that line, as it does with the straight line in Figure 8.1.

Regressions generate **equations** that we can think of as something like recipes for making a cake. A regression equation would follow a model like the statement below (using the convention in which an asterisk stands for multiplication):

$$0.5 * A + 0.7 * B + \text{some fixed value} =$$
$$\text{the predicted value of the target variable.}$$

In an equation like this, you add ingredients in certain proportions and they then forecast the values in the target variable. In Figure 8.1, the straight line represents the best estimate of the values of the target variable, based on values of one predictor. The dots show the actual values of the

FIGURE 8.1   The regression model

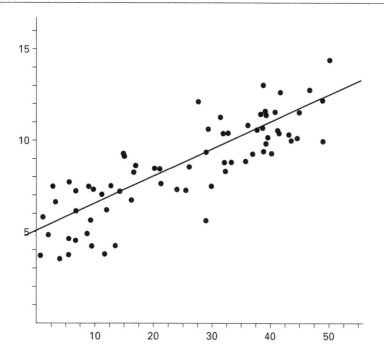

target variable (distances across) vs the predictor variable (distances up and down).

Regression-based methods have had a long and distinguished history of working well in many settings. Still, at times these methods perform indifferently, poorly, or even not at all. Also, regressions do not work with target variables that are categorical (such as which of several groups a person belongs to, or in which of several regions a person lives). You also must break down categorical predictors into sets of yes/no variables. You could not use a single variable holding many text codes as a predictor, as we did with classification trees in the last chapter.

Classification trees in fact take a different approach, allowing them to surmount these limitations of regression. Tree methods handle categorical, ordinal and continuous variables equally well. Beyond this, they find ways that variables **interact** with each other. An **interaction** occurs whenever the effects of two or more variables together differ from what we would expect based on the effects of the variable separately. In addition, tree methods even can handle missing values in data as another type of response, as we saw in the last chapter.

FIGURE 8.2   A portion of a classification tree

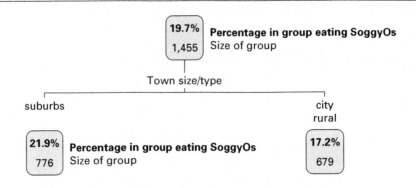

As a reminder, **classification trees** work by **splitting** the sample into contrasting groups and splitting those groups again and again, seeking to find small subgroups that differ as much as possible in levels of some target variable, such as preference ratings or levels of use. We can see a single split in a tree in Figure 8.2. This comes from the first example in Chapter 7.

With a classification tree, we have no equations, but rather a set of simple if-then rules. For instance, one rule that we showed in the last chapter read like this:

IF 'Put in more effort/did more' = No
AND 'dropped/lost an order' = No
AND 'Hoping to see/get more'= No
AND 'Behind the market/lagging' = yes
THEN average satisfaction = 7.07

Now, on to networks

You may well be wondering what kind of predictive model could differ from both this type of splitting routine and from regressions. And so we come at last to **Bayes Nets**.

The first clue to their nature comes in the term **network**. All the variables are connected and all influence the target **and** each other. A network can be as simple as two variables that relate to each other, or it can contain thousands of variables, as in, for instance, research into how genes interact.

Soon we will get to a simple example showing how remarkably these networks perform. First, though, we will pause to reassure you that they are very solid methods, with extensive use in aeroplane guidance systems, public safety, running nuclear power plants, cancer research, the genetic research we mentioned just above – and even national defence. We actually can say that they have been battle-tested. The social sciences and marketing sciences have been a little late to the party. Catching up now seems like a good thing to do.

What do these networks actually do?

The vast variety of problems these networks can solve may seem slightly bewildering. Applications range from brainstorming to highly sophisticated modelling and forecasting systems.

Here are some uses:

- Automatically finding meaningful patterns among variables;
- Getting accurate measures of variables' strengths;
- Screening large numbers of variables quickly, for data mining;
- Developing models of cause and effect (in the right circumstances);
- Incorporating expert judgment into data-driven models;
- Solving problems in **conditional probability**.

We will show three examples of networks in action following our small introductory model. One example will link responses to survey with actual marketplace behaviour with very high predictive accuracy. The other two will use text responses to predict intentions and 'intent to recommend' – also with exceptional levels of correct prediction. But first we need to go over some basics, because these networks do function differently from the methods we know. Once we have these ideas in place, the demonstrations will make sense.

What makes a Bayesian Network Bayesian?

Everything Bayesian refers back to the work of the reverend Thomas Bayes, who lived an apparently quiet life in Tunbridge Wells, England, in the 18th century. Bayes is the contemplative-looking fellow in the illustration. He published two books in the 1730s, but never anything he called 'Bayes Theorem'.

Bayes' formulation itself is simple. Any reasonably literate person can easily understand it in its entirety, once we step aside from the nearly blinding formula often used to represent it. Starting from Bayes' straightforward assertion and arriving at many of the types of analyses that bear

IMAGE 8.1   Thomas Bayes

SOURCE: Portrait of Thomas Bayes, no date given, artist unknown. Source identified as T O'Donnell, 1936, *History of Life Insurance in its Formative Years*, American Conservation Co, Chicago. http://en.wikipedia.org/wiki/Thomas_Bayes.

his name is likely to have caused the good reverend to take on a strange hue. This perhaps is the inevitable price of progress.

We can formulate Bayes' idea in a variety of ways. Let's start with this more practical formulation:

> We start with **prior** (existing) beliefs that we can then update or modify by using information which we get from data we observe, and this gives us a new and more accurate **posterior** estimate. From this posterior estimate, we draw conclusions.

That's really all there is to it. However, it is usual to encounter this headache-inducing representation:

$$P(B_i|A) = P(A|B_i)P(B_i)/\Sigma_i\{P(B_i)P(A|B_i)\}$$

This equation has the property (unfortunately not novel for statistics) of requiring a page or so of explanation to lay out verbally all the minutiae of its mathematical details – yet we handled the sense of it without notation in the modest paragraph above.

So far we have managed to describe the Bayesian approach without explaining the idea of **conditional probability**. This appears prominently in many discussions. However, a probability that is **conditional** is no more than what we just described – an estimate of probability that takes into account some information from some earlier (prior) information or estimate. Our first example, involving a taxi cab getting into an accident, will show how earlier information affects an outcome. Just a little more discussion needs to come first.

The ground rules for networks

Diagrams of variables are key

A diagram of how variables fit together is integral to a Bayesian network. Somewhat more formally, these networks are based on **graph theory** and on **probability theory** – they fall under the heading of **graphical analytical methods**. Grasping their workings fully requires both a diagram and the calculations that underlie it. Networks in fact are called **directed acyclic diagrams (or DAGs)** because all the variables connect, all must point somewhere – and none can point back to itself, or form a **cyclic** structure.

A Bayes Net may be a familiar type of diagram if you are one of the lucky fraternity/sorority having experience with structural equation models (SEMs) or with partial least squares (PLS) regression path models. As in those types of models, variables are connected with arrows, showing pathways between them, and finally these lead to a target variable.

Arrows matter, but not as you might think

The arrows have a specific meaning in these diagrams; however, this is not entirely intuitive. We can say that a variable at the start of an arrow **leads to** another variable, and in certain conditions we even can say that the starting variable **causes** the variable at the end. However, if we change the variable at the end of an arrow, the variable at starting point will change as well. So effects run in both directions in a network.

Dealing with the data we typically encounter, connected variables in a network almost always have an equal chance of being the cause and being the effect. Strong influences go both ways. It is very rare indeed that we can prove one variable in fact **causes** another, dealing with the messiness inherent in behaviour, opinions and commentary.

Terms and phrases: it's all in the family

There is of course some terminology to learn. Fortunately, this part largely goes down easily, being (for statistics) warm and fuzzy. Some of the relationships are shown in Figure 8.3.

- The variable at the start of an arrow is called a **parent**;
- The variable at the end is called a **child** of the parent;
- Children can have several parents and parents can have several children;
- If there are two or more parents, they are called **spouses;**
- A parent of a parent is a **grandparent**, and so on;
- Variables are **dependent** only if they are directly connected;
  - Children and parents are dependent on each other;
  - Children are independent of grandparents and other variables further away.

Whether variables are **dependent** on each other becomes important when screening variables for inclusion in a model. One powerful screening technique involves including only those variables that are **dependent on the target variable** (its parents and children) and any other co-parents of

FIGURE 8.3   What to call the nodes in a Bayes Net

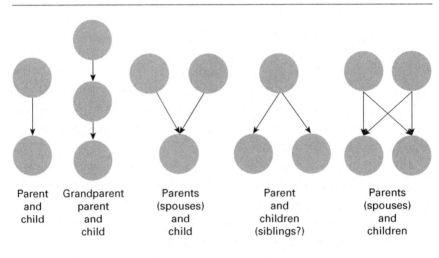

| Parent
and
child | Grandparent
parent
and
child | Parents
(spouses)
and
child | Parent
and
children
(siblings?) | Parents
(spouses)
and
children |

the children. This quickly eliminates less important variables where there are many – as in data-mining applications. This set of variables has a name also: the **Markov blanket**.

Everything is connected: changes move through the whole network

It is important enough to restate this: in whichever way the arrows point, **all variables in a network change when one changes**. The whole network is connected. And indeed, understanding networks as **conveying information across all the connected variables** is critical to all practical applications.

Network construction ranges from simple to complex

When we are attempting to understand relationships among variables, the way we fit the network together is of prime importance. Networks can build themselves automatically – something akin to a classification tree building itself on autopilot. However, networks typically are far less prone to taking on different shapes based on small changes in the data.

There are many ways that you can choose for a network to assemble itself. The simplest methods fit all the variables directly to the target variable. This is very much like a standard regression – all the variables are put into the mix and each one connects only to the target variable, and not to any of the other predictors.

At their most complex, networks have many branches and result from countless attempts to develop a best model – testing and retesting how variables best fit together to predict the values in the target. These methods use sophisticated tests to ensure that the network does not seize upon a connection that is good 'locally' (where a variable is being added) but not good for the overall network.

You also can put a network together yourself, and if you do not violate any basic rules, it will return answers about variables' effects based on the way you have chosen to assemble everything. There are various intermediary strategies as well, such as letting the network form an initial shape and then modifying it based on your understanding of the questions that need to get answered.

Understanding conditional probability

Bayesian networks take into account **conditional** probabilities. In practical terms, this simply means they consider how all the values in each variable relate to the values in all other variables. The workings of conditional probability can be difficult to grasp, but let us try this in the small example we have been promising, namely *the yellow taxi-white taxi problem*. (This example is from Kahneman and Tvresky. If you read further, you may encounter it in texts or courses about Bayes Nets.)

Let us start. The answers are surprising!

The yellow taxi-white taxi problem

IMAGE 8.2

SOURCE: Uploaded 2010, anonymous author 'zombieite.
http://www.flickr.com/photos/zombieite/4987163977.

Here is the situation. There is an accident involving a taxi cab.

- A witness reports that the cab involved was white in colour.

- In this city, 85 per cent of cabs are yellow and 15 per cent are white.

- The police actually test the witness out on a street corner and find that he is 80 per cent accurate at getting the cab's colour.

What are the odds that the cab actually was white, if the witness says it was white? We can solve this with a simple Bayesian network.

Setting up the taxicab problem is simple in a Bayes Net

Recall that we can make a network ourselves by linking up variables. Here, we will form a tiny network by linking two events: the colour of the cab and what the witness reports as the colour. Each event is called a **node**.

We understand that the witness's report of the cab's colour depends on its actual colour, so we will draw a small network with the colour of the cab leading to what the witness says, as you see in Figure 8.4. You must always have a direction between variables in a network.

FIGURE 8.4   A very small Bayesian network

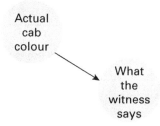

This depiction has little meaning until we can see what it inside each **node**. Each node actually holds a table representing numerically the situation we described. First we set up the node showing the odds of a taxicab being each colour, which we have called 'actual cab colour'. We see this in Figure 8.5.

FIGURE 8.5   Inside the first node

Node	Actual cab colour ▼		Apply	OK
Chance ▼	% Probability ▼		Reset	Close

Yellow	White
85.0	15.0

FIGURE 8.6   The second node set up as a table

Node	What the witness says ▼		Apply	OK
Chance ▼	% Probability ▼		Reset	Close

Cab	Yellow	White
yellow	80.0	20.0
White	20.0	80.0

Next we set up the second node showing the odds of the witness being right about each type of cab. We see that in Figure 8.6. Whether the colour is yellow or white, the witness gets it right 80 per cent of the time, and says the other (wrong) colour 20 per cent of the time.

Now what happens when the witness says he definitely saw a white cab? We will turn to the network diagram in the Bayes Net software (showing the two nodes), and change the type of display so that it does not show tables, but rather bar charts representing the probabilities we just entered. We will then reach into the diagram itself and change the value of **white** in the witness node to **100 per cent**. This corresponds to the witness saying 'white'.

The actual cab colour and what the witness says are linked (as we saw in Figure 8.4). Therefore, if we change the values in one node, the other will change along with it.

Now for the surprising answer

We have pushed the 'What the witness says' node to 100 per cent in Figure 8.7. As we can see, the odds of the cab actually being white is **about 41.4 per cent,** given that 85 per cent of cabs are yellow and the witness is 80 per cent right in identifying colours.

This is far from what most people would guess. Many guess either 80 per cent (seeing the 80 per cent accuracy figure) or 12 per cent (multiplying the 15 per cent of the cabs that are white by 80 per cent).

FIGURE 8.7 The unexpected answer

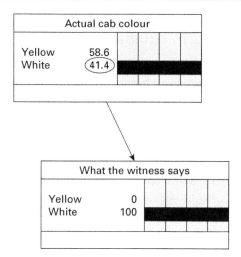

Why is the correct answer so different?

This happens because the odds that the cab truly is white (as the witness says) **depends on**, or **is conditional upon**, the percentages of cabs that are white and yellow. Let's take a minute to see how this plays out.

The witness will say that 12 out of 15 white cabs actually are white, because he is 80 per cent accurate at identifying white cabs. That part probably is obvious. However, there are 85 yellow cabs, and the witness also will say that 17 out of these 85 are white. (That is because he also is 80 per cent accurate with yellow cabs).

This means that the witness will say a total of **29 cabs out of 100** are white, but he is right only **12 times out of 29**. And 12 out of 29 indeed means the odds of the colour being correct is indeed 41.4 per cent!

This problem has been solved elegantly with a tiny network that took less than five minutes to assemble and that then gave the answer instantaneously. But nearly nobody would guess this correctly.

Here we come upon an issue with Bayesian networks. We have just neatly and simply unravelled a problem that would have eluded most of us. And yet, the answer seems strange until it is explained. We simply do not think in these terms, even when we should do so to solve a problem. As an expert on this subject (Yudkowsky) points out, thinking in these terms is a difficulty for 'novice students and trained professionals alike'. In sum, we have an approach that is truly powerful and that does things we cannot guess intuitively. With that in mind, let us take a deep breath, and learn more about these remarkable methods.

More about networks compared with regressions and classification trees

Bayes Nets look at the whole pattern of scores or responses in the variables it is analysing. For instance, comparing two variables that we will call **A** and **N**, this method creates a chart, or matrix, that shows how the scores relate. We can see this in Figure 8.8. In this chart, each box represents how often scores coincide. At the top right, for instance, we see that 33 people gave a score of 10 on variable A and 10 on variable N, that 44 gave a score of 9 on variable A and 10 on variable N, and so on. The darkened boxes are where the scores on the two variables align most often.

FIGURE 8.8 Bayes Net aligning two variables

Score on variable N	Score on variable A: 1	2	3	4	5	6	7	8	9	10	Totals
10			1	1	1	6	4	45	44	33	135
9				2	1	5	31	6	5	12	62
8			1	3	4	29	11	5	7	8	68
7			2	4	28	9	4	4	4	2	57
6			3	4	21	7	5	3	2	2	47
5			2	2	34	6	5	2			51
4					32	5		1			38
3				28							28
2			31								31
1	32	40									72
Totals	32	40	40	44	121	67	60	66	62	57	**589**

Bayes Nets will pick up the basically S-shaped relationship that you can see in those highlighted boxes. Regression, on the other hand, seeks how well the relationship between the two variables falls into a straight line, as we can see in Figure 8.9. In that figure, for readability we have substituted dots for the numeric values, with larger dots corresponding to larger numbers.

FIGURE 8.9   Linear relationship as estimated by a regression

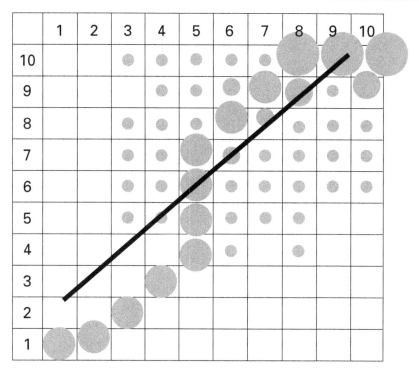

The straight line is key, as the **correlation** that standard linear rely upon is a **single number** describing how well pairs of variables conform to a straight line. As a reminder, correlation can range from zero, where the two variables cannot be fitted to a straight line at all, up to 1, where the two variables fall perfectly on a straight line. This is a much less detailed understanding of how variables relate than the whole pattern captured by Bayes Nets. And in some instances, the Bayes Net will also provide a more accurate model.

Turning to classification trees, these take a step towards looking at the whole distributions of variables, but in a different and more restricted way than Bayes Nets. Classification trees seek to split apart the scores in the target variable based on scores in the predictors. One way to express this is that classification trees look for **situational relationships**, as in saying, 'When variable N is like this, THEN variable A is like that.'

On a practical level, the **splitting** done by classification trees means that relatively few variables will get chosen as predictors. As we talked about in Chapter 7, that is because with each variable, groups get split. The subgroups become smaller at each step. Finally, the groups become too small to split further, and then there is no room for further predictors.

Differences in predictions: networks take the more realistic view

It is worth underlining that in networks, when one variable changes, all the other variables change as well. Any given variable has the most influence on variables with which it is closely connected, but effects from changes travel through the network like ripples going across a pond. Another, more formal way to say this is that **information propagates across the network.** Measurements of effects take into account all the other variables.

> **Predictions from Bayes Nets** take into account all the variables' relationships, and how every variable must change if any one changes. This sometimes is referred to as **information propagating through a network**. This is a much more realistic view than in regression, where effects from changing one variable assume all other variables remain the same.

This is very different from the basics of regression-based models, where any variable's effect assumes that **all other variables remain the same**. This is a particularly unrealistic view when dealing with data such as opinions, beliefs or purchasing patterns, as these all tend to be highly interrelated. Indeed, some authorities on regression (for instance Wilkinson), bemoan the tendency of regression-based models to fail in real-world applications, in particular setting policy. In the real world, when we change one factor, many other factors always change along with it – leading to the downfall of some precise-looking forecasts that regression delivers.

Drivers, causes and what works in which situation

Bayes Nets ultimately lead us to rethink what happens when we model effects of variables. Many of us have become accustomed to talking about the independent variables as 'predicting' or 'driving' the independent. Your author doubts that we ever will change the preferred terminology, but in a regression, the independent or predictor variables actually **explain** something about the target variable.

This may seem puzzling (this is becoming a refrain), but each independent variable accounts for (or explains) some of the **variance** or **pattern** in the dependent variable. You can see this clearly when you think again about a regression equation. In the equation, you multiply the score in each variable by some amount, add everything up, and you have the predicted score for the target variable. Each predictor variable actually is a part of the target's score.

Nonetheless, the term **driver analysis** is likely to be with us for the long term. (For the record, this is common but not learned usage: 'driver analysis' apparently is not covered in texts on statistics.) Concerning Bayes Nets, you may encounter more accurate terminology for what happens to a target variable when you change another variable. This is **sensitivity of the target to changes in another variable**. If you see that, and it seems confusing, just think of drivers.

FIGURE 8.10   Bayes Nets vs regression and which works well in which situation

Type of relationship	Straight line	Decreasing returns curve	S-shaped (growth) curve	Rapid saturation curve	Best in middle ('just right') curve
Bayesian network	Works well	Works well	Works well	Works well	Works well
Regression (All linear varieties)	Works well	Works well	Misses something*	Basically wrong	Basically wrong

Legend	Works well	*Can be helped by doing special 'transformations'
	Misses something*	before the analysis. These typically are not
	Basically wrong	done, due to difficulties in explaining results.

We will leave the topic of linear regression vs Bayes Nets with one last summary chart. In the hope that a slightly eccentric graphic can encourage recall, Figure 8.10 shows the type of relationships in which each method is likely to find success.

Our first example: Bayes Nets linking survey questions and behaviour

We will start with a relatively simple example of Bayes Nets showing a predictive relationship between responses to survey questions and behaviour. We will get to a larger example with text immediately after this. We show small examples of each method addressing questions other than analysing text because this underlines the general applicability of these predictive methods. While the types of analyses we are reviewing can be used to build predictive models with text, they all have much broader usability.

In this example we will see Bayes Nets addressing an important set of questions:

- What the relative effects are of several variables on the dependent variable;
- How strongly changing each variable affects the dependent;
- How these variables relate to each other and to the dependent.

In this example the predictor variables were heavily weeded. As mentioned, Bayes Nets can cut out the variables that have little direct relationship to the target variable, restricting them to those in the **Markov blanket** that we mentioned earlier. (Mr Markov and his blanket could be the subject of an entirely different discussion, but we will skip this today.)

Now on to the actual network

We will discuss a survey done among professionals using an information technology (or IT) product. It entailed a very long questionnaire. We will leap forward past the variable screening phase, to just seven key variables. Figure 8.11 shows how these variables relate to each other and to the target variable, which is **the per cent of services each corporate customer signed up to use again**.

Before we describe how the variables relate to each other, we should say that this network assembled itself. That is, the Bayes Net building software sought out the strongest patterns of relationships in the data and created a diagram of how the variables relate. The arrangement definitely passes the test of common sense.

Starting at the top in Figure 8.11, you can see that all predictor variables other than 'gives me a competitive advantage' connect with the target variable **through** this one. This means that all the other variables explain something about the way in which this company is seen as giving such an advantage.

FIGURE 8.11 A small Bayes Net

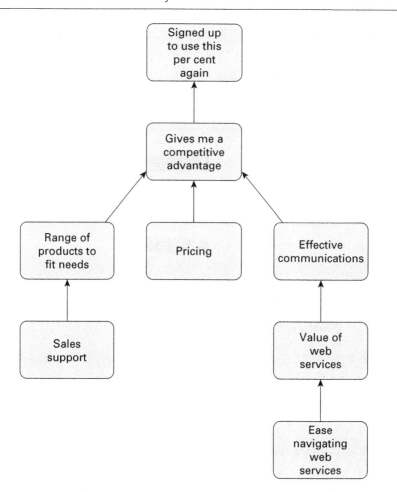

Three variables link directly at this point. They are ratings for range of products, pricing and effective communications. Sales support in turn links directly to range of products, a very logical connection.

Finally, effective communications is supported by value of web services, which in turn is supported by ease of finding web services.

The network, as a reminder, will also determine the importances of the variables and sensitivity of the dependent variable to changes in the independents. The sensible-seeming arrangement of the network gives us some confidence that these effects are measured accurately. Correct prediction levels, which we discuss soon, are high, and so give us more confidence that we have an accurate picture.

Figure 8.12 shows perhaps the best variable importance measurement in chart form that your author has seen. It compares the effects of changing each variable to what would happen if we could directly change the dependent variable. This chart shows that, for instance, changing 'gives me a competitive advantage' has about 45 per cent of the effect of directly changing the dependent.

FIGURE 8.12   Variables' effects in the network

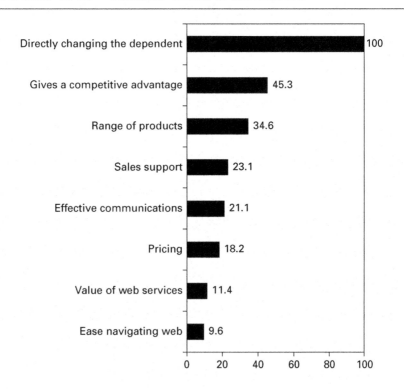

These values are somewhat similar to the Beta values that a regression provides. However, they summarize a more complete understanding of the data, where changes in the predictor variables actually can have different levels of impact for different values of the target variable. This is the full detail about **sensitivity of the dependent variable** to changes in the independents. We can develop another chart allowing us to see this.

While we skip this second chart in this short example, it does indeed show that effects on the target variable change depending on the values of the predictor variable and the target variables. That is, over some ranges of the values of each, the target variable changes more. This is another level of information beyond what we can see in a simple regression coefficient.

> In a Bayes Net, variables that are closest together typically have the most influence on each other. However, any change will spread across, or propagate, through the entire network.

And there is still more to what we can learn. We can look at the network diagram itself and see how every variable in the network changes when we change any one variable. Variables that are closely connected (such as parent nodes and children nodes) have strong influences on each other. The further the variables are from each other in the diagram, the less impact they tend to have on each other. However, all changes propagate through the whole network.

This whole-network understanding of the data makes any prediction of real-world effects much more realistic than the estimates from a regression-based model. In regressions, we must assume that all other things remain the same if we change any one variable.

Correct prediction levels were very strong indeed for fitting question-naire questions to behaviour. The model level of correct prediction of percentage of business signed for was 84 per cent, and this was using a stringent form of **testing** or **validation** of results, called **cross-folded validation**. (More on **validation** follows.) Without any validation, predic-tions were a stellar 93 per cent correct.

Those of us who have tried to fit questionnaire questions to actual behaviour know that this almost invariably has poor results when using regression-based models. Networks do not always do as well as this one, but so far have usually outperformed regression-based models on overall measures of model fit with a behavioural target variable, such as actual use levels, or buying the item in question.

In this case, the best regression-based model, a very complex variant of regression called a partial least squares (PLS) path model, turned in a paltry performance, with a weak 11 per cent correct prediction.

What precisely is validation?

We have not yet discussed **validation**. So perhaps this is the time. **Validation** is not a new idea, but the notion that you should use it regularly has gained support as data sets have gotten larger and models have grown more complex.

> **Model validation**: Holding aside some of the data when you build a predictive model, then trying out the model on that portion of the data. This is supposed to give you a better reading of how well the model will perform in the outside world, when it is actually applied. It aims to help you avoid over-fitting your predictive model.

The idea behind validation is that you should build the model on part of the data, **holding aside** the rest of it. You then try out the model on the part of the data that you held aside. When you try the model on this **hold-out sample**, predictive accuracy usually comes in at a lower level than when you simply look at the how the model performed where it was made.

Even the best predictive modelling technique will fit some random bumps and fluctuations that are found only in the data set on which a model was built. Trying out the model elsewhere, even on another part of the same data that you set aside, gives you some safeguards against **over-fitting** to seeming patterns that you will not find the outside world. Validation often comes built in by default in Bayes Nets programs, as the method is newer than regression and classification trees.

Why is it good to validate? As mentioned in earlier chapters, larger datasets often lead to many effects seeming to be meaningful, simply because you have so much data. Statistical tests start to break down, because with enough data everything seems significant. When you have a massive dataset, it is entirely feasible to put some of it to one side and have ample amounts left for building a complex model. So validation often is a prudent step in assessing how well predictive models actually will perform.

Using a Bayes Net with text

This example comes from a large online community of IT professionals, discussing issues related to hardware, software and their service experiences with the corporation hosting the community. They also were asked one question about intent to continue using services: would they be continuing next year at or above the level of the current year? Answers could be 'yes', 'maybe (undecided)' or 'no'.

Their verbatim comments were encoded using a large automated coding system. Although the system was automated, people also spent about a week modifying and refining the coding.

This led to a set of **79 encoded responses** that addressed concerns ranging from account management to brand presence to the cost/value relationship of consulting, to software services, to integrated software solutions, and so on. (We will spare you the full rundown of the 79 codes.)

These responses were encoded used a 'yes/no' (or 0/1) coding scheme. If a person mentioned an idea, he or she was given a code of '1' for that item, and otherwise was given a code of zero. A person could have as many '1' codes as the number of ideas that he or she mentioned.

We weeded the variables first, then assembled them seeking to find the best model. Figure 8.13 shows the model in its final form.

Trimming the 79 codes down to 20 was done by using a method called the **augmented Markov blanket,** which is somewhat more inclusive than **Markov blanket** mentioned earlier. That is, it contains another layer of connections following those to the target variable's children and their co-parents.

Bayes Nets allow you to remake the model using slightly different methods for connecting variables. You can see the models and select one that has logical-seeming connections and strong predictive power.

FIGURE 8.13   A network based on encoded text comments

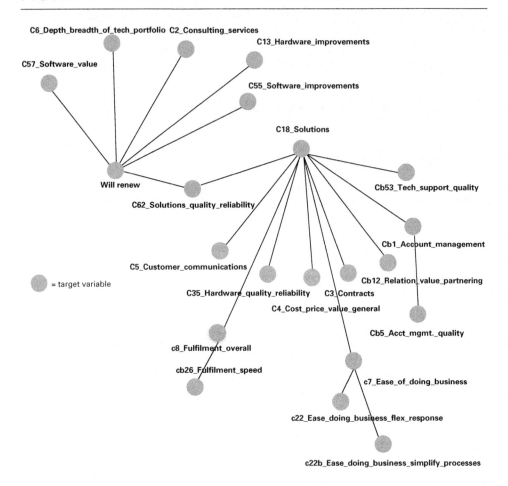

The final model also shows the ability of Bayes Nets to modify results from an initial method to improve predictive accuracy. We took another step after first using a fast method of network construction to prune the many coded variables, selecting the ones with the strongest connections with the target. Next we had the program rerun the model with a slightly more sophisticated (and computationally intensive) network-building technique, using the reduced set of variables. This improved our predictive accuracy and gave us an arrangement of variables that looked intuitively sound.

Careful reading of the model in Figure 8.13 shows that the connections indeed pass the test of common sense. We see a number of variables relating to broad topics that connect directly to the target variable ('will renew'). One variable, comments related to **solutions quality [and] reliability** (next to the target variable in the diagram), in turn connects to a variable about **solutions**. This latter variable is a focal point for many other concerns. Note how variables related to a specific topic (ease of doing business, account management, or fulfilment) were automatically grouped together. We understand that these should go together, and that is precisely what the network did.

How well did the model perform?
Overall performance was impressive for using text comments alone to predict intended behaviour. That is, knowing just the types of comments made, we could predict stated intentions correctly 63 per cent of the time, with the model doing particularly well in predicting 'yes' responses (82.8 per cent correct). We see the comparison of predictions vs actual intentions in Figure 8.14.

The principal area in which the model did not predict correctly was among the 2,902 who were undecided. Based on their comments alone,

FIGURE 8.14 Correct prediction levels in the Bayes Net model based on encoded comments

		Actual response		
		No	Maybe	Yes
		(n = 5,142)	(n = 2,902)	(n = 9,651)
Predicted response	No	70.5%	20.8%	4.4%
	Maybe	6.8%	12.9%	12.8%
	Yes	22.7%	66.4%	82.8%

the model misidentified some 66.4 per cent of them as saying 'yes' to renewing. Still, the level of correct prediction overall is high enough to give us confidence that the variables' importance levels produced by the model also are accurate.

Variables' importance levels

Figure 8.15 shows the variables' relative importances. When we have many variables (say, 20 or over), we have found displays of **relative importances** easier to read and interpret than displays like the one in Figure 8.12, where everything is pegged to what might happen if you could move the target variable directly.

FIGURE 8.15 Importances from the encoded comments network

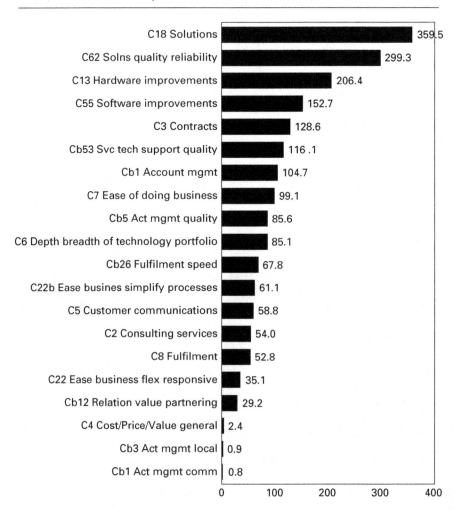

This chart uses an index that sets the average effect of a variable to be 100. The most important variable, with an index of 359.5 is therefore 3.59 times as important as these variables are on average. The weakest variable, with an index of only 0.8, is less than 1 per cent as important as the average.

The variable '**solutions**', a focal point for many other concerns, is the most important. It is followed directly by 'solutions quality and reliability', which served as a bridge between this variable and the dependent.

Another very detailed sensitivity chart, which we have not included here, shows that **hardware improvements** and **software improvements** relate more strongly to 'no' responses than to 'yes' responses to the target question. Careful reading of results therefore shows not only what needs most attention, but also which areas are most likely to lead to not intending to renew. The prioritization of concerns is very clear.

It bears repeating once more that measures of variables' effects arise from taking into account the entire pattern of relationships that we saw in the diagram. That is, any effect attributed to any one variable takes into account all the other variables and how they relate. This should lead to higher confidence in the accuracy of the importances than in a regression model, where we must assume that if one variable changes, all others remain the same.

A brief comparison to our earlier regression-based example

In Chapter 6, we saw a regression-based model that included encoded text responses along with scaled rating questions. In that regression model, as a reminder, combining text commentary with scaled ratings had better predictive accuracy than the regression models based either on scaled ratings alone or text alone. This model had a very good correct prediction level of 61 per cent.

However, the regression started producing clearly inaccurate measures of variables' effects after we entered 20 variables into the model. The remaining variables, while still passing tests of statistical significance, had coefficients that clearly ran in the opposite direction from what we knew to be correct. This is a well-known problem with regression, coming about from variables being too closely correlated, or even too closely related in their ideas, for the regression to process them correctly.

We also saw that some variables' coefficients shrank as other variables were entered into the model. For instance, the first variable to enter started with a coefficient of 0.7 when it was the only variable in the model, but then its coefficient shrank as each additional variable was added until it became less than half its original size in the final model (down to 0.3). This shrinkage in effects is another well-known problem with regressions. (Please take another look back at Chapter 6 for particulars.)

FIGURE 8.16   Bayes Net importances using data from the regression example

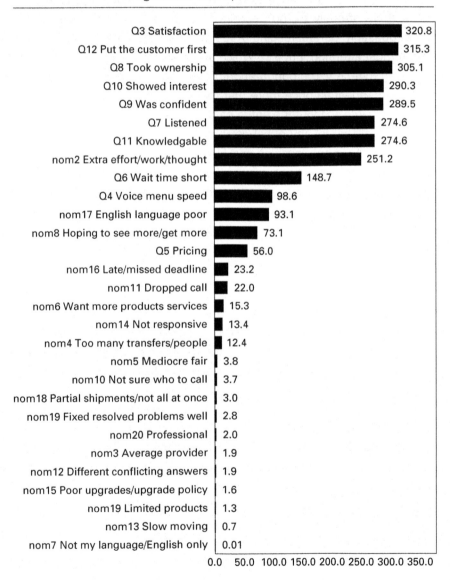

Q3 Satisfaction	320.8
Q12 Put the customer first	315.3
Q8 Took ownership	305.1
Q10 Showed interest	290.3
Q9 Was confident	289.5
Q7 Listened	274.6
Q11 Knowledgable	274.6
nom2 Extra effort/work/thought	251.2
Q6 Wait time short	148.7
Q4 Voice menu speed	98.6
nom17 English language poor	93.1
nom8 Hoping to see more/get more	73.1
Q5 Pricing	56.0
nom16 Late/missed deadline	23.2
nom11 Dropped call	22.0
nom6 Want more products services	15.3
nom14 Not responsive	13.4
nom4 Too many transfers/people	12.4
nom5 Mediocre fair	3.8
nom10 Not sure who to call	3.7
nom18 Partial shipments/not all at once	3.0
nom19 Fixed resolved problems well	2.8
nom20 Professional	2.0
nom3 Average provider	1.9
nom12 Different conflicting answers	1.9
nom15 Poor upgrades/upgrade policy	1.6
nom19 Limited products	1.3
nom13 Slow moving	0.7
nom7 Not my language/English only	0.01

0.0   50.0 100.0 150.0 200.0 250.0 300.0 350.0

Based on these concerns, we should not have overly much confidence in the regression's ability to pinpoint the strengths of variables' effects – and the earlier example underlined this. As we discussed, regression was developed as a forecasting tool, aiming to get the best possible estimate of the target variable's values – even if this means distorting some coefficients. Coefficients ideally should reflect the basic, underlying relationship of a predictor variable with the target. However, in practice, coefficients often are shaped most strongly by the presence or absence of other variables in the model.

Bayes Nets do not suffer from either of these problems. We tried the same variables in a Bayes Net, and it performed at essentially the same level as the regression (63 per cent correct for the network vs 61 per cent for the regression). However, **all the variables** could appear in the Bayes Net model.

Also, as we can see in Figure 8.16, the effects make intuitive sense. Scaled measures in a survey tend to be closely related, and in particular, we would expect **willingness to recommend** (the target variable) and **satisfaction** to be most closely related of all. Logically these concepts are tightly intertwined, and countless studies have borne out their close relationship empirically. (The regression estimated that the verbatim comments had stronger effects than the scaled ratings.)

In the Bayes Net, the verbatim comments with higher levels of importance than some of the scaled measures are therefore particularly noteworthy. On the positive side **putting in extra effort or thought** has a very strong impact, just as it does in the scaled measures. **English language problems**, an issue not captured in the scaled measures, has a noticeable impact on the negative side. This clearly is an important concern that the text commentary alone revealed.

Bayes Net software: welcome to the thicket

Software for Bayes Nets is problematic. Programs present a confusing world of choices, and seem inconsistent, perhaps not surprising for a relatively new set of methods. Applications range from free to incredibly expensive, and from remarkably capable to nearly useless. Not all the free programs are of the 'nearly useless' type, though, which is good. Unfortunately, since some of the truly expensive ones do not provide trial versions, we cannot say certainly whether higher costs always bring more capabilities. (The top end is *really* expensive, running into six figures.)

Surveying the choices in software, we find that most programs allow you to build networks by hand, as we did in the tiny taxi cab example, and to use those networks to answer specific questions. However, there are many programs with salient limitations. For instance, this author has encountered these difficulties in some of the many programs that could be given a trial run:

- Some cannot make networks, only allowing the editing of networks made elsewhere;
- Some have very steep learning curves;
- Some cannot find the structures in data;
- Some can only make networks that are grossly over-connected, leading to unintelligible thickets;
- Some only search for structures and say nothing about variables' effects.

Some do not even accept data files. They are just for solving logic problems.

You can find lists of software applications by typing 'Bayesian networks' into a web search engine. The software used in the examples here include the free programs Weka and Tetrad, and the pay-for programs Netica and BayesiaLab. Both free programs require some reading and struggling before you get to useable results. Both of the pay-for programs are highly capable, providing many useful analyses. BayesiaLab is the more expensive of the two. It also has more features and does more to automate production of output. This is a simple statement of programs that your author has found useful, and again not an endorsement. As with classification tree programs, it will be your needs that dictate which program is the best choice.

Summary, conclusions and cautions

Bayes Nets or Bayesian Networks are a remarkable set of methods with strong predictive powers. They typically do better than regressions in several areas, in particular getting an accurate fix on variables' importances and including all the variables of interest in a predictive model. Networks take into account all the interrelations of all variables when estimating importances, unlike regressions, which assume that when one variable is changed all others remain constant.

Like classification trees, Bayes Nets give us an insight into how variables interact, but the understanding in Bayes Nets extends to a holistic view of the ways in which all the variables in a model fit together. Classification trees' view of interactions is **situational**, that is, any variable beyond the first one in the model will have an effect **only if** the other variables have specific values. Bayes Nets models see the patterns across all values in all variables. They also are more comprehensive than classification trees, in that trees tend to produce simple models with relatively few predictors. You can enter a great many variables into a Bayes Nets model, and it will include and evaluate all of them.

Bayes Nets are newer methods that use analytical approaches quite different from more traditional methods. They can solve problems easily that may entirely elude other analytical procedures. However, they require some new terminology and their unfamiliarity may make some audiences less willing to accept them.

Bayesian Networks fall under the heading of **graphical analytical methods.** Diagrams are key to understanding their workings. You can get a great deal out of networks – such as variables' relative importances and effects – without ever looking the network itself (which some may find confusing). However, to understand whether the outcome makes sense, somebody needs to look at how the variables connect to each other.

Bayes Nets do not involve **equations** (as regressions do) or sets of **if-then rules** (as classification trees do). Every now and then, you might encounter somebody who needs to see equations, and for that person, networks might not provide a satisfying answer.

To see the effects of changing more than one variable at a time, you either need to go back to the network diagram itself, or (with some software) construct a stand-alone program that allows you to run **simulations**. (Simulations are no more or less than seeing the effects on an outcome of changing several or many factors at once.)

Even with a single variable being changed, effects can be different depending on the values of the target variable and the predictor variable. Effects from changing several variables at once requires taking many factors into account and certainly are nothing we could see intuitively, even though the network will handle as many changes as you want with aplomb.

IMAGE 8.3   Worth the effort to explore

SOURCE: 1935, uploaded 2006, National Undersea Research Program (NURP) Collection, OAR/NURP. Image ID: nur06017.
http://commons.wikimedia.org/wiki/File:Tritonia_Lusitania_1935.jpg.

Software unfortunately is a confusing terrain, even more so than for classification trees. Some programs are free, although they follow the general rules that free software generally is harder to use and more limited in what it can do than programs you must buy. You can spend a really great deal on some Bayesian Network software. But you may not have to, because there are some very powerful choices among the more reasonably priced options. As with any software, it is best for you to find a list and try as many as seem reasonably likely contenders. Because Bayes Nets operate differently from other methods, even if you use regular statistical software, there will be at least some learning curve. Ultimately, only you know what works best for your needs.

We have covered a good amount of new material in this chapter, and using Bayes Nets requires still more in terms of hands-on experience and learning about the details of the software you choose. Like any method you apply to a mass of unstructured data such as text, Bayes Nets are not guaranteed to develop useful output every time. However, these are among the most powerful of analytical methods, typically producing very strong predictive models that can address your informational and strategic needs, even with unstructured data such as text. Any learning that they require definitely will be more than repaid.

References

Cooper, G F and Herskovits, E (1992) A Bayesian method for the induction of probabilistic networks from data, *Machine Learning*, **9**, pp 309–47

Heckerman, D (1995) Tutorial on learning with Bayesian Networks, in M Jordan, *Learning in Graphical Models: Adaptive computation and machine learning*, MIT Press, Cambridge, MA

Jensen, F V and Nielsen, T D (2007) *Bayesian Networks and Decision Graphs*, 2nd edn, Springer-Verlag, New York

Kahneman, D, Slovic, P and Tversky, A (eds) (1982) *Judgment under Uncertainty: Heuristics and biases*, Cambridge University Press, Cambridge, UK, pp 156–58

Korb, K B and Nicholson, A (2010) *Bayesian Artificial Intelligence*, Chapman & Hall (CRC Press), New York

Mackay, D (2003) *Information Theory, Inference and Learning Algorithms*, Cambridge University Press, Cambridge, UK

Pearl, J (1986) Fusion, propagation, and structuring in belief networks, *Artificial Intelligence*, 29 (**3**), pp 241–88

Pearl, J (1988) *Probabilistic Reasoning in Intelligent Systems: Networks of plausible inference*, Representation and Reasoning Series, 2nd edn, Morgan Kaufmann, San Francisco, CA

Pearl, J (2000) *Causality: Models, reasoning, and inference*, Cambridge University Press, New York

Russell, S J and Norvig, P (2003) *Artificial Intelligence: A modern approach*, 2nd edn, Prentice Hall, Upper Saddle River, NJ

Wilkinson, L, Blank, I and Gruber, P (1999) *Desktop Data Analysis with Systat*, SPSS Inc, Chicago, IL

Witten, I and Frank, E (2005) *Data Mining: Practical machine learning tools and techniques*, 2nd edn, Morgan Kaufmann, San Francisco

Yudkowsky, E [accessed 17 February 2015] An intuitive explanation of Bayes' Theorem, *Eliezer S Yudkowsky* [online] http://yudkowsky.net/rational/bayes

Zhang, N and Poole, D (1994) A simple approach to Bayesian network computations, *Proceedings of the Tenth Biennial Canadian Artificial Intelligence Conference*, **AI-94**, pp 171–78, Banff, Alberta

LOOKING FORWARD AND BACK 09

KEY QUESTIONS

Where might things be going? What roles does text analytics play? And most importantly, where have we just been?

This chapter first takes a look at possible next directions, calling on several expert opinions. However, most of the material is devoted to a summary and synthesis of the topics we covered. These fall into several broad areas: best practices in text analytics; software and you; and analytical methods and their uses. In that area, we include a chart comparing and contrasting the approaches, their uses and expected outputs.

Where we may be going

'It is very possible that . . . one [computer] would suffice to solve all the problems that are demanded of it from the whole country'

This was said in 1943, and serves as a warning to anybody seeking to make predictions. It also serves as a caution: do your research. It is commonly ascribed to Thomas Watson, former head of IBM, but he never said it. (The person responsible for the quote was Sir Charles Darwin, grandson of **the** Darwin and then head of Britain's National Physical Laboratory.) That is just one of those myths that keep getting spread after being completely debunked, and we need to watch for those too. With these caveats in mind, let's go forward and somewhat gingerly discuss predictions – and maybe even have some fun along the way.

The experts speak

Authors Miner, Delen, Elder, Fast, Hill and Nisbet teamed up into a massive editorial 'I' and offered a few predictions in their still more massive *Practical Text Mining* (2012) running to 1,053 pages. They started by observing that text analytics really is in its infancy, or perhaps early teens (but gave no guidelines on how to handle a pubescent area of analysis when it became recalcitrant). They looked back to a similar period in the early days of data mining and drew some likely inferences. Data mining then was a morass of methods and algorithms, all claiming to perform very special feats, just as text analysis is now awash with dozens of competing approaches.

A weeding process took place with all the proposed data mining tools and vendors then, and it is reasonable to assume that this will happen with text analytics in the next few years. Their projection is that we will emerge from the current phase, with its plethora of competing programs and their sellers, and will settle on a smaller number with proven performance.

Let us hope that we will come to a world where the better applications win and the lesser ones diminish. Tom Reamy, chairing a gathering called 'Text Analytics World' also noted that this field is just starting to grow up in a 2014 presentation. He said that things yet to come will involve asking more of the right questions, in particular, where is the value? It is our hope that this book will give the field a small shove in this direction.

Many other experts look forward to a future when we all will use whatever they are doing, but in a better form. Some call for better indexing of documents and some for more efficient retrieval. Some talk about better meshing of text commentary and other data, such as stock prices. Nearly all agree that we need better processing of shades of meaning, which seems to mean that the future of text lies in better guessing what people really intend to say. It is of course important to give computers a more accurate sense of semantics, and indeed we can expect machines to get much stronger in understanding the ambiguities and multiple meanings inherent in the way we use language.

Yet, from your author's perspective, it is strange how many proposals seem to come from an assumption that we never can ask people what they mean, but must always rely on comments we more or less overhear. It is likely many of the problems of disambiguating text can be resolved by asking a representative sample of the people offering comments what

IMAGE 9.1   We may have come up with something

SOURCE: Archimedes taking a warm bath, circa 1850, G A A Beckett, from The Comic History of Rome, Bradbury, Evans & Co, London.
http://posner.library.cmu.edu/Posner/books/book.cgi?call=937_A138C_1850.

they meant, what they are doing and planning to do, and then applying what has been learned to many thousands of other comments. Yet this approach does not seem to get any mention. Let us be the first to suggest then, that a future direction could involve the scoring and categorizing of a great deal of text by asking a strong, representative sample of users some good questions.

Closer to home (for this author, in any event), Professor Jehoshua Eliashberg of the Wharton School offered likely the most sensible predictions and suggested directions for text analytics. Professor Eliashberg has been working on a highly advanced topic, analysing movie scripts to assess their box office potential. He says,

> 'Text analytics becomes useful in particular when applied to understand consumer sentiments, linguistic styles, and forecast behaviour. The future of text analytics is going toward gaining better understanding of actual meaning so that this meaning can be used to inform and drive decisions. Deep semantic and linguistic understanding and their linkages to the choices that people make, as well as to the experience they obtain based on their choices, is in my mind the direction which text analytics needs to pursue in the future.'

Artificial intelligence and text

Of course, some authors look forward to a brave, new world including artificially intelligent machines which will be completely fluent with language and perhaps even think for themselves. What precisely 'artificial intelligence' and 'think for themselves' may mean is open to some debate. The so-called Turing test proposes to answer the question, but it would be helpful if we could have a general agreement on what goes into a Turing test.

Alan Turing, a genius involved in inventing computers, felt that a machine would be intelligent if it could fool people who could not see it into thinking it was a person. He apparently meant this included everything a human does with language, including getting insulted and making human-seeming mistakes. That strikes some as a great deal to ask. Many Turing tests have taken place (and a good number of related ones), and continue to take place, using a variety of criteria for what makes a passing grade. So far no machine has passed to everybody's satisfaction.

Some are not looking forward to the dawning of true machine intelligence, should that ever arrive. Stephen Hawking reiterated a theme common in science fiction when he speculated that any truly intelligent machine that we managed to invent could very well be the last, and the last of mankind.

Even assuming things never become dire, the occasional uncanny ability of a machine to interact can give us pause. For instance, here is a transcription of a recent interchange this author had with his telephone:

'Phone, where can I find coffee?'
'Oh – interested in a late afternoon snack, Steven?'

This was a terribly shrewd guess for something you could hold in your hand. One can only wonder what the future will bring.

What role does text analytics play?

A wise recent quote about big data also applies to text analytics. As Lazer *et al* (2014) have pointed out:

'Big data hubris' is the often implicit assumption that big data are a substitute for, rather than a supplement to, traditional data collection and analysis.

Throughout this book, we have shown examples where linkages to other data, gathered by 'traditional' methods, gives text analytics true gains in usefulness for guiding decisions. Text analytics can be seen as part of a continuum of data gathering activities. We can make taxonomies in many ways. Figure 9.1 shows one of those that may be useful.

Text analytics, like data mining and its descendant big data, focuses in on what has happened or takes a current market pulse. Because you are looking at history – even if very recent history – rather than inquiring into

FIGURE 9.1 One way to see where text analytics fits with other types of data collection

Designed experiments	Scaled and other direct questions	Sales tracking	Text analytics Data mining

Looking forward
Forecasting

Looking backward
Taking market pulse

what could happen, these are in fact the least forward-looking of the various data-gathering activities.

Every now and then, you may come across an academic type who says somewhat hopefully that the day may come when spontaneous customer comments will drive new product development. If you do not already know how unrealistic this is, then take a strong recommendation never to believe that.

Keeping expectations realistic

Customers and prospects will not develop new products and services for you. They also cannot name your products or develop catchy communications ideas. They can respond to your ideas if you ask in the right way, but even then are sharply limited in telling you what they truly want. It really is your job to come up with the concepts and the right ways to test them.

While we are discussing this, simple direct questions to people about what they find important also do not work well. That is the reason **designed experiments** are over on the left of the continuum, as the most forward-looking of data collection activities, and **direct questions** are nearer to the middle. For many years, marketers struggled with unreliable forecasts and botched new product and service introductions based on direct questions.

Finally, about 1975, better forecasting methods which actually used designed experiments, like experiments in a lab, were developed. In these, people were exposed to a series of systematically varying product or service descriptions or **profiles** and asked to evaluate them. In these, products were broken down into discrete features that varied in very specific ways. Everything was completely controlled so that, when the data came back, the relative desirability of each variation of each feature could be determined, and good estimates of actual demand for many different product or service features could be made. This was called **conjoint analysis**. It was later extended to evaluating the performance of hypothetical products and services in the context of competitors, and this is called discrete **choice modelling**.

Many articles and books have been written on these methods. We will not be discussing them further here, and include them solely to underline the importance of putting text analytics to its best uses. You should not be pressing it into service instead of other methods that perform excellently in different areas of inquiry.

Where text excels

Text, particularly in connection with other data, can give you a sharply-honed sense of the marketplace, and can help you diagnose problems and concerns. At times, you will find an issue that you can remedy quickly, as in the example (using classification trees) in which spontaneous comments were linked to ratings, showing unexpected problems with language in a call centre. In many other instance, text analytics can clearly highlight areas that will repay in-depth investigation with other methods.

Summing up: where we have been

Best practices for text analytics

In an ideal world, we would always do whatever is the very best. If we cannot in reality, we still can shoot for doing things as well as we can. We discussed a good number of pointers throughout the book, and here are the more important ones. If you would like a fuller explanation, many of these are found in Chapter 1 and some in Chapter 5. Please refer back if anything seems confusing.

Perhaps one of the most important pieces of advice was to make sure you had a **really good reason to do the analysis**. At first, this might seem like little more than Gerald Ford's statement, mentioned in the introduction: 'When a man is asked to make a speech, the first thing he has to decide is what to say.'

However, it is critical to underline because so much in text analysis seems to get done 'just because' – that is, just because it could be done, because it seems 'interesting', because somebody needed something to show some progress, or because some data-scientist type was due to make a report.

Another critical notion is that **text analytics needs sponsors**, people who can take actions based on what the text reveals. Even the most brilliant insights, if not asked for, typically lead nowhere. As important, text analytics is not free – on the contrary, it requires considerable expertise and investment. Somebody who can make that investment needs to be behind the effort.

In spite of many claims to the contrary, **meaning does not spring un-bidden from data**. No amount of flailing around will make this more likely to happen, either. Some stories that circulated for years about serendipitous finds have finally emerged as not reflecting real events, or even as being jokes. Just recall (from Chapter 1) those beer promotions in the diaper aisle (or perhaps that was that vice versa). They never happened. The story was supposed to point out how ridiculous claims of this type can become.

Another absolutely wrong assertion that we reviewed is the notion that more data is always better. **Data is not information**, and the distinction is critical. Anything that can be gathered or measured in any way is data, including printed materials thrown away because of errors, misinformation spread by spy bureaus, and recordings of the hum given off by neon lights. **Information** is something that you can use to make a better decision or that prepares you for an unusual contingency.

More data that has been collected for no particular purpose, other than to have the data, does not make it easier to find the information you need. It makes this harder.

Data has even been compared with pollution. According to security expert Bruce Scheiner, we are dealing with data at our stage in the information age much as machinery was dealt with early in the industrial

IMAGE 9.2   More of this does not make life better

SOURCE: Guiyu-ewaste, uploaded 2014, by anonymous author 'bleahbleahbleah'. Licensed under CC BY-SA 3.0 via Wikimedia Commons.
http://commons.wikimedia.org/wiki/File:Guiyu-ewaste.jpg#mediaviewer.

age. That is, we are spewing a lot of trash into the environment, and our grandchildren will look back at our activities, and our inability to clean ourselves up, with horror. Whether this will become a reality or not, realizing that we need to be selective definitely is the best way to go.

One point that also amply bears repeating is to be careful about where you get the text that you analyse. Any place you find text is a **sample frame**, and this frame limits how accurate your conclusions can become. You need to focus on the comments of people who actually use and value your product or service, or at least might use it. If you get people from the wrong frame, it does not matter how many of them you find or how elegantly you perform your analyses. Your conclusions can be disastrously wrong.

We have already dragged out poor Alf Landon twice, but this is such a key cautionary tale that we will call on him one last time. A huge sample of 2.4 million, but 2.4 million drawn from the **wrong sample frame**, was used to predict a victory for him in the 1936 US presidential election. He actually lost in a landslide, getting 38 per cent vs 62 per cent for Franklin Delano Roosevelt. This has been called the largest error ever in a major public opinion poll.

The organization running the poll should have known better, even back in 1936. **Reliance on large numbers alone is not enough.** George Gallup knew this, used the right sample frame and a much more modest sample, and called the election correctly. We definitely have had enough time since to absorb this lesson.

Worse, getting data from the wrong people can work one time and then stop working for mysterious reasons. We saw that with Google flu trends, which correctly predicted an outbreak of the flu, but then completely missed the swine flu epidemic of 2009. It went on missing forecasts for years following.

Social media: proceed with caution

Because social media sites, even the largest, such as Facebook and Twitter, have uncertain populations, you need to stay particularly wary about statements based on what happens on them. Unless you are advertising on one of these sites, you should not assume that the comments there come from the people who need or may need your product or service. Social media commentary can serve usefully as a rough kind of temperature-taking, particularly if your organization is sensitive to any negative mentions. It is not clear whether adverse social media attention does any lasting harm, if the response is thorough. We saw this in the example with Domino's Pizza, in Chapter 5. However, it is best to stay informed – although if your only interest is in staying alert to any disparagement, you might want to consider a service that monitors the web.

A topic we need to recap

One last area needs a summing-up before we get to our next topic, the methods themselves. In Chapter 1, we went over the generally chill-inducing topic of **statistical significance**, and a related area, **statistical power**. We cautioned that it is best to look at significance but not to rely on it automatically. Especially with larger batches of data, nearly anything can appear significant. When you start looking at many thousands, statistical significance certainly puts a floor underneath what you should consider. Non-significant results with large samples definitely mean that nothing worth noting is happening.

The methods we have discussed and their applications

Figure 9.2 is a large chart that should point your towards methods you can use to solve specific problems. This is a listing and comparison. For each method, we point to the chapter where it was discussed, the application, any sub-methods or specific applications we discussed, and key points that require extra attention. If you need more detail, please refer back to the chapters listed with each.

Software and you

As we mentioned earlier, text analytics software is a kind of morass, with dozens of applications and many conflicting claims. Keeping track of this all is quite a daunting task. You would need a large team of people just to review all the different products and approaches. Also, these lists are in flux, with software appearing, mutating or disappearing. Even now, it seems that the Advisor program mentioned in Chapter 3 is changing from a desktop application to part of an 'enterprise' level service called Skytree Infinity. We can expect many other changes.

FIGURE 9.2   A summary of methods, their applications and key cautions

Preparation and Description				
	Chapter 2: Getting Words Ready		Chapter 3: Words in Pictures	Chapter 4: Clustering Words and Documents	Chapter 5: Sentiment Analysis
Method	Text preparation	Gathering words	Pictorial representations	Clustering and scoring models	Counting and sentiment analysis
Specific Applications	• Regularizing text • Removing stop words • Correcting misspellings • Lemmitization	• Sliding windows • Automated coding • Factor analysis	• Wordles • Word clusters • Word treemaps • Word clouds • Graph layouts • Heat maps	• Clustering via hierarchical, K-means and TwoStep methods Classification using classification trees	• Simple counting • Centrality of words • Sentiment analysis
Watch out for	• Exclusion of words you need as stop words	• Size of the sliding window • Choices made by automated coding: expect changes • Automatic selection of number of factors: always check	• Over-reliance on a single method; try many and compare to see which best conveys patterns	• Using only a single method	• An onslaught of terminology • Incorrect sample frames

Predictive Models		
	Chapter 6: Linear Regression	Chapter 7: Classification Trees	Chapter 8: Bayes Nets
Method	Regression	CHAID and CART	Bayesian Networks
Specific Applications	• Regression using words • Regression using words made into factors • Models that create equations	• Optimal recoding of variables • Discovering interactions among variables • Capturing non-linear relationships • Creation of predictive models that can be described with simple if-then rules • Models for scoring documents	• Predictive models linking text and actual behaviour • Capturing linear and non-linear relationships • Accurate measurements of variables' effects • Models to score documents but only in a special simulation program
Watch out for	• Missing non-straight line relationships among variables • Changes in regression coefficients based on putting more variables into the model; good predictions at the expense of accurate readings of effects • Problems with missing data	• Over-reliance on automatic growing of classification trees	• Non-intuitive nature of conditional probability • Difficulty in explaining to some audiences • Many software solutions to consider with wildly varying capabilities

That said, we can break the software into four broad categories:

- Free software, including open-source software where you can see and modify the programming code;
- Moderately priced software, which seems fairly thin on the ground in text analytics;
- Expensive software, where we found several capable programs;
- Enterprise software and custom solutions, which are indeed quite expensive.

Free applications

You need to bear in mind that even if some software comes free of charge, all of it will end up costing you something. **Applications you can download free of charge**, of which there are dozens, typically are harder to use and generally less tractable than software you must purchase. Free programs may have severe limitations in what they can do, and their output often is rudimentary. Some free programs simply break down and refuse to work.

Worse, these programs typically come with no technical support beyond a user community. These can disappoint you. You may have a problem, go the user community, and see a 'thread' containing many comments. On inspection, this will turn out to be somebody mentioning the same problem, and a couple of dozen people saying, 'That happened to me also. Who can fix this?'

We do not recommend software but will mention a few free offerings that seem relatively well-known and widely-used among serious data-analytical types. The set of programs called **R** is largely the work of serious academics, and so usually does what it says it will, eventually. Most people find **R** hellishly difficult to use, as its default mode of operation uses an old-fashioned typed set of commands. The syntax can be very arduous. At times it seems as if some practitioners find making it hard part of the fun.

However, in addition to working on your desktop, **R** now can be found on 'the cloud', meaning you can solve very large problems if you buy enough cloud capacity. We can expect other programs to get there in the next few years. **RapidMiner,** a formerly free program, has adopted a multi-tier pricing structure, depending on how much computer memory you need to use. The most expensive version, which claims to be able to address 'unlimited' memory, does not have a listed price. That's expensive.

If you can find **RapidMiner 5**, that will handle problems that your computer can hold in its memory. Typically you can process many thousands of records or documents before memory becomes an issue with most modern PCs. Some analysts like the RapidMiner interface, which asks you to hook various program elements together on a 'canvas', but most users will need to watch a few tutorials to get it to work.

Another free program, **Weka**, is highly capable, and can do text analytics and numerous machine-learning applications. It has four alternative interfaces, three of them graphical. Some users find this easy and others are more puzzled. An excellent book by Witten, Frank and Hall (2011) will give you a lot of pointers on using this program. For now, it is limited to problems that can be handled within your computer's memory.

Enterprise-level software

At the other extreme of the pricing continuum, we have **enterprise-level software**. These programs typically require an initial investment in the six figures, and some require expensive yearly licences. These are typically offerings from well-known software providers, including SAS Enterprise Miner, IBM SPSS Data Miner, and Statistica Data Miner, and about a dozen others. They normally are easier to run (that is a relative term) than the free offerings, are very large and comprehensive, handle plenty of data, can gather data from the web, and offer a host of analytical functions.

If you do not get one of these massive programs, you will need to get statistical software if you want to do predictive analyses. We mentioned regular SPSS in the text, but there are many capable alternatives. Again, this is not a recommendation, but a pointer towards something worth considering. One of the best bargains in full-featured statistical software is a program called **NCSS**. It does a vast range of analyses and has a superb help system. Assuming you run a Windows computer, this may meet all your needs.

The best bet in software

This may sound like a truism, but the best programs will be ones that you try and find to do the kinds of analyses you require. Many programs offer free trial versions. If you are truly interested, you may be able to arrange for one even if nothing is explicitly presented. There are numerous lists online. One of the better ones is run on a site called **kdnuggets.com**. This at least has an identifiable curator and tries to vet the content. You should be wary of unsigned 'best of' lists as these can be terribly out of date and inaccurate in their basic information.

In conclusion

Text analytics can provide remarkable insights and help guide actions. But because text is unstructured data, you really need to follow good practice and always remain cautious. This is particularly so if the text comes from a source on the web that you do not control. Using the comments of an incorrect set of people can lead to spectacularly wrong conclusions.

Following the key guidelines we have covered, text has worked particularly well when combined with other data, such as ratings. The combination of text and other data can provide more insights and better directions for action than either the text alone or the other data alone. Many of you may have noticed that an example running through this book was a survey done by a major social media site. They do a great deal of monitoring of public comments, of course, but when they really want to improve something, they put that aside and engage in talking directly to their customers and prospects.

We have come a long distance from the preface and covered a wide range of topics. We could not even touch on all possible areas related to analysing text, but you should now have a formidable armamentarium to use while doing battle in this arena.

This leads us to an appropriate sentiment from boxing announcer Jim Watt: 'At the finish, it was all over.' And thank you for following this voyage.

IMAGE 9.3

SOURCE: 1884, Winslow Homer, photo courtesy of Colby College Museum of Art. Accession number 2013.142. http://commons.wikimedia.org/wiki/File:Winslow_Homer_-_A_Fishing_Schooner.jpg.

References

Armstrong, J S (2001) *Principles of Forecasting*, Springer, New York

Bell, G (1999) The folly of prediction, in P J Denning, ed, *Talking Back to the Machine*, Copernicus (Springer Verlag), New York, pp 1–15

Cellan-Jones, R (2014) Stephen Hawking warns artificial intelligence could end mankind, *bbc.co.uk*, 2 December 2014 [online] http://www.bbc.com/news/technology-30290540 [accessed 17 February 2015]

Lazer, D, Kennedy, R, King, D and Vespignani, A (2014) The parable of Google flu: traps in big data analysis, *Science*, **343**, pp 1203–205

Maynard, D [accessed 17 February 2015] Practical opinion mining for social media, slideshare.net, 2013 [online] http://www.slideshare.net/dianamaynard/opinion-miningtutorial

Miner, G, Delen, D, Elder, J, Fast, A, Hill, T and Nisbet, R (2012) *Practical Text Mining and Statistical Analysis*, Elsevier, Waltham, MA, pp 991–1004

Reamy, T [accessed 23 February 2015] Future directions in text analytics, October 2012, *KAPS Group* [online] http://www.kapsgroup.com/presentations.shtml

Schneier, B [accessed 17 February 2015] Data as pollution, *Schneier on Security*, blog, 30 January 2008 [online] https://www.schneier.com/blog/archives/2008/01/data_as_polluti.html

The Economist (2003) Thomas Watson quoted in Punching the card, *The Economist*, 8 May 2003 [online] http://www.economist.com/node/1763632 [accessed 23 February 2015]

Train, K E (2002) *Discrete Choice Methods with Simulation*, Cambridge University Press, Cambridge, UK

Turing, A (1950) Computing machinery and intelligence, *Mind* LIX (**236**) (October), pp 433–60

Turing, A (1952) Can automatic calculating machines be said to think?, in B Copeland, *The Essential Turing: The ideas that gave birth to the computer age*, Oxford University Press, Oxford

Wikipedia [accessed 17 February 2015] Turing test, *Wikipedia* [online] http://en.wikipedia.org/wiki/Turing_test

Witten, I, Frank, E and Hall, M (2011), *Data Mining*, Morgan Kaufmann (Elsevier), New York

GLOSSARY

Bayes Net or Bayesian Network: a highly accurate method of modelling how variables relate to each other and their effects on each other. Readings of effects take into account all the variables' relationships, and how every variable must change if any one changes.

Big data: a broad term without a consistent and concise definition for datasets so large or complex that traditional data processing applications are inadequate.

Classification tree rules: a set of simple if-then statements describing the combinations of predictor variables that lead to different values of the target variable. See also *classification trees*

Classification trees: a method within data-mining, when the task is classification or the prediction of outcomes and the goal is to generate rules that can be easily understood. This method labels records and assigns them to discrete classes, and excels at finding interactions. See also *classification tree rules, interaction, regression*

Clustering: grouping of people, objects, documents or words, based on how similar they are to each other. See also *hierarchical clustering, k-means clustering, TwoStep clustering*

Correlation: a simple summary measure of how closely two variables fall compared to a perfect straight-line relationship, called the 'R' value in statistics.

Descriptive analytics: text analytics that show broad patterns, count items, or reveal what is near another item but not what influences an outcome and by how much. See also *predictive analysis*

Descriptive methods: showing patterns and similarities but not effects on any outcome or behaviour. See also *predictive methods, descriptive analytics, predictive analytics*

Eigenvalues: a mechanical means for deciding on the number of factors, or groupings of variables, you should elect to have. See also *factor analysis*

Entity extraction: identifying a set or group of words so that the computer understands they have a single meaning, often used to identify people or organizations.

Factoids: incorrect or inaccurate statements presented in the press that seem likely to be true.

Factors analysis: a way of combining words that have similar meanings into a group where each word has a weight relative to the other words grouped with it. Factors reflect some underlying idea or point out which words tend to appear together.

Hierarchical clustering: a clustering method that seeks to build a hierarchy of clusters, which can be visualized as being like a tree with a lot of branches – the most similar words are on the branches that are closest together. See also *clustering, k-means clustering, TwoStep clustering*

Information extraction: the task of automatically extracting structured information from unstructured and/or semi-structured machine-readable documents, often through natural language processing. See also *natural language processing*

Interaction: when the effect of two or more variables working together to produce an outcome is different from what we would expect based on the effects of the variables separately.

K-means clustering: a clustering method that partitions observations into clusters in which each observation mean groups around a central value serving as a prototype of the cluster. See also *clustering, hierarchical clustering, TwoStep clustering*

Multidimensional scaling: a way to generate a visual display of a table of similarities among words.

Natural language processing: a field of computer science, artificial intelligence, and linguistics concerned with the interactions between computers and human or 'natural' languages, and hence related to the area of human-computer interaction. See also *information extraction*

Optimal recoding: the ability of classification trees to split the codes in a variable in the best possible way to predict an outcome variable. See also *classification tree*

Predictive analytics: shows what leads to a change in some target variable, such as liking, preference or behaviour, and how strong those influences are likely to be. See also *descriptive analytics*

Predictive methods: those that show effects on any outcome or behaviour but not patterns and similarities. See also *descriptive methods, descriptive analytics, predictive analytics*

Regression analysis: a statistical process for estimating the relationships among variables; in most regressions, this estimates how well this relationship conforms to a straight line.

Sample frames: the locations where you gather data. Using the wrong sample frame can lead to grievously wrong predictions, no matter how much data you gather.

Scree plot: a visual display of the eigenvalues associated with a factor in descending order versus the number of the factor to help you assess which components or factors explain variability in data. See also *eigenvalues*

Sentiment analysis: analysis that tries to find the positive or negative tone in documents, typically by comparing the words in documents to words tagged as positive and negative.

Sentiment scores: the balance of positive and negative words in documents after a sentiment analysis.

Significance testing: testing the probability that what we think is a relationship between two variables is really just a chance occurrence.

Statistical power: a measure of how likely it is you are to be missing something real in a statistical exercise.

Statistical significance: the degree to which you can be confident that you are not making a false claim as a result of a statistical exercise.

Supervised learning: methods of learning with a target outcome or pattern they are trying to reach, such as regression. See also *regression analysis*

Target variable: the variable that we are trying to forecast or predict using the other variables. The target is called the dependent variable and the other variables the independents.

Tokens: the words taken from a block of text once it has been cleaned in a process sometimes called tokenization.

TwoStep clustering: a clustering method designed for large datasets in which records are pre-clustered into sub-clusters which are then, in turn, combined into fewer groups. See also *clustering, hierarchical clustering, k-means clustering*

Unsupervised learning: methods of learning that try to find a pattern rather than match or predict one, such as clustering and factor analysis. See also *clustering*

INDEX

Note: Chapter references and chapter summaries are indexed as such. Page numbers in *italics* indicate Figures or Images.

CPSIA information can be obtained
at www.ICGtesting.com
Printed in the USA
BVOW05s1511110117

473254BV00007B/24/P